RAMBUTAN
RAMBUTAN
RAMBUTAN
RAMBUTAN
RAMBUTAN

RAMBUTAN

Recipes from Sri Lanka

Cynthia Shanmugalingam

BLOOMSBURY PUBLISHING

LONDON · OXFORD · NEW YORK · NEW DELHI · SYDNEY

For Mum and Dad, for everything.

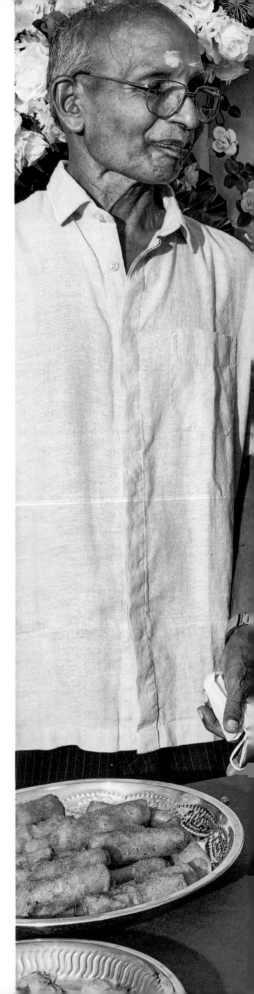

Introduction 12

Vegetables & Fruit 26

Fish, Seafood & Meat 90

Cool, Raw & Pickled Dishes 160

Rice, Roti, Hoppers & Dosas 204

Drinking Snacks & Shorteats 242

Drinks & Sweets 284

Introduction

At the top of Point Pedro market, a few miles on a noisy bus from my parents' house at the northern tip of Sri Lanka, you will find a whole storey of vegetable sellers. In the large, airy building, some feet away from the black and gold sand, you can still hear the Arabian Sea, ferocious with fish, crabs and catamarans. Beside the shouting in the fish market and above the rice guy with his nineteen different kinds of rice, the vegetable sellers sit cross-legged on a cement floor. Each one is surrounded by beautiful piles of fruit and veg, with slightly different specialisms and prices. When you walk past the okra guy, he says 'yes! okra?' in Tamil as if you had asked him a question. And if you glance at him in response, he starts snapping the ends off his okra with a serene smile on his face.

The first time I saw this I was like, dude what are you doing? And my mum started giggling. Snapping okra this way demonstrates how fresh it is, she explained to me. Fresh okra should not be soggy or soft. It has a taut body and it will snap clean.

This is the kind of cooking knowhow that Mum – alongside almost everyone else in my Sri Lankan family – has always seemed to *just know*. Like all the great cooks from the island, they tend to prod, sniff, shake and listen to their ingredients with the kind of concerned familiarity of a chiropractor. They seem to have been born knowing just what fruit, veg, fish, meat, spices and rice to buy, when everything is in season, and how to turn it all into the wonderful Sri Lankan fare that they eat every day.

Unlike them, I have had to learn a different way. When my parents left the island in the 1960s to live in England, they didn't know that on the flight, thousands of years of culinary knowledge would be evaporated into thin air. Alongside my brother and sister, I could never quite pick up everything they knew 'back home', no matter how many withering looks my father gives me

when he asks me to go over to that vendor to pick out a pumpkin, and I return with a shit one.

And yet, I have learned how to make Sri Lankan food that is both exciting and rewarding, and I know that by the end of this book, you will too.

Rambutan is the story of an immigrant kid in England trying to cook her way out of the profound sense of loss about the place her parents called home. It contains the best recipes from my mum, grandmother and all the other generous aunties and friends who gave them to me, sometimes modified a little to make them easier, or because they seemed more fun that way, but always retaining the ancient spirit of Sri Lankan cuisine.

Like Point Pedro market, this book is led by delicious fruit and vegetables, and half the recipes are vegan (see page 333 for a full list of the vegan and vegetarian recipes in the book). There are one or two rules that require a little effort, but the recipes are designed to deliver as much edible Sri Lankan joy as easily as possible. And at the same time, *Rambutan* is about my sense of the island, pieced together through a lifetime of travels, myths and memories.

———————

Warning: I have not shied away from the country's often painful history of war, colonial oppression, slavery, spice trading, poverty and proselytising in these pages. These chapters, too, are part of the story of our food. Rather than dimming the ingenuity and creativity of the island's cooks, in successive generations our ancestors created Sri Lanka's culinary songbook. They combined the Javanese, Malay, Indian, Arab, Portuguese, African, Dutch and British influences that came into the island with Tamil, Sinhalese and indigenous cooking. Using both ingredients native to the island (like cinnamon, curry leaves and cassava) as well as ingredients brought in by its visitors (like chillies, tomatoes and cashew nuts), the result has been a delicious, unique food tradition that is completely our own, and – if I do say so myself – one of the world's most unsung cuisines.

Today, a Sri Lankan table might include: crispy bowl-shaped hopper pancakes made of fermented rice and coconut milk, or fresh sambols made with green mango, raw carrots, or bright green chillies. There might be spicy red curries of roast aubergine or braised breadfruit cooked in coconut milk and smoky spices. There could be black curries, like pineapple or pork, cooked with toasted coconut, sugar and vinegar. There might be pillowy, crispy rotis; flaky, folded *parathas;* fragrant coconut rice porridges *pongal* and *kiri bath*; and epic sharing dishes, like a sticky chicken *buriani* or a complex *lamprais*. There should be lots of vegetables – perhaps a lemongrass and kale dal, a plantain curry, a cashew nut curry. There could be spicy fried things to drink with a beer or some tea – perhaps fried *vadai* doughnuts studded with shrimp, cumin, shallots and green chillies, or a nice crispy mutton roll with a dollop of hot sauce. There could be many of the island's famous seafood and fish dishes, like a turmeric fish curry, tamarind prawns or most revered of all, crab curry; plenty of meat dishes like pickled pork curry or black pepper beef or a fried chicken and *pol sambol* sandwich and a host of street snacks like spicy *malu* buns. And if you have a sweet tooth, you could finish off with a fruit and rose *falooda*; a *watalappan* jaggery and cardamom custard tart; some cashew-studded milk toffee, or to wash it all down, a cool drink or two.

I have been lucky to stuff my face with this food all my life, cooked for me, before I learned to cook it myself, by my mum, my grandmother and other absurdly hardworking Sri Lankans like them, almost always women. Sri Lanka's different communities – Tamil, Sinhala, Muslim, Burgher and others – and its different regions, all have different cooking styles and specialities, and over a lifetime of travelling back to Sri Lanka and eating at home, I have been able to sample almost all of them, and to learn their recipes. My family is Tamil, from Nelliady right up in the very northernmost tip of the Jaffna peninsula, and my mum's dad ran a set of shops in the Sinhala heartland of Hambantota, right down in the deep south. Which is like being from both John O'Groats and Land's End, and eating everything in between.

————

I don't think being Sri Lankan in itself qualifies you as being a great cook or an authority on Sri Lanka (you only need to pop into my brother's kitchen to be able to prove *that*). But I do think that learning to taste and cook Sri Lankan food the way I have, from all the Sri Lankans who have taught and loved me, has given me a kind of special perspective on the island and its food.

I was born in Coventry, England, in 1981 as the youngest child of my Sri Lankan immigrant parents. In 1983, Sri Lanka's long civil war between Tamil rebel fighters and the Sinhala majority government began, and over the next few years almost all my family fled. My grandmother moved into our house in England, to snore loudly in my room, after our house in Sri Lanka got bombed when I was about seven, and she and Mum together passed onto us their obsession with food.

Despite the fighting back in Sri Lanka, Dad was careful to teach us about the country, and against Mum's better judgement, during the height of the civil war, to take us there in our summer holidays. A poor farmer's son, Dad made sure we got buses and ate street food, trying to get us to be more like regular Sri Lankan kids than spoiled Westernised imports, while we sweated, scratched our mosquito bites and longed for cornflakes.

We got to spend summers in the hill country with our cousins, climbing guava trees and chasing butterflies. We went up to Jaffna before the war became too intense, to see our family and eat home-cooked food. We travelled down into the belly of the deep south to see my grandfather's old shops and the family members that still ran them, eating as we travelled, taking in the big cities of Colombo and Kandy, where Mum and Dad use to study and live.

When I went to university, my parents moved back to Sri Lanka and I began a tradition of going back each year, trying to forge my own adult relationship with the place, with my own friends and nights out and food experiences and opinions. And I began developing these recipes. It has not always been easy. In fact, it has been a universally maddening experience.

I've translated my grandmother's fastidious recipes from blurry iPhone scans of scribbled recipes in old exercise books. I have had instructions shouted down the phone by Mum from Sri Lanka, and I have been taught all over the island in the kitchens of friends of friends and aunties of aunties. Sri Lankans have almost no tradition of writing recipes down: cooking skills are passed down in families usually by watching and observing, so you can only learn by doing the same. Even then, in my experience, Sri Lankans tend to give you mysterious and quixotic instructions like 'cook it until it's cooked' or when you ask, 'should I put coconut milk in now?' respond 'yes, why not? Something new!' You get contradictory but declamatory statements like 'nobody puts egg in hoppers, who told you that?' and then 'yes, everybody in Sri Lanka puts eggs in hoppers, don't be stupid,' which have driven me close to giving up entirely.

This book is about paying homage to those amazing cooks, as well as demystifying some of the magic behind the food, and it contains a mix of traditional dishes and modern ones.

Sri Lankans frequently have different cooking habits that might not make sense in a typical kitchen in the UK. They cook meat and fish for longer than we do, probably because there's less refrigeration there and it's safer to nuke all germs with high heat, which makes it tougher than we're used to eating it. My mother's family all crack crab claws in their teeth and suck marrow from bones with gusto; they eat so expertly with their hands that serving food to be eaten with knives and forks requires a little adaptation. When I began cooking, I began switching things up a little bit: cooking meat more gently, experimenting with making an oil from prawn heads, making a jaggery custard in a silkier way, learning from books and cooking shows, and then from doing street food stalls and pop-ups in London with the help of chef friends.

Cooking Sri Lankan food has become a way for me to create a sense of home in London, to feed friends, cook at parties and introduce the people I love to the food I love. *Rambutan* isn't meant to be a comprehensive guide to every Sri Lankan dish out there, but is intended to be a mix of some of my reinventions and some treasured traditional dishes; part memoir, part manual, part travel guide. I hope that, as you cook the recipes yourself, you can step into my idea of Sri Lanka, one you can explore with the same wonder and excitement that I've had all my life.

9 Things About Sri Lankan Food

I have always loved the stories of Hindu mythology, with our allegorical tales of elephant heads, warrior-goddesses, sex positivity and divine flutes. The ancient idea of avatarams – or incarnations – has always seemed wonderful to me. For us, the same spirit could have the body of a fish, a tortoise, a boar, a woman, a playboy cowherd, a serious king, or – my favourite – a half-man, half-lion.

In Hindu mythology and in Sri Lanka, things often come in 9s: 9 fundamental emotions; the festival of 9 nights, Navaratri; 9 Sri Lankan provinces. And so there are 9 short essays in this book that each explain an idea in Sri Lankan cookery. I hope they will demystify or explain something useful to you about the cuisine: what's going on with 'tempers' for example? Do you really have to go out and find fresh curry leaves? Wait a minute, aren't many of these red curries identical? In a way, they form nine incarnations of the fundamental spirit of Sri Lankan cooking, and each idea comes with some stories and a recipe.

1. *Temper, Temper* (page 36)
Why do you sometimes fry spices at the start, or at the end of a curry?

2. *Curry Everything* (page 68)
A short guide to the main different styles of curry in Sri Lanka.

3. *Go And Get Fresh Curry Leaves* (page 100)
Why curry leaves are so important and what they taste like.

4. *The King of Sambols* (page 152)
What sambols are, and how to eat them.

5. *Puff Up Your Coconuts With Pride* (page 166)
Why I think freshly grated coconut is irreplaceable
(and how to crack your own).

6. *Eat Fruit With Salt And Chilli* (page 190)
Some of my favourite Sri Lankan fruits.

7. *Sri Lankan Muslim Street Food* (page 222)
The island's best street food, and the city it comes from.

8. *Shorteats Are Portable Snacks* (page 244)
How Sri Lankans eat at a party, and what a Tamil party really feels like.

9. *Cool Drinks* (page 314)
Some of my favourite drinks, and a little about cricket.

Sri Lanka

The North

Deep in ancient Tamil culture, Jaffna is both the name of a peninsula and a town. It is home to the roasted style of Sri Lankan curry powder used most in this book – which is the same red colour as its hard, red soil. The area is notorious for having the spiciest curries on the island, and the best mangoes, *karuthakolomban*. Largely Hindu, you can enjoy temple food like pongal and vadai doughnuts. With plenty of lagoon water, there is an abundance of crabs and shellfish, and the locals tend to cook with tamarind.

The East

The best surfing and among the most beautiful glimmering white beaches of the country, the east's food reflects its mix of Tamil and Muslim communities. It is the birthplace of the crispy, fried roti wonder that is kothu, and has deliciously inventive street food. Also known for great grilled meat and fish curries.

The West

Home to the metropolitan melting pot that is the capital, Colombo, with fancy restaurants, cool cafés and wonderful street food. It is the best place to try Burgher cuisine, like lamprais, Sri Lankan Malay delicacies like *puttu*, and Sri Lankan cocktails. It is also home to large Christian communities – and their great drinking snacks. With a shoreline of fantastic beaches and design, it includes the tropical modern architecture at Lunuganga.

The South

This is the Sinhalese heartland of Sri Lanka, the origins of celebratory coconut rice dish kiri bath, and a sour fisherman's fish preparation, *ambul thiyal*. It is known for its famously fantastic cricket, and Galle Fort Muslim cuisine, such as breadfruit and beef curry, and a unique spicy biriyani.

The Centre

Stuffed with ancient Buddhist monuments, including the great Lion Fortress Sigiriya, green tea plantations and the gorgeous mountains of Sri Lanka. The centre of the island is home to the Malayaha Tamil community, fertile juicy coconuts, wonderful fruit and vegetables, with rambutan, jackfruit and mangosteen trees, and more.

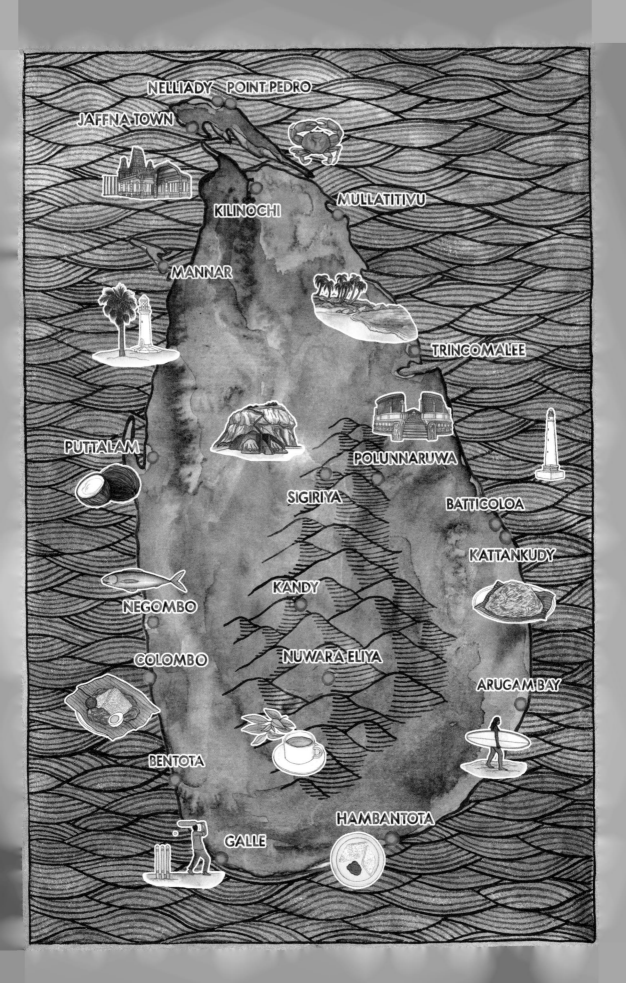

Essentials

This is a quick guide to equipment and ingredients you will need – plus some useful extras.

EQUIPMENT ESSENTIALS

The only special equipment I recommend for Sri Lankan cooking is:

A good electric spice grinder

Freshly toasted and ground spices are so earth-shatteringly great that you won't be able to go back to stale powders once you have tried them. You can use a coffee grinder (milling a few tablespoons of rice when you switch between the two cleanses it of smells) or I have a small spice grinder that lives on my kitchen counter that I got for £30. You can use a pestle and mortar instead, but it takes longer and is a lot more uneven. If you are making larger quantities, you can blitz in batches.

A coconut grater

These clip to your tabletop, they are around £10 to buy online (try coconutty.co.uk) and I personally think they look very cool on your shelf – like a hex was put on a tulip and now it's got evil metal teeth. Having one will mean you can produce freshly grated coconut in no time (see page 175). If you don't have one, frozen grated coconut is a reasonable substitute, but don't use desiccated (see page 166).

A hopper pan

You'll only need one if you want to make them – you can find them online at Amazon or Ceylon Supermart. If you can't find a non-stick hopper pan, season your pan by frying an egg in it before you try cooking any hoppers. You need one with a lid to cook your hoppers perfectly.

INGREDIENTS GUIDE

Most ingredients used in these recipes are available in your local supermarket or corner shop, especially if it's one of the better-stocked ones. For others – fresh coconuts, plantain, fresh curry leaves, pandan and Maldive fish – try to find a Sri Lankan, Indian or Pakistani shop near you. Caribbean, South East Asian or West African supermarkets often stock some of them too. Sometimes I find the owner may keep curry leaves behind the counter if they're not on display so don't be afraid to ask! If you're shopping online, you can also try Red Rickshaw, Ceylon Supermart and Amazon.

Fresh curry leaves

Fresh curry leaves are basically irreplaceable (see page 100 for more on why) and give cooking a wonderful zesty, aromatic flavour. Dried ones aren't a great substitute, but some friends have successfully grown a little plant at home, buying the seeds online. Curry leaves don't freeze very well, but they should last around a week in the fridge in an airtight container.

Cooking oils

Any neutral-tasting oil works well in Sri Lankan cooking. Traditional Sri Lankan cooking oils include cold-pressed untoasted sesame oil (known as 'gingelly' oil in the island) and coconut oil. Cold-pressed sesame oil is said to be very good for you, and has a high smoking point, but can be a little hard to find, so vegetable oil or sunflower oil are good substitutes. Coconut oil has a lower smoking point, but has a delicious sweet flavour, especially if you can get your hands on organic and Fairtrade coconut oil; the flavour is much richer and also it will support Sri Lankan farmers and their soil. For deep-frying, vegetable oil or sunflower oil is best.

Coconut milk

You can use either tinned coconut milk or coconut powder for coconut milk. For tinned, look for brands with a fat content of about fifteen per cent or higher – that's what will give you a thick, creamy milk and produce the desired glossy texture we are gunning for. Whether powdered or tinned, look for organic and Fairtrade brands that support farmers and workers, and ones that are free of guar gum or other stabilisers. I like Biona's, and their coconut milk comes from Sri Lanka. Give the tin a good shake before you use it.

Fresh root ginger

Fresh ginger has a kind of fiery, zesty warmth that you can't get from ground ginger. It's easy to peel with a teaspoon, and keeps in the fridge for a week or so.

Freshly grated coconut

You can't use desiccated for any of the recipes that call for fresh – unless you're toasting it for the black curries on pages 44 and 124 (for more on why, see page 166). You can use frozen coconut that has defrosted, if you can find it. Otherwise, there's a quick guide on page 175 to smacking open your own.

Tamarind

Tamarind is called 'puli' in Tamil which means sour, which makes sense because the delicious tangy pulp you get from the pods on a tamarind tree is wonderfully tart and acidic. You can buy it in two main ways: either as a tamarind block, or as shop-bought tamarind paste. The recipes in this book use the block, which you need to soak for 10 minutes and then squeeze out the liquid.

The shop-bought paste is generally not as good or consistent in flavour, but if you need to use it, use roughly 2 tablespoons for every golf ball-sized chunk of tamarind block.

Chillies

There are three types of chilli in this book: fresh green chillies, dried red chillies and chilli powder. For fresh green chillies, which give a kind of fresh, herby heat, I use a cayenne or serrano-type green chilli, as long and thin as my finger; they need to be kept in the fridge. They're sometimes called Indian green chillies, and they should be crisp and crunchy, with no black spots. For dried red chillies I use Kashmiri red chillies which have a great flavour and aren't too hot, but another hotter dried red chilli is fine to substitute if you prefer the heat. For either type, I don't remove the seeds, but you can if you are very sensitive to heat. For chilli powder, I use a hot one because it's usually used in my recipes to dial up the spiciness of a dish, but if you prefer, a mild one will be just as flavourful.

Pandan leaves

Long, straight pandan leaves are called *rampa* in Sri Lanka, and they can be a little tricky to hunt down here. They have a terrific warm, vanilla flavour that adds a layer of fragrance, tasting almost sweet when you use it. Buy them fresh from Asian supermarkets if you can find them, but if not, it's usually okay to leave them out entirely (wherever the recipe marks them 'optional').

Dried fish and shrimp

Sri Lanka has an ancient tradition of drying and smoking fish, which we call *karavaadu*. The most common type are the smoked, dried tuna flakes, called Maldive fish, or you can use bonito or finely shaved katsuoboshi flakes, which are essentially the same thing, from Japanese or Asian supermarkets. Dried shrimp is also used in a couple of dishes; you can use Thai or Vietnamese dried shrimp if you can find it. They're slightly bigger and crunchier than small Sri Lankan *kuniraal*, but they both produce great flavour.

Goroka paste

Goroka is a sour, yellow segmented fruit that looks a little like garlic. In the same family as mangosteen, the dried fruit is used in the south of Sri Lanka to add a fantastic punchy acidity and deep red colour to dishes. You can substitute *kokum* if you can get hold of that in South Asian shops, or tamarind, but neither are quite as good as the real thing.

Rice

We have about nineteen different kinds of rice in Sri Lanka. Dad is always trying to get me to smell them to distinguish the type and quality of rice when we buy it at the market together from a baffling array of buckets ('Um it smells like rice, Dad.' 'Stupid girl.'). Although I need the labels to know which is which, I know that if you can get hold of Sri Lankan rice, you are in luck. Look out for firmer long-grain rice like *suwandel*, which has an amazing milky flavour; starchier short-grain rice, like small pearl-shaped *muthu samba*, which has a delightful mouthfeel; and plump, more glutinous types of rice that are good for puddings and porridges. Among the island's many subtle varieties there are eight or nine different varieties of red rice, which have delicious nutty flavours, including *pachchaperumal*, black-red *kalu heenati*, and *kuruluthuda*. For most recipes I encourage you to experiment with any rice that excites you, but in these recipes I use two easy-to-find rice varieties: basmati and arborio.

Jaggery and jaggery syrup

Jaggery is the name for the Sri Lankan palm sugar you get when you tap palm trees and the sweet sap crystallises. There are different varieties: *palmyra* jaggery in the north which has a kind of full, deep flavour; *kithul* jaggery in the south that has a smoky quality; and coconut jaggery from all over the island, but especially the central region. It can come in hard blocks or in little discs, or you can buy it as a syrup. Jaggery has a complex, molasses-like flavour and rich dark brown colour. Muscovado sugar is a good substitute if you can't find it; but if you can, look out for Kimbula Kithul; it is a wonderfully flavoursome Sri Lankan brand, made the old-fashioned way.

Spices

You get the big bang of flavour from a spice when it is heated gently or freshly ground. This is the whole reason why you feel so happy when the waiter in an Italian restaurant offers you an enormous mill to grind pepper over your pasta right there: once ground, the oils are at their loveliest, but they soon begin to evaporate into the air, losing flavour. Buying ground spices means much of their fragrance and aroma might have long gone and they are stale.

So, my philosophy on spices is to buy them whole and, wherever possible, to cook with them whole. It saves time and effort, and the spices retain their power and punch much better that way. Ideally, you need about ten of them, but you can get them all in one go every two to three months and then you're all set. I go to an Asian shop and buy them up in packets of 300g or so, and then I decant a handful at a time into small jars and label the lids. You can keep the remaining packets in an airtight container in a cool, dark cupboard until you need to restock.

The ten most-used spices in this book are:

- Black pepper
- Cardamom pods (green)
- Coriander seeds
- Cinnamon sticks
- Cumin seeds
- Fennel seeds
- Black mustard seeds
- Nutmeg
- Turmeric (ground – the root is harder to find)
- Asafoetida (powdered – easier to use than resin)

There are, however, a number of dishes when powered spices are necessary because they can only emulsify together in that way: for red curries and black curries and for finishing off some other curries. For these I recommend making your own ground spices. It is so rewarding, and because you know when they were ground, you can make just enough for a month or so.

Sri Lankan (SL) curry powder

Since it's used in about half of the recipes in the book, it's worth making your own batch of Sri Lankan curry powder. It takes ten minutes and will keep in the fridge in a jar for three months, but feel free to scale the quantities up or down depending on your needs.

- 30g coriander seeds
- 15g cumin seeds
- 15g fennel seeds
- 15g black peppercorns
- 2 tbsp coconut or vegetable oil
- 8–10 fresh curry leaves
- 70g dried Kashmiri or medium hot red chillies
- ¼ tsp ground turmeric

Make sure the windows are open and the ventilation is on, because roasting the chillies will kick up an intense smell which carries through the house. In a dry pan over a low-medium heat, roast the coriander, cumin, fennel and black peppercorns for 1–2 minutes, stirring regularly, until they begin to be really fragrant, then pour them into a bowl. Add the oil to the pan, and cook the curry leaves and dried chillies for 2–3 minutes, stirring often. Remove from the heat and when cool, blitz in a spice grinder or mini food processor until fine – you can blitz it in batches if you need to. Stir in the turmeric, and put the whole lot in a jam jar.

Meat powder

This will keep in the fridge in a jar for two to three months.

- 4 whole cardamom pods
- 2 tsp fennel seeds
- 4 cloves
- 2.5cm piece of cinnamon stick
- ¼ nutmeg, grated

Crush the cardamom pods a bit with your fingers. Put a small pan over medium-low heat, and add the cardamom, fennel seeds and cloves, and roast for 1–2 minutes. Remove from the heat, tip into a spice grinder or mini food processor along with the nutmeg and cinnamon, and blitz until fine.

VEGETABLES & FRUIT

Potato white sodhi curry

Mum says that by the time she arrived to live in London on a soggy Tuesday in 1972, she had learned some English but no one seemed to be speaking it. The British accent she was hearing for the first time seemed to contain no starts or ends to any words. Floundering in a similar-sounding soup of noises, she was glad when slowly familiar phrases began to jump out at her. One of the first, to her surprise, was 'Yoganadhan' who seemed to dominate the news. Yoganadhan is a Tamil man's name – so who was *Yoganadhan*, Mum wondered? Why was he such a big deal in the UK?

Then, one day, Dad brought a white friend home for dinner who said that he was from *Yoganadhan*, and Mum was like, okay wait a minute, something is not hanging together. *Yoganadhan* it turned out was actually *Northern Ireland* and after they had all sorted that out, the friend was very happy to eat Mum's silky, mild *sodhi* potato curry, and tell her with really expert levels of appreciation about all the delicious varieties of potato you get in the United Kingdom and in Ireland. A *sodhi* or *kiri hodi* is a mild coconut milk broth of a curry, and potato *sodhi* is a lovely warming dish to make. I like to make this one with a waxy, nutty potato like Yukon Gold, or Cornish new potatoes, which lets the taste of the potatoes really shout. With just a little brightness from lime juice, curry leaves and fresh green chillies, it makes a golden, caramel-like curry, which I serve with rice and the parsley and lime sambol on page 176.

Serves 4

700g potatoes, peeled and cut into large chunks

Salt and black pepper

3 tbsp coconut or vegetable oil

1 large red onion, finely sliced

4 garlic cloves, finely sliced

10 fresh curry leaves

Optional: 5cm piece of pandan leaf

3cm piece of cinnamon stick

6 whole cardamom pods, lightly bashed in a pestle and mortar

3 green chillies

300ml coconut milk

1 tsp ground turmeric

½ lime

For the temper

1 tbsp coconut or vegetable oil

1½ tsp mustard seeds

1 tsp fenugreek seeds

1. Put the potatoes in a large pan of cold water with ½ teaspoon of salt. Bring to the boil and then lower the heat to a simmer for 10 minutes, or until the potatoes feel almost tender when you poke them with a fork. Drain and set aside.

2. In a separate large pan set over a medium heat, add 2 tablespoons of oil and the onion and let it cook, stirring regularly. When the onion is translucent, add the garlic, curry leaves and pandan leaf, if using, followed by the cinnamon, cardamom and green chillies, and stir for 1–2 minutes until fragrant.

3. Now add the drained boiled potatoes, coconut milk, another ½ teaspoon of salt and the turmeric and mix gently. Try not to break the potatoes into smaller pieces while mixing it through. Turn the heat down to a simmer, and let the potato curry cook over a low heat for 7–8 minutes, or until the potatoes are soft and the liquid is thickening up.

4. While it is simmering, make the temper. Place a separate clean frying pan over a medium-high heat and add the tablespoon of oil. When the oil is shimmering, add the mustard seeds and fenugreek seeds. Stir rapidly to avoid burning, for about 30 seconds–1 minute, until fragrant. Switch off the heat.

5. Dish up the potato curry, and pour the tempered spices and hot oil over it. Finish with a couple of generous grinds of black pepper and a squeeze of lime juice.

VEGETABLES & FRUIT

Roast pumpkin curry

This is the recipe for one of my favourite Sri Lankan white curries, roast pumpkin. It is a delicious simple vegetable dish, mild and fragrant. You can make it with any squash or pumpkin that has a dense, sweet texture; butternut squash, onion pumpkin, delica pumpkin and kabocha all work really well. Pumpkin curry is very traditional. I like to roast it first because lots of its natural sugars come through and it becomes sweet and nutty.

Serves 2–4

½ pumpkin (approx. 1 kg)

2 tbsp coconut or vegetable oil

Salt

½ tsp SL curry powder (see page 21) or 1 tsp chilli powder

1 medium red onion, peeled and thinly sliced

10 fresh curry leaves

3 garlic cloves, peeled and sliced

1 tsp mustard seeds

1 tsp cumin seeds

2 whole cardamom pods, lightly bashed in a pestle and mortar

200ml coconut milk

1½ tsp ground turmeric

4cm fresh root ginger, peeled and finely sliced or cut into matchsticks

1 lime

For the temper

1 tbsp coconut or vegetable oil

10 fresh curry leaves

1. First, roast the pumpkin. Preheat the oven to 220°C/Fan 200°C/Gas Mark 7. Scoop out the seeds with a spoon and discard. Cut the pumpkin into wedges around 2cm thick (leave the skin on). Place on a baking tray and toss in 1 tablespoon of oil and sprinkle with salt and ¼ teaspoon of the curry powder, mixing well. Roast for 20–25 minutes until tender and golden and starting to brown at the edges. Remove from the oven and leave to cool on the tray.

2. To make the curry, put a medium-sized wok or saucepan over a medium-high heat. Add the remaining tablespoon of oil, and when hot, fry the onion until translucent. Add the curry leaves and garlic, and about a minute later, add the mustard seeds, cumin seeds and cardamom. Fry the mixture for 1 minute, being careful not to burn the spices, stirring and adding a little more oil if necessary.

3. Pour in the coconut milk and add the turmeric and remaining ¼ teaspoon of curry powder, a teaspoon of salt and two pieces of the roasted pumpkin for flavour. Cook so that the curry is gently bubbling for 3–4 minutes, then turn off the heat.

4. Dish up by placing the roasted pumpkin wedges on a plate, and spooning the curry liquor over and around the pumpkin.

5. Heat up the oil for the temper in a small pan and add the curry leaves, letting them crisp up.

6. Scatter the tempered curry leaves over the pumpkin curry, add the fresh ginger and finish with squeezing over the lime.

Roasted aubergine red curry

Traditionally, this is made with fried slices of aubergine, but tossing them in a little oil and roasting them in the oven gives just as good results and is much easier. This recipe is spicy and gets its lovely red colour from smoky roasted red curry powder, as well a couple of good tomatoes for a little acidity. Don't skimp on the coconut milk: it cuts through the heat to give the curry a silky mouthfeel and plenty of thick curry liquor that you can mop up with roti or rice. It will also gently cook the garlic, which is a big element in this curry. I like to temper this one with curry leaves and it makes it a pungent, spicy, soft, delicious dish.

Serves 2

2 medium aubergines, cut into 1cm-thick discs

1½ tsp salt

3 tbsp coconut or vegetable oil

1 red onion, peeled and finely sliced

10 fresh curry leaves

1 tbsp sliced garlic

1 tbsp sliced ginger

250ml water

2 tomatoes, roughly chopped

2 tbsp SL curry powder (see page 21)

50ml coconut milk

1 lime

1. To roast your aubergines, preheat the oven to 240°C/Fan 220°C/Gas Mark 9. In a large bowl, mix the aubergine slices with ½ teaspoon of salt. Line two baking trays with baking parchment and put a generous tablespoon of oil on to each one. Toss or mix lightly with your fingers to coat the salted aubergine in the oil and arrange the slices so they are flat next to each other. Bake for 30–45 minutes, until golden and cooked through, then remove and set aside to cool.

2. To make the curry, fry the onion in the remaining tablespoon of coconut oil over a medium heat until soft. Then add the curry leaves, and after 30 seconds – when sizzling and bright green – add the garlic and ginger. Add a teaspoon of salt, the water, tomatoes and SL curry powder. Cover with a lid and turn the heat down to a simmer. After 5–6 minutes, add the roasted aubergine slices and cook, without stirring too much, for 2–3 minutes.

3. Finally, gently stir through the coconut milk, and cook through for 2–3 minutes. Serve with a generous squeeze of lime.

VEGETABLES & FRUIT

Temper, Temper

When my sister turned thirteen, she cropped her hair like our idol Princess Diana and we got MTV. I did everything she did, and so we sang songs nonstop in the car which must have driven our parents nuts. It meant at five years old I was shouting '*shamon!*' at unpredictable times, and according to Mum, doing Tina Turner-inspired dances for anyone who would watch me.

Wise-cracking male friends of my parents noticed these developments in my sister and started to ask her – never my brother – 'What can you cook? Rice? An egg? Dal?' before collapsing into insulting giggles. Mocking her for being too Westernised to know even the most basic of dishes, she would roll her eyes, admit she couldn't cook dal, and go back to listening to *Whitney* on her Walkman. All cultures contain sexists, but each culture gets their sexists in their own unique ways. Because we were between two cultures, we got a strange hybrid. Tina, Whitney and Lady Di were getting harassment and abuse. And at home, some of the friends who visited us felt they could be mean to us while we were still children.

From all this, we can learn three things. One: listen to Whitney, not to gross dudes. Two: hair is freedom. And three: Sri Lankan dal, or *parippu* as it is called in both Tamil and Sinhala, is considered an idiot-proof recipe, the hardest to mess up of the Sri Lankan repertoire, and one of the first dishes a young cook learns to make.

My sister is now a doctor, a mum of three, she has her own swimming pool and she's a fantastic cook. She didn't let the sexist trolls get her down on dal and you shouldn't either. It might be child's play, but Sri Lankan dal is one of the most delicious and most nutritious of our island dishes, and one of the best to experiment with and adapt.

Whatever you put into it, the heart of *parippu's* deliciousness lies in the temper, an easy and essential Sri Lankan cooking technique that layers up flavour and gives a humble bowl of cheap boiled red lentils complexity and depth. In Sri Lanka and all over India, a temper is kind of last-second play, added in the final moments of whatever you're cooking, and which transforms the game entirely. In this case, you will have been simmering a pan of lentils for a while, and it will all smell and look and taste lacklustre and you will be feeling worried and underwhelmed, until the final minutes of cooking – during which you add the temper.

To make a temper, you take out a second pan, heat up a little oil with whole spices and curry leaves, and let everything sizzle and crisp up for a couple of minutes. That's it! It is unbelievably low-effort, high-reward cooking, for when you stir this hot fragrant oil – spices and all – into your cooked lentils it will be magically and completely transformed. You can do it with any curry you make, infusing the contents of your pan with spicy deliciousness.

This last-minute step is a kind of flavour re-up, where a little hot oil acts to brighten and sharpen the noise of the spices, curry leaves, onions and other aromatics before serving.

The point of the temper is this: typically, if you are cooking anything for any length of time, much of the brightness of the base of the curry (which might variously include curry leaves, green chillies, onions, spices, garlic, ginger and the like) get sort of dulled down, rendering them the quiet backing vocals for whatever you're cooking. In the recipe on the next page, and the others that use a temper, this last-minute step is a kind of flavour re-up, where a little hot oil acts to brighten and sharpen the noise of the spices, curry leaves, onions and other aromatics just before serving.

I've included tempers in this book in all the recipes I think need them. There's usually an order to the temper because I am scared of things burning. It's unorthodox, but this is what I have found works: add the onions first, then aromatics (curry leaves or green chillies or ginger or lemongrass or pandan leaves), then the whole spices, and if you're tempering garlic, that's the last because it burns so quickly. I never temper with ground spices as they burn too easily and are so delicate, but other people do – they only need a few seconds. You can try adjusting the temper you make – perhaps with slightly different spices or different oils – and see how it rebalances and changes the dal or whatever else you are cooking.

Coconut dal with kale

In war or other times of national crisis, dal is rationed out by the Sri Lankan government as one of life's essentials. Cooked with lemongrass and, if you can get it, pandan leaf (which adds a warm, vanilla flavour) as well as coconut milk, turmeric, curry leaves, garlic and lime, this dal is distinctively light and restorative, and is worlds away from its Indian counterparts like black dal makhani made with cream, or tarka dal made with butter. There is no other dal quite like it, and I encourage you to try adding roasted squash or pumpkin or roasted sweet potato. This one is one of the ways my mum would cook it when she was too short on time to make a separate kale curry. She'd simply stir the leaves in very close to the end of cooking so they retained their bright green flavour and nutrients.

Serves 4

For the dal

300g red split lentils or toor lentils

3 garlic cloves, peeled and halved lengthways

1 lemongrass stalk, bruised

1½ tsp salt, or to taste

½ tsp SL curry powder (see page 21)

Optional: 4cm piece of pandan leaf

1 tsp ground turmeric

100ml coconut milk

3–4 small handfuls of kale (approx. 200g)

½ lime

Optional: 1 tsp chilli flakes

For the temper

1 tbsp coconut or vegetable oil

1 small red onion, peeled and finely sliced

10 fresh curry leaves

½ tsp mustard seeds

½ tsp cumin seeds

1. Pour the lentils into a saucepan and rinse loosely under the tap then drain well. Cover the lentils with water until they're submerged by about 5cm. Add the garlic, lemongrass, salt, SL curry powder and pandan leaf, if using. Bring to a boil over a medium-high heat.

2. Skim off any scum and turn the heat down, so the lentils are simmering. Add the turmeric and simmer for 12–15 minutes until the lentils are tender. There's no need to stir here, you can basically forget about them except to check they're not bubbling too vigorously.

3. Drain off about eighty per cent of the liquid. You don't want it to be too wet and soupy because you're adding coconut milk.

4. Stir in coconut milk and kale and allow to simmer gently for 2–3 minutes until the kale is bright green. Take out a little kale to try; it shouldn't taste raw but should be soft with a firm bite. Remove from the heat and transfer to your serving bowl.

5. In a small frying pan, make the temper. Heat the oil over a medium-high heat (careful, it will splutter a little). When hot, add the onion and cook, stirring occasionally for 3–5 minutes until it starts to turn golden brown. Add the curry leaves, mustard seeds and cumin seeds and cook for a couple of minutes until the curry leaves are bright green. Be careful not to burn the spices!

6. Pour the whole temper, oil included, onto the cooked dal. Squeeze lime over it and sprinkle over the chilli flakes, if using, just before serving.

Fried sweet plantain curry

Plantains come thick and fast in Sri Lanka. You often see enormous bunches of green ones beside their cute little brothers, small yellow bananas, hanging in shops or by the side of the road. My friend Lara's mum, Ingrid, is from Trinidad, and when Lara and I used to live together in London, I learned about letting your plantains get so ripe the skins go almost completely black; so ripe that you think surely these are off and I must throw them away. Ingy and Lara taught me that it's only from frying super-ripe plantain in hot oil that you get that crispy on the outside and sweet, gooey inside deliciousness you find in plantain cooking from all over the islands. I curried them like we would in Sri Lanka, with a little coconut milk, whole spices and curry leaves, and the result was a stone-cold banger, a kind of love child of Trinidad and Sri Lanka – and it tastes very lovely with fresh pol rotis (page 218).

Serves 2–3

1–2 tbsp coconut or vegetable oil

2 ripe, almost completely black plantains, peeled and sliced

1 red onion, peeled and finely sliced lengthways

2 garlic cloves, peeled and sliced

10 fresh curry leaves

2 green chillies, slit lengthways

1 tsp mustard seeds

1 tsp cumin seeds

½ tsp coriander seeds

1 tsp salt, or to taste

1 lemongrass stalk, bruised

100ml coconut milk

½ tsp SL curry powder (see page 21)

½ tsp ground turmeric

1. Start off by shallow-frying the plantain. Get ready by setting aside a large baking sheet with a wire rack on top to place the fried slices when they're done. Heat 1 tablespoon of oil in a frying pan over a medium-high heat. When hot, lower in the plantain slices and fry until golden brown, then flip them over and fry on the other side. This should take around 30 seconds on each side. Allow them to dry on the rack so they stay nice and crispy.

2. To make the curry, fry the onion in the same pan you cooked the plantain using the remaining oil, over a medium-high heat. When it starts to brown, add the garlic, and about 30 seconds later add the curry leaves, chillies, mustard seeds, cumin seeds, coriander seeds, salt and the lemongrass. Stir-fry for about 1 minute until fragrant, then add the coconut milk, SL curry powder and turmeric. Cook over a high heat for 3–5 minutes so that the coconut milk has had time to thicken slightly.

3. To plate up, mix two-thirds of the fried plantain into the curry, and dish out the whole curry into a bowl. Finish by arranging the remaining fried plantains on top so they remain crispy.

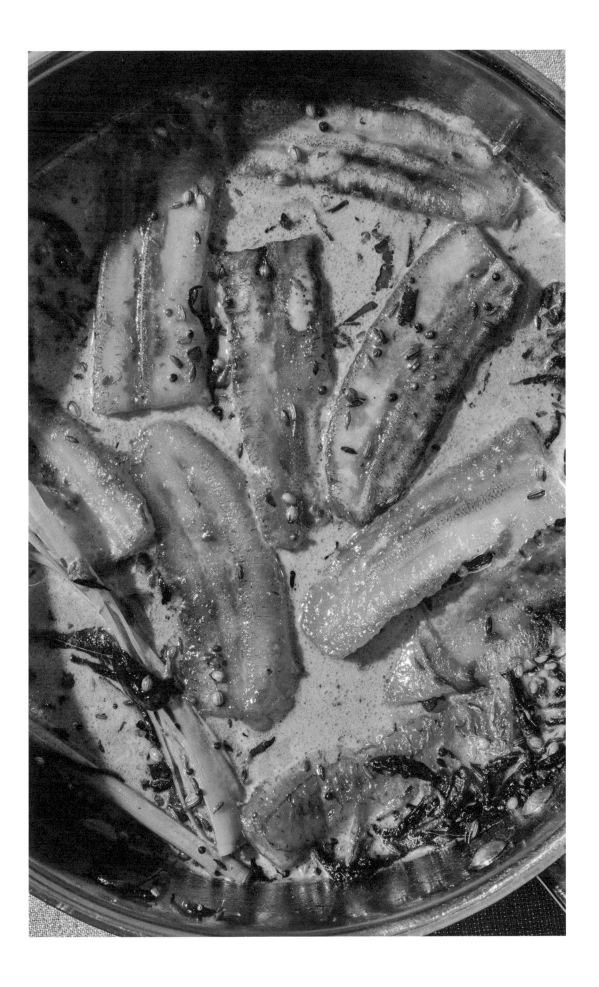

Black coconut pineapple curry

Sri Lankans curry fruit as an everyday event, and loads of it: mango, pineapple, sweet plantain, a tart tropical fruit called *ambarella*, jackfruit, breadfruit. Here, the resulting pineapple curry is spicy, tart and sweet, with a kind of jammy consistency. I like to start off by getting the pineapple a little blackened in a hot pan because it caramelises up so beautifully and adds flavour.

Pineapple curry is delicious in all its incarnations, but my favourite is black pineapple curry, a dish I first had at that lovely oasis of tropical modernism that is Lunuganga, hidden in the trees and gardens of west Sri Lanka. In the old house of our most celebrated architect, the great genius that was Geoffrey Bawa, I surveyed his extremely cool windows, his delicate frangipani trees, his fluffy-tailed mongeese and ate this profoundly delicious curry, apparently one of his faves. 'Black' curries or more properly 'black coconut' – *kalu pol* in Sinhala – is a delicious style of Sri Lankan curry, whose blackness comes from three sources: you start off with earthier, darker spices of the Sri Lankan repertoire; you then toast them so well they go almost black; and, finally, you separately toast some desiccated or fresh coconut with some plain white rice and grind it up, which adds a lovely smoky flavour. There is no coconut milk in this dish and its brightness comes from vinegar; with the natural sweetness of pineapple it makes for a sweet-and-sour wonder.

Serves 2–4

For the black spice mix

5 or 6 fresh curry leaves

Optional: 5cm piece of pandan leaf

2.5cm piece of cinnamon stick

3 whole cardamom pods, lightly bashed in a pestle and mortar

1 tsp coriander seeds

1 tsp black peppercorns

1 ½ tsp mustard seeds

1 tsp cumin seeds

½ tsp fenugreek seeds

½ tsp fennel seeds

5 or 6 cloves

1. First, make the black spice mix (which you can do as much as a few days ahead if you like). In a medium frying pan over a medium heat, dry toast the curry leaves and pandan leaf, if using, for 2–3 minutes, stirring as you go, until they begin to turn brown. Add the cinnamon, cardamom, coriander and black peppercorns and toast it all, stirring every so often, for about 1 minute. Now add the more delicate spices that need less time: the mustard seeds, cumin seeds, fenugreek seeds, fennel seeds and cloves. Keep toasting and stirring for a further 1–2 minutes, by which time everything should be smelling fragrant and toasty, but not burnt. Switch off the heat, spoon it all into a bowl and leave aside to cool. When cool, blitz in a spice grinder or mini food processor until fine.

2. Next, make the toasted rice coconut powder, which will give the curry its dark colour and smoky, toasty flavour. Wipe down your frying pan and set it over a medium heat. Pour the rice into it, stirring it every few seconds so it toasts evenly – this should take 4–5 minutes until it starts to go golden. Then, add the desiccated or fresh coconut and keep stirring every so often for about 5 minutes, until the coconut and rice grains are golden brown, which means they are toasted. You don't want anything fully black or burnt! Spoon into a bowl and leave to cool. When cool, blitz in a mini food processor to a coarse powder consistency.

Continued overleaf

For the pineapple curry

25g rice (I use basmati or a short grain, whatever I have in the house)

25g desiccated coconut or freshly grated coconut (see page 175)

2 tbsp coconut or vegetable oil

1 pineapple, peeled and sliced into chunks about 2.5cm wide (discard the core)

1 medium red onion, peeled and finely sliced

4 green chillies, sliced

4cm fresh root ginger, peeled and finely sliced

20 fresh curry leaves

Optional: 5cm piece of pandan leaf

1 heaped tbsp black spice mix (see previous page)

1 tbsp apple cider or coconut vinegar

3. To make the curry, heat the oil in a medium frying pan over a medium-high heat. After a minute, when the oil is nice and hot, add the pineapple chunks to the pan, letting them go golden brown on one side, which will take around 4–5 minutes, shaking the pan often. Spoon the pineapple onto a plate. Turn the heat down to medium, add the onion, and let it cook, stirring occasionally so it doesn't stick to the pan. After 3–4 minutes, when translucent, add the green chillies, ginger, curry leaves and pandan leaf, if using. Stir-fry for 2–3 minutes until the curry leaves are bright green.

4. Add all the pineapple, and any juices, to the pan. Then add 1 heaped tablespoon of black spice mix (if you have any excess, it will keep in an airtight container for up to a month), the vinegar and just enough water to half-submerge the pineapple. Stir well to mix together and bring to a gentle boil, then lower the heat and leave to simmer for 20 minutes, with the lid slightly ajar, stirring 2–3 times throughout. Serve hot.

Breadfruit curry

Breadfruit really does taste like toasty, freshly baked bread. Green and spiky on the outside and white and fleshy on the inside, it comes from the same family as the notoriously funky durian fruit and jackfruit. When you crack open the skin, the insides are gloriously fleshy with a single white stone in the middle; the smell like someone has smashed bread pudding into a tropical green body. Although it's hard to find good-quality, fresh breadfruit in the UK, tinned breadfruit cooks beautifully in curries, and is widely available in the UK because it is eaten in the Caribbean and in West Africa, too. This is a mild, coconutty, light curry for it.

Serves 2–3

2 tbsp coconut or vegetable oil

1 red onion, peeled and finely sliced

3 garlic cloves, peeled and chopped

5 fresh curry leaves

4 whole cardamom pods, lightly bashed in a pestle and mortar

½ stick of cinnamon

1 tsp fennel seeds

Optional: 5cm piece of pandan leaf

2 x 400g tins of breadfruit, drained and cut into large chunks, roughly 5cm

1 tsp salt, or to taste

½ tsp SL curry powder (see page 21)

1 tsp ground turmeric

150ml coconut milk

½ lime

For the temper

1 tbsp coconut or vegetable oil

10 fresh curry leaves

2 green chillies, sliced

½ tsp mustard seeds

½ tsp cumin seeds

1. Get a saucepan or wok over a medium-high heat and add the oil. When hot, cook the onion for 4–5 minutes, until translucent. Add the garlic, curry leaves, cardamom, cinnamon, fennel seeds and pandan leaf, if using. Cook for 3–4 minutes, stirring sparingly just to stop anything from sticking, until the curry leaves are bright green and the spices smell fragrant.

2. Add the breadfruit and salt to the mix, along with the SL curry powder, turmeric and enough water to almost cover the breadfruit. Lower to a low-medium heat and cook, stirring, for 8–10 minutes.

3. Pour in the coconut milk, bring up to a gentle bubble and then lower the heat to a simmer and cook for 5–6 minutes, stirring, until the sauce has thickened and reduced.

4. To make the temper, heat the oil in a separate pan and, when hot, add the curry leaves, which should crisp up and go bright green, along with the green chillies. When crispy, add the mustard seeds and cumin seeds and stir so that nothing burns. Cook for 30 seconds–1 minute, until the mustard seeds release their aroma, then pour all the hot oil, curry leaves and the seeds onto the curry. Finish with a squeeze of lime juice.

Green mango curry

Sour green mangoes make for a sweet, sour, spicy curry, which has a sticky, jam-like texture with just a little coconut milk. This curry is sort of a hybrid between a red curry and a white curry (see page 72), and comes out a kind of glowing amber colour. I think the secret to this dish is a delicious mustard-heavy temper – those little bullets pack pungent flavour and heat into the curry – as well as cinnamon which gives it sweetness. If the mango flesh is soft enough to easily sink a finger into, it's too ripe. The mango skin is kept on, so that it holds the mango flesh together as it softens; but you don't have to eat the skin when you dig into the curry. Keep the seed, it goes in the curry and will be great fun for someone to fish out and eat.

Serves 4

1 tbsp coconut or vegetable oil

½ red onion, peeled and finely sliced

5 fresh curry leaves

2 garlic cloves, peeled and chopped

1 tsp cumin seeds

½ tsp fennel seeds

3 green (unripe) mangoes, sliced into 2cm wedges

1 tsp salt, or to taste

300ml water

½ tsp SL curry powder (see page 21)

3cm piece of cinnamon stick

¼ tsp ground turmeric

1 tsp caster sugar

¼ tsp white vinegar

100ml coconut milk

½ lime

For the temper

1 tbsp coconut or vegetable oil

10 fresh curry leaves

1 tbsp mustard seeds

1. Heat the oil in a wok or medium-sized saucepan over a medium heat. When hot, fry the onion for 4–5 minutes, until soft and starting to go golden. Add the curry leaves and after 1 minute, when they are soft and bright green, add the garlic, cumin seeds and fennel seeds. Fry the spices and curry leaves for 1–2 minutes more, stirring occasionally, until the spices are fragrant.

2. Add the mango slices, salt, water, SL curry powder, cinnamon, turmeric, sugar and vinegar and bring to a simmer, making sure everything is mixed together but not stirring too much. Turn the heat down to simmer for 8–9 minutes. You want the mango to be soft and cooked through but not mushy. Taste, and adjust the sugar, salt and vinegar to what feels right depending on how tart your mangoes are: it should be tart with a little sweetness, and be jammy and spicy.

3. To finish the curry, stir in the coconut milk, mixing it just enough to combine, and cook through for 2–3 minutes, keeping it on a gently simmering heat. Take the pan off the heat and dish up into a serving bowl or dish.

4. Finally for the temper, heat a separate small frying pan over a medium-high heat. Add the oil and, when hot, add the curry leaves, which should crisp up and go bright green. When crispy, add the mustard seeds and stir so that nothing burns. Cook for about 30 seconds–1 minute, until the mustard seeds release their aroma, then pour all the hot oil, curry leaves and the seeds onto the mango curry. Finish with a squeeze of lime juice. Serve hot.

Coconut milk greens curry

There are more than 110 native varieties of spinach-like greens in Sri Lanka. My great-uncle came by the house once and gave me a bouquet of *ponnangani* from the garden as if it were roses. You get moringa leaves, which are slightly bitter, red amaranth or *pulicha keerai*, and flavoursome *ara keerai*. There are hundreds of recipes, but this is the most common and my favourite. It is a wet, fragrant mix of spinach – or any greens, such as chard, kale, spring greens – cooked in thick coconut milk, turmeric, black pepper and cumin. It's very simple and healthy. I like to cook it quite quickly, so the greens retain some chlorophyll and nutrients.

Serves 4

2 tbsp coconut or vegetable oil

1 red onion, peeled and finely sliced

3 garlic cloves, peeled and sliced

1 tsp ground turmeric

1 tsp cumin seeds

Salt and black pepper

3 green chillies, sliced

4 handfuls of baby spinach or kale, washed (approx. 400g)

200ml water

200ml coconut milk

½ lime

1. Heat the oil in a wok or frying pan over a medium heat. Add the onion and garlic, stirring occasionally until the onion is translucent and starting to brown at the edges. Sprinkle in the turmeric, cumin, about a teaspoon of salt, and the green chillies. Give it a good mix, then cook for about 1 minute until the spices are fragrant.

2. Add the spinach, the water and the coconut milk, and cook with the lid on over a high flame for 3–7 minutes, depending on what greens you are using (baby spinach cooks faster than kale). You want them to be bright green but soft when you bite into it.

3. Remove from the heat, taste the curry and adjust with salt if needed. Plate up and finish with a generous squeeze of lime and a couple of generous grinds of black pepper.

Roast beetroot dry varai curry

Beetroot is thought to have been brought over by European colonisers sometime in the 1700s, and is a common, everyday vegetable. Earthy and sweet, beets take to Sri Lankan spices really well. There are so few ingredients in this fragrant, quick, spicy delicious dish that each one matters. I like to roast the beets in the oven first, which isn't a traditional step, but it brings out their natural sugars and caramelises them a little at the edges. Using a good organic coconut oil makes a big difference for this one. A generous squeeze of lime just before serving brings it to life.

Serves 2–3

A bunch of 5 or 6 beetroot (approx. 500g)

3 or 4 tbsp coconut or vegetable oil

1½ tsp salt, or to taste

Optional: 1 tsp white mung dal or chana dal

15 fresh curry leaves

1 tsp mustard seeds

½ tsp fenugreek seeds

½ tsp cumin seeds

2 green chillies, sliced

50g freshly grated coconut (see page 175)

½ lime

1. Preheat the oven to 200°C/Fan 180°C/Gas Mark 6. Peel the beetroot and slice into 1–2cm thick wedges. Place on a baking tray and coat in 2 tablespoons of oil and ½ teaspoon of salt. Roast for about 20 minutes, until tender and they can be pierced easily with a knife.

2. If you want to include fried lentils, soak the lentils in a small bowl of water for 10 minutes. When soaked, drain and spoon out the lentils onto a tea towel or some kitchen roll, and pat well to them dry. Heat 1 tablespoon of oil in a small frying pan on medium-high and when shimmering, add the lentils. Stir-fry for 2 minutes, until nutty and golden on all sides. Spoon the lentils onto kitchen roll to dry.

3. Heat the remaining 1 tablespoon of oil in a medium frying pan over a high heat. When hot, add the curry leaves, mustard seeds, fenugreek seeds and cumin seeds. After about 1 minute, when the mustard seeds have started to pop and the curry leaves are looking crispy, add the green chillies and the freshly grated coconut, as well as the fried lentils if using. Add the remaining salt and stir-fry rapidly for 1–2 minutes, until everything is nicely coated. Serve, finished with a squeeze of lime.

Burnt cabbage varai

This is a slight twist on a traditional cabbage *mallung* or *varai*. Cabbage develops a lovely nutty flavour and makes for a pretty, delicate dish if you slice it into wedges and blacken it in a hot pan. You then cover the lot with a traditional fragrant, crunchy mix of fried lentils, coconut, curry leaves, chilli flakes and some tempered whole spices.

Serves 2–3

2 tbsp urad dal, rinsed and soaked for 10 minutes

2 tbsp coconut or vegetable oil, plus 1 tsp

2 tsp black mustard seeds

1 tsp cumin seeds

1 green chilli, sliced

10 fresh curry leaves

½ onion, peeled and sliced

1 tsp ground turmeric

50g freshly grated coconut (see page 175)

1 small (250g) hispi or pointed spring cabbage, cut into wedges around 3cm at the widest part

½ tsp chilli flakes

1. Drain and dry the lentils very well with a tea towel or kitchen roll. Heat 1 tablespoon of oil in a frying pan over a medium heat. When the oil is shimmering, add the dried lentils, mustard seeds, cumin seeds, green chilli and curry leaves. Fry for 4–5 minutes, until the lentils are golden. Spoon the mixture out into a small bowl and set aside for later.

2. Add the onion to the pan, with another tablespoon of oil. Fry for 4–5 minutes, until soft and translucent. Add the turmeric and grated coconut, cook for 30 seconds or so, stirring occasionally, then add to the bowl with lentils and spices.

3. Set a clean frying pan over a high heat and add the 1 teaspoon of oil. When the oil is shimmering, add the cabbage wedges to the pan. Do not move them for 2 minutes; keep cooking until blackened. Then flip them over and repeat the process, ensuring the stalk is cooked through.

4. Plate the cabbage, and spoon over the spiced onion-crunchy lentil mix. Garnish with chilli flakes.

Squash sambar spicy wet curry

Sri Lankans who have emigrated tend to have something of a little sister complex when it comes to India. No, we're not Indian, we have to tell people every day.

When my sister was eight, she came home from school one day to my parents and announced we had got it all wrong. She was, in fact, an Indian. Apparently, Miss Bartlett – a well-meaning and very nice teacher at her school – had insisted on this conclusion that afternoon, between playing the recorder and Tidy Up Time. I guess Miss Bartlett hadn't heard of Sri Lanka and my sister had tried to speak up, but she was eight and Miss Bartlett was the boss. So Vathany arrives home to the Supreme Court of Dad to make the announcement, and Dad promptly overturns the decision.

'I am, I am, Daddy, I'm Indian! She's the teacher! She said it!' My parents delight in telling people this story, complete with a very sad impression of my sister, who apparently had little fat tears rolling down her face.

'I don't care who said it! I'm not Indian and also you are not Indian and that's the end of it!' Dad shouted back.

My sister was, apparently, inconsolable but she has happily since got over it. And if there was any lingering doubt in your mind, so should you.

To just clear it up once and for all, Sri Lankans are not Indians, the country was never colonised by India, and has never been a part of India. The kingdoms that are now Sri Lanka, formerly Ceylon, were governed separately to the kingdoms that are now India for 450 years of European colonisation, until the two nations separately achieved independence from the British Empire in 1948 and 1947.

That said, there are some links between the nations, most strongly between the Tamil people of Sri Lanka and the people in the southern state of Tamil Nadu, India. There were once kingdoms that included some of South India and Northern and Eastern Sri Lanka, which is why there is some commonality. Although the 4,000-year-old Sri Lankan Tamil community is distinct, with our own dialect, our own unique culture and history, we watch South Indian movies, we listen to their songs, and there is a crossover in some of our dishes.

And this is one of the best crossover hits. This is a Sri Lankanised sambar, that is a delicious mixed tangy vegetable and lentil stew. Unlike its Indian predecessor, it is made with Sri Lankan curry powder and coconut milk. You can chuck any veg you have lying around into it; it is very forgiving and light and nutritious. It's great with rice or, best of all, with dosas (page 236).

Ingredients & method overleaf

Serves 4

200g red lentils

150g pumpkin, peeled and chopped into 2.5cm cubes

150g carrots, peeled and chopped into 2.5cm pieces

150g cauliflower, cut into florets

2 golf ball-sized pieces of tamarind block, soaked in 120ml warm water for 10 minutes

3 green chillies, finely sliced

2 garlic cloves, peeled and chopped

1 tsp SL curry powder (page 21)

1 tsp salt, or to taste

½ tsp ground turmeric

125ml coconut milk

For the temper

2 tbsp coconut or vegetable oil

10–12 fresh curry leaves

1 tsp cumin seeds

1 tsp black mustard seeds

1. Pour the lentils into large pan and rinse loosely under the tap then drain well. Add the vegetables to the lentils and cover in 1–2cm water. Place over a medium heat and cook for 15–20 minutes. If the water starts to boil, turn it down to a simmer. Test a carrot to see if it's ready – you want them cooked through but still with a slight bite, so they don't turn to mush in your mouth.

2. Squeeze the tamarind with your fingers, then discard the seeds and skin, leaving behind the pulpy water. Reduce the heat and add the tamarind water, green chillies, garlic, SL curry powder, salt and turmeric to the pan. Mix well and simmer for 5–7 minutes. Add a little water if it looks like it's drying out; it should have a stew consistency.

3. Add the coconut milk and let it cook for 3–4 minutes, stirring it through. Transfer to a serving bowl while you make the temper.

4. Heat the oil in a small frying pan over a medium heat. Add the curry leaves, cumin seeds and mustard seeds and fry gently for 2–3 minutes, until the seeds start to pop and the curry leaves are crispy and green. Pour the whole lot into the sambar.

Carrot, parsnip and peas avial curry

This is a mild, simple, coconut broth, which gives rise to almost laksa-like feelings.
My grandmother used to make it as a quick, light side dish to ensure we were getting
in our vegetable quotient. You can use any combination of vegetables, but this works
particularly well to provide a balance of creamy starchiness from the parsnips, the
brightness of the carrots, and the sweet pop! of peas. It also works well with frozen
veg if you have some stashed in the freezer. The dish's deliciousness lies in its temper.
I use cardamom, mustard seeds and cumin for this one as it's warm and fragrant,
and the carrots especially seem to really like it.

Serves 4

2 tbsp coconut or vegetable oil

1 red onion, peeled and
finely sliced

5 fresh curry leaves

225ml water

2 parsnips, peeled and chopped
into sticks

½ tsp ground turmeric

½ stick of cinnamon

1 lemongrass stalk, bruised

2 green chillies, sliced

2 medium carrots, peeled
and sliced

200g peas

200ml coconut milk

Salt

1 lime

For the spice mix

¾ tsp coriander seeds

2 whole cardamom pods, lightly
bashed in a pestle and mortar

¼ tsp fennel seeds

For the temper

1 tbsp coconut or vegetable oil

5 fresh curry leaves

½ tsp cumin seeds

½ tsp mustard seeds

1 or 2 whole cardamom pods,
lightly bashed in a pestle
and mortar

1. First, make the spice mix. Put the coriander seeds, cardamom
and fennel seeds in a small dry pan over a medium heat. Stir for
3–4 minutes until fragrant. Let cool, then put in a spice grinder
or mini food processor and blitz until fine.

2. To make the curry, heat the oil in a medium saucepan or wok
over a medium-high heat. Fry the onion for 5–6 minutes, until just
translucent; it's nice to have some bite to the onions too. Add the
curry leaves and cook until the leaves are bright green. Add the
water, parsnips, spice mix, turmeric, cinnamon, lemongrass and
green chillies. Stir, and then allow to cook for 10 minutes.

3. Add the carrots and peas, and cook for a further 10 minutes.
You want the vegetables to still have a little bit of bite.

4. Stir in the coconut milk and a little salt and cook through for
4–5 minutes.

5. In a small frying pan, make the temper. Heat the oil over a
medium-high heat and, when sizzling, add the curry leaves,
cumin seeds, mustard seeds and cardamom. Cook for about a
minute, being careful not to burn anything, then pour the whole
lot, oil and all, onto the mix. Finish with a generous squeeze of
lime and serve.

Cucumber and turmeric white curry

This is a cooling, mild, silky Sinhalese curry, especially good on a hot day. The cucumber is cooked gently, retaining some bite and crunchiness. It tastes best when peeled of its thin green rind, so that the curry contains only the white flesh and the seeds. Usually in Sri Lanka, you cook this with a bright, spongy, white-skinned *Kalpitiya* cucumber variety. It's great with small, flavoursome, crunchy Persian cucumbers, or equally with salad cucumbers you get everywhere. Try it with aubergine vinegar moju (page 198), red chicken curry (page 138) and perhaps a fresh sambol like daikon (page 164).

Serves 4

1 tbsp coconut or vegetable oil

½ red onion, peeled and finely sliced

5 fresh curry leaves

½ tsp cumin seeds

½ tsp coriander seeds

2 cucumbers (approx. 400g), peeled, cut in half lengthways and sliced into 2cm half-moons

1 tsp salt, or to taste

125ml water

½ stick of cinnamon

½ tsp ground turmeric

100ml coconut milk

For the temper

1 tbsp coconut or vegetable oil

5 fresh curry leaves

1 tsp mustard seeds

1. Heat the oil in a wok or saucepan over a medium heat. When hot, fry the onion for 5–6 minutes, until soft and starting to go golden. Add the curry leaves, and after 1 minute when they are soft and bright green, add the cumin seeds and coriander seeds. Fry for 1–2 minutes, stirring occasionally, until the spices are fragrant.

2. Add the cucumber wedges, salt, water, cinnamon and turmeric. Mix it all up and bring to a simmer. Keep simmering gently for 6–8 minutes; you want the cucumber to still have a fair bit of bite and crunch to it.

3. Pour in the coconut milk and stir it through, cooking everything for 3–4 minutes on a gently simmering heat. Remove from the heat and dish up into a serving bowl or dish.

4. Finally, for the temper, heat the oil in a small frying pan set over a medium-high heat. When the oil is shimmering, add the curry leaves, which should crisp up and go bright green. When crispy, add the mustard seeds, and as the mustard seeds release their aroma in about 30 seconds, pour the whole lot, including all the hot oil, onto the cucumber curry. Serve hot.

Curry Everything

I blame Madhur Jaffrey. As a young, hip cook in 1973, Ms Jaffrey wrote a book called *An Invitation to Indian Cooking.* An instant classic, full of witty writing and reliable recipes, she became a cooking sensation. She went on to present dozens of shows for the BBC and PBS, and to write many more bestselling cookbooks. On Indian food, *The New York Times* declared her 'the final word on the subject'. 'Madhur Jaffrey is the true queen of curry' proclaimed Tom Parker Bowles, a guy whose mum might be the queen of England one day.

Jaffrey might be a queen and a legend, but I have beef with her, curry beef to be precise. She did trailblaze for several generations of South Asian cooks – including me – but nearly fifty years of trash-talking curry began with that book and it's time to set the record straight. On page twenty-six of my edition, MJ writes: 'To me, the word "curry" is as degrading to India's great cuisine as the term "chop suey" was to China's'. She goes further: 'Of course when Indians speak in their own languages they never use the word at all.' And ever since, all sorts of people have extended the Queen of Curry's proclamation. No, they insist, the word doesn't exist in India, the dish doesn't exist in India, and the dish *was invented by the British*, as a kind of Britsplaining of disparate foods while they were in the area colonising things anyway.

Listen up curry deniers: curry *is* a word, it is a Tamil word, it is used by at least sixty-nine million Tamil Indians and three million Tamil Sri Lankans and the word is over 3,000 years old. In Tamil, the word is written கறி which is pronounced exactly as 'curry' is pronounced in English. It is used to refer to wet, braised curry dishes like fish curry (*meen*-curry) or aubergine curry (*katharikai*-curry) which is to say 'curry' is used exactly as it is in English. It need not be transliterated as 'kari' because then it could read as if it ought to rhyme with 'sari', 'safari' or 'calamari' (and these pronunciations would all be very, very wrong). Tamil references to curry show up in literature from the great golden age of Tamil ancient civilisation, the *Sangam*. Curry appears in the poem *Perumpanatruppadai* from 100 CE (made of pomegranates and butter); and in a *Purananuru* by Kapilar, an anthology of poems from 100 BCE (made of meat, with 'flower-fragrant smoke', apparently). Archaeological evidence dating to 2600 BCE shows pounded spices – including mustard, fennel, cumin and tamarind pods – have been in use for 5,000 years[1], so curry powders are very ancient too.

---

[1] Iyer, Raghavan. *660 Curries*

The Tamil word is also used for curry leaves (*karu-veppilai*), for curry powder (*curry thool*), and more perplexingly, for raw vegetables (*maru-curry*). Curry means a lot of different things in poetic Tamil; just like the dish itself, it is a shape-shifting, magical thing. Fittingly, it has now travelled the globe, and is made in many different ways, from Bali to Barbados, from Japan to Vietnam. Curry exists, curry is magnificent and curry is one of the most brilliant and varied culinary inventions of all time. After everything they did to us, we are definitely not giving the *British* credit for it, please! Here is the last word on the subject: Tamil people invented curry, and look everyone, you're welcome.

Curry means a lot of different things in poetic Tamil; just like the dish itself, it is a shape–shifting, magical thing.

It was a cold, wet January day in London when I received my own exciting invitation to cook curry. I had started cooking one-off Sri Lankan feasts as a way to recreate what my mum and all the other aunties had been teaching me on the island. My experience of hosting them had been fun to plan but increasingly terrible in reality, making my back ache and leaving me with little loose change. Generous and encouraging friends like Asma Khan and Selin Kiazim had let me borrow their whole restaurants; I had sold out; the menus I was proud of. But the experience of lugging huge crates of ingredients around London had left me cold. I'd spent enough days trying to brief chefs in broken Tamil who had no idea what I was on about. Every time, I would have some kind of last-minute pandemonium, my friends coming through to rescue me. Pop-ups, I can reveal exclusively, are a pain and I was over them.

This invitation was different. It was an email out of the blue from someone I had never heard of. Would I like to cook a curry at an impossibly sexy hotel in – could it be right – the Cayman Islands? I blinked. What was happening? Had they mixed me up with someone else? Would I like to be *flown out* to cook, they were asking? Alongside a brilliant family of chefs from Trinidad and a British-Pakistani chef from London?

I excitedly typed out yes and felt beyond thrilled. I received my tickets, got to the airport, and arrived at the breezy, white sands and sparkling ocean of Palm Heights. At last, I had made it, I thought. All those horribly stressful events and scrubbing on my hands and knees were past me now. There was a whole team of lovely, talented chefs to help me, a kitchen of tropical ingredients I could pinch, and everything seemed easy and light. Someone was there to take pictures, someone else to make us drinks. Feeling giddy, I spent the days before the pop-up in a fever dream, absently noticing that

Anya, Numra and the other guest chefs were doing a lot more preparation than me. Sure, we were technically supposed to be prepping, but what about taking selfies on the beach, I thought? Or in the different amazing armchairs. Perhaps I should try out my room's beautiful bathtub? Yes, I would like another piña colada! Usually, I'd have to cook a whole dinner, but this was just a few dishes from each of us. Easy! I thought from my stylish stripy sun lounger.

Before I knew it, it was the day of the dinner. A long, beautiful table was set up with flowers and polished glasses against the backdrop of the waves. Another glorious pink sunset was shaping up, more glamorous guests getting ready to sit down. A beautiful Somali boxer came by to wish me luck; a Trini DJ was getting set up to play all night. A *Zoolander*-looking fashion guy from American *GQ* asked me how the cooking was going.

'Oh, the cooking!' I replied. Oh fuck, I thought. I was nowhere near ready. What had I been thinking? Having been flown out and put up so generously with the simplest prep job of any pop-up I'd done, had I blown it? I began rushing, trying to do too many things at one time. I was busy smushing up shallots for lunu miris (page 208) very last minute, and trying to figure out if hibiscus could sub in for goroka for the grilled fish (page 96), when, oh dear. I smelled the burning.

From an enormous pan over the fire pit came the acrid smell of burnt onions, blackened along with spices and curry leaves: a foundation for my prawn curry. Panic rose quietly. Cherry and Silver, the charming, fast-working American chefs who were assigned to help me, saw the freakout in my eyes. They asked me what goes in next. Tamarind, spices, coconut milk, prawns, lime, was the answer. So we poured it all in. Spooning a mouthful of the blackened onion curry mix into their mouth, Cherry said in the way I imagine American schoolteachers speak to children: 'Cynthia, I want you to listen to me, it's still delicious.' Oh, have a word, Americans, I thought. Classic hyping me up. Well, I know what burnt is, the curry was lost, it was all over. Cherry wasn't letting me have it and held out a spoonful for me as if I was their baby. 'You're here, you deserve to be here,' they said, 'your food is delicious.' American schoolteachers are probably lovely, I thought as I swallowed. Cherry was right. The curry liquid was charred and fabulous. It tasted exactly like Mum's kitchen, cooked over fire. Despite everything I had done to get in the way, I had stumbled on a better method than the one I usually use. A perfect prawn curry.

Curry is forgiving, it is simple, it is kind. It has survived thousands of years and will be here long after we are gone. It is what a Sri Lankan fisherman will cook with his leftover catch, over a fire, under the stars, with just a pan, a knife and tin of spices. Curry is full of possibility and hope – that someone like me or you could happen upon a delicious way of doing things, perhaps a new ingredient or new technique. This guide is to pass on what I have learned about the flavours that make for a great Sri Lankan curry. I hope it gives you the freedom to invent some yourself. My mother did, and so did her mother, so you are in very good company if you do, too. You just might come up with a curry masterpiece.

A QUICK BREAKDOWN OF SRI LANKAN CURRIES

To start with, the easiest, quickest and probably oldest Sri Lankan curries are **white curries**. For these, you make a base (usually of fried onions, curry leaves and salt), add whole spices (like cumin, mustard seeds or cardamom), whatever it is you're currying, and then turmeric powder, black pepper, coconut milk and lime. You can make powdered spice mixes for these (called *thuna paha* in Sinhalese, or *sarakku* in Tamil), but I find whole spices work just as well, and whole spices are much better to store as they retain more bright flavour than powdered ones. White curries are gentle and mild. Some lovely dishes to cook this way are those with delicately flavoured ingredients, including green mango (page 50), cucumber (page 64), spinach (page 52), tinned breadfruit (page 48), fish (page 92), chicken (page 142), roast pumpkin (page 30) and cashew nut curry (page 74).

Then there is another quick style called *varai* or *mallum*. Equally simple, they are effectively dry coconut curries, where you roast, grill or stir-fry vegetables or perhaps some fish, and then separately toast curry leaves, spices, freshly grated coconut and sometimes a handful of crunchy fried lentils, then mix it all up together with a little salt and lime juice. Fast and painless, this style preserves the nutrients in vegetables and their fresh texture, and in my experience, is the best way to cook roast beetroot (page 54) or charred cabbage (page 56) and would be great with green beans or stir-fried kale.

One notch harder are spicy **red curries**. The trickiest step here is making your own roasted curry powder, which takes less than five minutes and requires a spice grinder (or mini food processor). Different communities have different recipes, and this book contains the Jaffna Tamil style, because it's what I grew up with. You can make your roasted Sri Lankan curry powder (SL curry powder, page 21) in batches and use it for three months, as long as you keep it airtight. The redness in the curry comes from dried red chillies, which you toast alongside whole spices before blitzing them up, and so these curries pack more heat than their white cousins, and have a distinctive smokiness. Because they're bigger in flavour, red curries will often be the main event at a mealtime. I promise that the first time you make the freshly ground stuff you will be blown away at how crazily fragrant it is, and will wonder why you ever bought any ready powdered stuff before. Red curries are essentially made the same way as white curries, except you don't usually bother adding many whole spices, and you might vary the element that gives it a tart zing: sometimes it's lime, sometimes it's tamarind, sometimes it's tomatoes. My favourite red curries are roasted aubergine (page 32), soft-boiled egg (page 130), prawn (page 106) lamb (page 120) and possibly the crowning glory of Tamil cooking in the north of the island: crab curry (page 108). For one or two red curries, there's an extra step of making a separate, gloriously warm spice mix that I call meat powder (or *eraichithool*) with fennel and nutmeg (page 21), to sprinkle in generously at the end of cooking, but this too takes less than five minutes and makes a pleasing cheffy racket in the kitchen.

I hope it gives you the freedom to invent some yourself. My mother did, and so did her mother, so you are in very good company if you do, too.

Finally, there are **black curries**, or *kalu pol* in Sinhalese. These curries require the most complicated toasting and grinding steps, as you basically spend five minutes making your own earthy black spice mix, then spend another five minutes making a black coconut mix of uncooked rice and coconut toasted smokily in a pan. These curries don't contain coconut milk, they get their tartness from vinegar, usually feature a spoonful of sugar and lend themselves well to fatty or sweet ingredients. It is a delicious way to cook pineapple (page 44) and my favourite dish of all Sinhala dishes: black pork belly curry (page 124).

There are other island curries that of course don't fit this taxonomy, like lamprais curry (page 146) and pickled pork curry (page 128), as well as Sri Lankan satay, a 'padre' curry made with duck and arrack, and various other amazing curries I have tried. But in essence, this covers about eighty per cent of the traditional Sri Lankan curry repertoire, and I hope is enough to get you started.

Cashew nut curry

Cashew nuts (called *cadju* in Sri Lanka) are very beloved in the island, and were introduced by the Portuguese from Mozambique and South America. This is one of the only nut curries I know of in the world. It is gently cooked in coconut milk, which gives the curry a luxurious, silky texture.

Serves 2–4

225g raw cashew nuts

2 tbsp coconut or vegetable oil

1 onion, peeled and finely sliced

3 garlic cloves, peeled and halved

5 fresh curry leaves

Optional: 5cm piece of pandan leaf

2 green chillies, sliced

½ tsp fenugreek seeds

½ tsp fennel seeds

2 whole cardamom pods, lightly bashed in a pestle and mortar

½ tsp SL curry powder (see page 21)

½ tsp ground turmeric

½ stick of cinnamon

125ml water

200ml coconut milk

¼ lime

For the temper

1 tbsp coconut or vegetable oil

10 fresh curry leaves

2 whole cardamom pods, lightly bashed in a pestle and mortar

½ tsp cumin seeds

1. Soak the cashews in a bowl of water for 1 hour. Drain well.

2. Place a wok or medium-sized saucepan over a medium heat and add the oil. When hot, add the onion, garlic, curry leaves, pandan leaf, if using, green chillies, fenugreek, fennel and cardamom, and cook for 3–4 minutes until soft and the curry leaves are still bright green.

3. Add the cashews to the mix, stirring in the SL curry powder, turmeric, cinnamon and the water. Reduce the heat to low-medium, and simmer for 5 minutes.

4. Add the coconut milk, bring to a gentle bubbling boil and then lower the heat and simmer for about 10 minutes, stirring until the sauce has thickened and reduced.

5. To make the temper, heat the oil in a small frying pan set over a medium heat. When hot, add the curry leaves, which should crisp up, cardamom pods and cumin seeds, and cook until they splutter. Pour the whole lot, oil and all, onto your cashew curry and serve. Finish with a squeeze of lime juice.

Chickpea spicy red curry

In my village in Sri Lanka, the weddings are lovely affairs, until lunch is announced and then you are in a stampede. It's unclear why everyone is so violently and suddenly hungry because from the minute you arrive you are being continually served food, in the manner of boxes and bags of wedding shorteats and *palaharam*, a mix of savoury and sweet snacks to crunch on while you are chatting loudly with the people sitting next to you. Perhaps all the stampeding is because lunch is mad delicious. This chickpea curry is dark, spicy and earthy, and is usually made with fried aubergines, and is very fashionable these days at Jaffna and Tamil diaspora weddings from Wembley in London to Scarborough in Toronto. I've skipped the aubergine for simplicity; the curry is wonderful without.

This dish cooks fast, so after the wedding, if the bride is a working Jaffna woman and she likes a cooked breakfast in the morning, these chickpeas can come out of a tin and Bob's your uncle: her new husband can cook his sweetheart a quick, delicious spicy breakfast before she boards her motorbike and drives to work. Try it with puttu (page 80), godamba roti (page 220) or alongside a sambol and some rice for a quick dinner.

Serves 2–3

2 golf ball-sized pieces of tamarind block, soaked in 120ml warm water for 10 minutes

1 tbsp coconut or vegetable oil

1 large red onion, peeled and finely sliced

4 garlic cloves, peeled and sliced

2 tsp fenugreek seeds

10 fresh curry leaves

2 x 400g tins of chickpeas, drained

1 tsp salt, or to taste

2 tbsp SL curry powder (see page 21)

200ml coconut milk

For the temper

1 tbsp coconut or vegetable oil

10 fresh curry leaves

1 1/2 tsp mustard seeds

1. Squeeze the tamarind with your fingers, then discard the seeds and skin, leaving behind the pulpy water.

2. Heat the oil in a saucepan over a medium heat. Add the onion and cook for 4–5 minutes until translucent. Add the garlic, and fry until the onion is starting to turn brown. Add the fenugreek seeds and curry leaves, and fry, stirring occasionally, for 1–2 minutes until the curry leaves are bright green.

3. Add the drained chickpeas, tamarind water, salt and SL curry powder. Bring to a gentle boil, then reduce the heat to simmer for 20–30 minutes with the lid ajar. Stir in the coconut milk and cook for 2–3 minutes to warm through.

4. Dish up the curry, cover to keep warm, and then finally make a temper. Heat the oil in a small frying pan over a medium-high heat, and when the oil shimmers add the curry leaves and mustard seeds. After about 30 seconds–1 minute, when the curry leaves are crispy, pour the whole lot onto the curry.

Green beans white curry

I love tender, sweet green beans and this mild, aromatic coconut milk curry is a great weeknight way to cook them. Different varieties of succulent green beans grow all over Sri Lanka: long, skinny snake beans, dramatic-looking wing beans, and *bonchi* or runner beans. I like to cook them in a light, coconut milk curry broth, just long enough for the beans to get tender and retain some grassiness. There's also a gentle kick from fresh green chillies and black pepper, and the temper is with fenugreek, which makes for a kind of caramel-like finish.

Serves 2

1 tbsp coconut or vegetable oil

1 red onion, peeled and
    finely sliced

¾ tsp coriander seeds

½ tsp cumin seeds

¼ tsp fennel seeds

5 fresh curry leaves

125ml water

250g green beans,
    sliced diagonally into
    3cm-long pieces

1 tsp ground turmeric

2 green chillies, sliced

100ml coconut milk

Salt

½ lime

For the temper

1 tsp coconut or vegetable oil

10 fresh curry leaves

1 tsp fenugreek seeds

A generous couple of grinds
    of black pepper

1. Heat the oil in a pan over a medium-high heat and fry the onion for 5–6 minutes, until translucent. Add the coriander, cumin, fennel and curry leaves, and cook for 4–5 minutes until the leaves are bright green.

2. Add the water and sliced green beans, along with the turmeric and green chillies. Cook for 5–7 minutes, until the beans are bright green.

3. Stir in the coconut milk and add a little salt. Bring to a gentle boil, then turn down and simmer for 3–4 minutes, until the beans are tender and just cooked through. Switch off the heat.

4. In a small frying pan, make the temper. Heat the oil over a medium-high heat, and when sizzling, add the curry leaves, fenugreek and black pepper. After about 30 seconds–1 minute, when the curry leaves are crispy, pour the whole lot onto the curry and stir through. Finish with a squeeze of lime.

Spinach puttu with fenugreek milk

Puttu is traditionally a hot, steamed rice flour crumble, sprinkled with freshly grated coconut. It is especially beloved by Tamils and Muslims alike, eaten as a replacement for rice, to soak up other curries.

Puttu is also the nickname of the young man from our village who picks me up from Kodikamam Station whenever I take the train up to Jaffna, I guess because he eats a lot of it. I usually greet him at the seat of his tuktuk after a seven-hour train journey, on a day that began at 4.30 a.m. at Wellawatte in Colombo, when bleary-eyed and in darkness I lugged around my parents' maddeningly heavy luggage. The train journey itself, although spectacular, will have been hot and prone to delays. What I am saying is, whenever I see the guy, my nerves are frayed. Puttu the man is a stylish guy with a big fluffy pile of glamorous hair. He is also always late (presumably because hair like that doesn't fix itself), usually stops to catcall irritated girls on the way home, likes to rakishly smoke cigarettes the whole drive, and then always ends the journey by overcharging me.

My father doesn't let me complain about the Puttu experience, as job opportunities, romance and hair gel can be hard to come by in Jaffna, and good on the young man for trying to make his way. This recipe is probably the best meal to eat after you have been driven to the house by Puttu, partly because you have been shouting 'Puttu!' to admonish his behaviour the whole time, and now the food has been programmed in your mind. Also, it's a quick, filling, Jaffna specialty.

Instead of rice *puttu*, this is a non-traditional instant couscous *puttu*, invented by my mother, who made it sometimes when she needed a store-cupboard quick dinner to fill a lot of hungry mouths. Guilty Sri Lankans, listen up: you do not need to get that *puttu* cylinder your mum gave you out of your cupboard for this recipe. We are not making those neat *puttu* pillars. Instead, we are going to make pretty little piles of *keerai puttu* – made with kale or spinach. The sticky grains of *puttu* are usually flooded with a laksa-like coconut milk broth called *sodhi* in Tamil, or *kiri hodi* in Sinhala, so this recipe includes my grandmother's fenugreek-heavy *sodhi* recipe. Of all the island's various *sodhi* recipes, this one is unbelievably fragrant and simple. It is made by simmering slightly bitter fenugreek seeds and curry leaves in coconut milk and finishing it all off with a bright squeeze of lime. You can eat this combo on its own for breakfast, or accessorise it with a Sri Lankan turmeric omelette (page 132), some pol sambol (page 156) and any curry you like, perhaps spicy chickpea curry (page 76) or a rich lamb curry (page 120).

Ingredients & method overleaf

Serves 2

For the puttu

150g couscous

150ml boiling water

Salt

1 tbsp coconut or vegetable oil

250g spinach, spring greens,
  or kale, finely chopped

1–2 green chillies, finely
  chopped

½ red onion, peeled and finely
  diced

1 tsp caster sugar

75g freshly grated coconut
  (see page 175)

For the fenugreek milk (sodhi)

10 fresh curry leaves

½ tsp salt, or to taste

2 tsp fenugreek seeds

½ red onion, peeled and sliced

250ml coconut milk

½ lime

1. Pour the couscous into a saucepan, and pour the boiling water over it. Sprinkle with a pinch of salt and stir. Cover with a well-fitting lid or clingfilm and leave aside for 12 minutes until the couscous is tender. When it's done, use a fork to fluff it up and set it aside.

2. Meanwhile, add the oil to a frying pan or wok, turning the heat to medium-high, and sauté the greens, chillies, onion and a pinch of salt for 3–4 minutes until the onion is soft. Remove from the heat.

3. Gently fold together the greens mixture, couscous, sugar and grated coconut and keep aside.

4. To make your sodhi or fenugreek milk, put the curry leaves, salt, fenugreek seeds and red onion in a small saucepan and cover with about 4cm water. Bring to the boil, and after 2–3 minutes, when the fenugreek and curry leaves are fragrant, add the coconut milk and stir well until it is heated through. Remove from the heat and just before serving, squeeze over the lime juice.

5. To serve, pour the fenugreek milk over the puttu.

Tomato rasam broth with leek and coriander

Rasam is just out-of-this-world delicious. A healing, ancient dish with South Indian Tamil roots, Sri Lankan rasam is a hot, clearing broth of tamarind, black pepper and cumin, with different variations depending on your feelings. 'Rasa' in Tamil means the essence, the mood, the taste, the jam, the thing that makes you feel something and it gets to something deep inside. You can flood rice with it, you can drink it down in a clear broth, you can have it as a side for your other dishes in a cute little bowl like you would with miso soup. I like to have it with a dollop of yoghurt and plain rice on cold days, and I like to add leeks because it's a way to eat more vegetables and their sweet greenness is so good in the tangy broth.

Serves 2

3 golf ball-sized pieces of tamarind block, soaked in 240ml warm water for 10 minutes

2 tbsp coconut or vegetable oil

2 medium tomatoes (approx. 200g), roughly chopped

1 tsp salt, or to taste

1 leek, light green parts halved and sliced into 0.5cm-thick slices

½ a small handful of fresh coriander leaves, roughly chopped

For the rasam spice mix

3 tsp cumin seeds

2 tsp black peppercorns

3 dried red chillies

5 garlic cloves, peeled and halved

For the temper

2 tbsp coconut or vegetable oil

10 fresh curry leaves

1 tsp mustard seeds

1. First, make your rasam spice mix. Set a small frying pan over a medium heat and add the cumin seeds, black peppercorns, chillies and garlic. Heat, stirring occasionally for 1–2 minutes until fragrant, being careful not to burn the spices. Once cool, put all the ingredients in a spice grinder, mini food processor or pestle and mortar and blitz to a coarse paste, adding a little water if necessary.

2. To make the rasam, squeeze the tamarind with your fingers, then discard the seeds and skin, leaving behind the pulpy water. Heat the oil in a small saucepan, and when hot, add the tomatoes. Sauté for about 4 minutes, until they begin to soften. Then add the tamarind water, salt, rasam spice mix and leek. Simmer gently over a low heat for 4–5 minutes; it should be very fragrant. Remove from the heat and pour into serving bowls. Add a couple of tablespoons of cold water, and stir in the coriander leaves.

3. To make the temper, heat the oil in a small frying pan set over a medium heat. When hot, add the curry leaves, which should crisp up, and mustard seeds, and cook until they splutter. Pour the whole lot, oil and all, onto your rasam and serve.

Tempered crunchy fried potatoes with turmeric

Sri Lanka has many different *kilangus*, or potatoey root vegetables: cassava, taro, sweet potato and one of my favourites, a vibrant purple yam called 'rasa valli kilangu' which means King's Jewel.

This quick dish, made by tempering hot spices, curry leaves and onion in oil and adding soft potatoes so they crisp up in the pan, is great made with new potatoes that you don't need to peel. I roast the potatoes a bit crispier than is strictly traditional. If you can get Maldive fish or bonito, it makes a big difference.

Serves 2–4

500g new potatoes, washed

½ tsp ground turmeric

2 tsp salt

2 tbsp coconut or vegetable oil

½ lime

For the temper

2–3 tbsp coconut or
  vegetable oil

1 medium red onion, peeled
  and finely sliced

10 fresh curry leaves

1 garlic clove, peeled and sliced

1 green chilli, finely sliced

1 tbsp Maldive fish flakes,
  bonito flakes or katsuoboshi

Optional: 2.5cm piece of
  pandan leaf

1 tsp chilli powder (or
  3 dried red Kashmiri chillies,
  crushed up in your hands)

1 tsp black mustard seeds

1. Put the potatoes in a saucepan and cover with cold water. Add the turmeric and salt. Bring to the boil, then turn down to simmer and cook for 15–20 minutes, until the potatoes are just tender enough to insert a fork. Drain well.

2. In a large frying pan over a high heat, heat the 2 tablespoons of oil. When the oil is shimmering, add the potatoes. With a fork, gently press down on each potato, breaking the skin and smashing them a bit. You don't want to break them up, just smush them up a little. Cook for 2–3 minutes and when they are nice and golden brown, turn each potato over. When they are brown on both sides, transfer to a bowl while you make the temper.

3. Pour 2 tablespoons of oil into the frying pan. When hot, add the onion and cook until it starts to go translucent. Add the curry leaves, garlic, green chilli, Maldive fish and pandan leaf, if using. Stir-fry for 2–3 minutes, until the curry leaves are bright green. Add the chilli powder or dried red chillies, mustard seeds and add a little more oil if necessary to keep everything bright and moving. After 1–2 minutes, when the seeds start to pop, return the potatoes to the pan and stir through, coating thoroughly in the spicy mixture. Finish with a squeeze of lime juice.

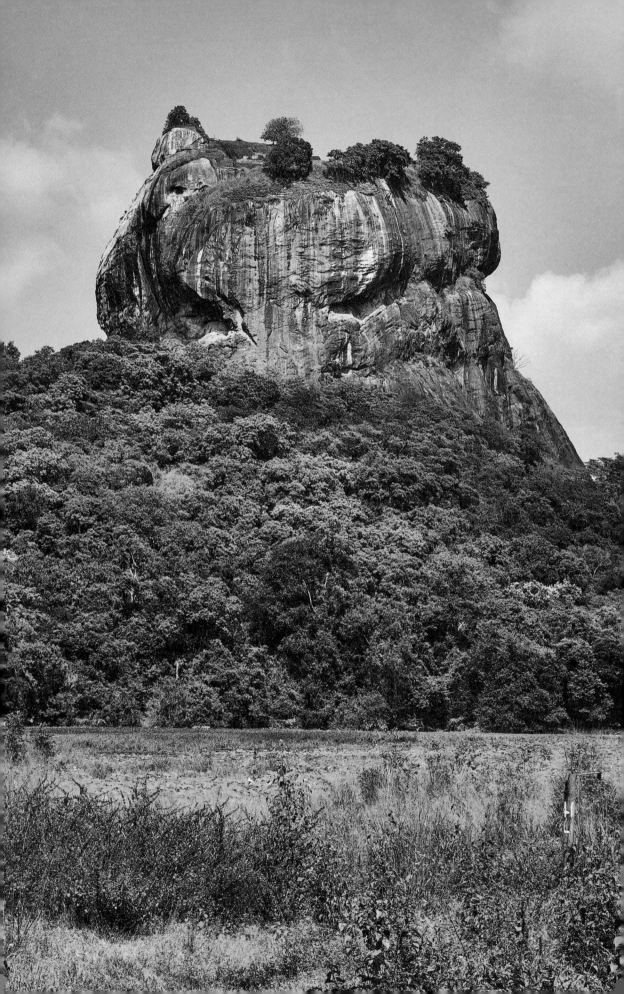

FISH, SEAFOOD & MEAT

Turmeric and coconut fish curry

This light coconut milk curry is my version of a great superhero of Sri Lankan curries: Medicine Curry (or *sarakku* in Tamil). A healing riff on a classic white curry, it has a slightly different spice mix, and is quick and easy to make. When we are ill, Tamil folks eat *sarakku* curries, meant to heal you from the inside out.

Spices are medicinal, I have no doubt, but I harbour a vagueness about exactly how. Coriander seeds in this curry give it a kind of peppery kick, and I think are said to bring your temperature down, like nature's paracetamol. Turmeric gives it a bright yellow colour, and contains something called curcumin, which is either an antiseptic or reduces inflammation and almost definitely makes your skin glow. The cloves and cinnamon are probably full of antioxidants. I hope it makes you feel good.

Serves 4

2 tbsp coconut or vegetable oil

½ red onion, peeled and finely sliced

5 fresh curry leaves

4cm fresh root ginger, peeled and sliced

2 tsp coriander seeds

1 tsp black peppercorns

2 tsp cumin seeds

2 golf ball-sized pieces of tamarind block, soaked in 125ml warm water for 10 minutes

1½ tsp salt, or to taste

4cm piece of cinnamon stick

6 cloves

1 tsp ground turmeric

200ml coconut milk

450g white fish (e.g. haddock or bream), cut into chunks

1 lime

For the temper

2 tbsp coconut or vegetable oil

½ red onion, peeled and finely sliced

10 fresh curry leaves

1. In a wok or medium pan, heat the oil over a medium heat. After 30 seconds or so when the oil is hot, add the onion and fry for 4–5 minutes until soft. Add the curry leaves, and then after 30 seconds when they have turned bright green, add the ginger, coriander, peppercorns and cumin. Cook, stirring occasionally, for about 1 minute, until the spices are fragrant.

2. Squeeze the tamarind with your fingers, then discard the seeds and skin, leaving behind the pulpy water. Add to the pan, along with the salt, cinnamon, cloves, turmeric, coconut milk and fish chunks. Bring to a gentle boil, then reduce the heat and simmer gently for 20 minutes, or until the fish is cooked. To test a piece, fish it out and twist a fork into it; it should be opaque all the way through and flake easily when it's done. Switch off the heat, and dish up.

3. To finish, make a temper. In a small frying pan, heat the oil over a medium-high heat. When shimmering, add the onion, shaking the pan occasionally to stop it sticking. After 5–6 minutes, when the onions are turning golden brown, add the curry leaves, and stir occasionally for about 30 seconds. Pour the whole lot, including the oil, over the curry. Finish with a generous squeeze of lime.

Red fish curry

This curry wants a meaty, fleshy fish with plenty of flavour. Fish has very little connective tissue which means it is delicate, cooks fast and makes a great quick weeknight dinner. The onions on top aren't traditional but I think they make it crunchy and tasty. Try it with parsley sambol (page 176) or green mango sambol (page 178) and perhaps a bean curry (page 78), a greens curry (page 52) or cucumber curry (page 64).

Serves 4

1 golf ball-sized piece of tamarind block, soaked in 125ml warm water for 10 minutes

1 tbsp coconut or vegetable oil

½ red onion, peeled and finely sliced

7 fresh curry leaves

2 garlic cloves, peeled and halved

4cm fresh root ginger, peeled and sliced

2 medium tomatoes (approx. 200g), roughly chopped

½ tsp ground turmeric

2 tbsp SL curry powder (see page 21)

1 tsp salt, or to taste

450g hake or firm white fish fillet, cut in half lengthways then into 6cm chunks

250ml water

100ml coconut milk

1 lime

For the temper

1 tbsp coconut or vegetable oil

½ red onion, peeled and finely sliced

8 fresh curry leaves

1. Squeeze the tamarind with your fingers, then discard the seeds and skin, leaving behind the pulpy water. In a medium-sized saucepan or wok, heat the oil over a medium heat and fry the onion for 8–10 minutes until soft. Add the curry leaves and after 30 seconds, when they are bright green, stir in the garlic and ginger. After about 30 seconds, when the garlic is beginning to turn golden, add the tomatoes and tamarind water and cook for 3–4 minutes, stirring occasionally.

2. When the tomatoes have cooked down a little, add the turmeric, SL curry powder and the salt. Slide the fish into the pan, and pour in the water. Allow to come to a gentle boil, then turn the heat down to a simmer, cover the pan with a lid and cook for 10 minutes.

3. Stir in the coconut milk and allow to come back to a simmer, then cook for a further 10 minutes or so, until the fish is cooked through. You can test it by gently flaking a piece with a fork: it should be opaque all the way through, and flake easily.

4. To make the temper, heat the oil in a small frying pan over a medium-high heat. When the oil is shimmering and hot, fry the sliced onion for 5–6 minutes, shaking the pan occasionally, until the onion is beginning to turn golden. Add the curry leaves and after about 30 seconds, when they are crispy, remove from the heat.

5. Serve the fish with the temper, and all its oil, spooned over the top. Squeeze over the lime.

Grilled ambul fish

Sri Lankan fishermen have one of the hardest existences of the many poorly paid skilled workers in Sri Lanka. Able to fish from stilts, swim through high tides like Olympic surfers and operate a catamaran in rough seas, they make very little and have survived war, tsunamis, torrential rains and floods.

This dish is an homage to Sri Lanka's fishermen from the south of the island. They make a kind of cured fish with a pungent, acidic flavour called *ambul thiyal* to sustain them through the season when the sea is too rough for fishing. The sourness comes from goroka, a wild mangosteen, which gives the dish its deep red colour and is a great foil for its earthy spices, cloves and cardamom. I find the original recipe to be very strong, so this is a lighter, grilled version of it. I cut the goroka with yoghurt to lighten the flavour and then cook it under a very hot grill. If you can't get hold of goroka, bought tamarind paste will do as an inferior substitute (tamarind paste you make yourself would be too watery). If you're a fish novice, this is a great one for you. It's an easy, quick fish dish to make, requires no knives, and pairs wonderfully with green mango sambol (page 178).

Serves 4

500g thick white fish fillets
(e.g. cod), with skin on,
cut into 6cm-wide slices

1 tbsp coconut or vegetable oil

1 lime

For the marinade

8 cloves

8 whole cardamom pods, lightly
bashed in a pestle and mortar

4cm piece of pandan leaf

10 fresh curry leaves

6 tbsp thick Greek yoghurt

1 spoonful of goroka paste
(or tamarind paste)

4 garlic cloves, peeled
and grated

5cm fresh root ginger, peeled
and minced or grated

1 ½ tsp salt, or to taste

1 ½ tsp freshly ground
black pepper

1. For the marinade, toast the cloves and cardamom together in a small dry frying pan over a medium heat for 1–2 minutes until fragrant. Tip into a bowl to cool, then crush in a pestle and mortar or blitz in a spice grinder along with the pandan leaf and curry leaves, until fine.

2. In a large bowl, mix all the marinade ingredients together. Add the fish and turn to coat well on all sides. Place in the fridge, cover so it's airtight and leave to marinate for a minimum of 20 minutes and up to 24 hours.

3. When you're ready to cook the fish, grease a wire rack with a little oil and set it over a roasting tin. Preheat the grill to high for 8 minutes so it is really hot. Place the fish on the wire rack and pat over a little extra marinade. Cook under the grill for 8 minutes, until just cooked, basting with a little more coconut oil halfway through cooking. To test it is cooked, insert the point of a small knife into a piece of fish and hold it there for 5 seconds. Put the knife on the back of your hand and it should feel between hot and warm. Serve with a wedge of lime.

Tempered kunisso dried shrimp and onion

Dried fish and the star of this recipe, tiny dried shrimp (*kuni-raal* or *kunisso*), are an acquired taste, so you have been warned. I have grown to absolutely love the flavour; it positively brims with umami. This dish is so quick and simple to make. It's just dried shrimp stir-fried in oil with golden onions, crispy curry leaves, lime, salt and a little punch of heat from chilli flakes. It's a fantastic addition to, say, a mild potato or dal recipe (pages 28 or 40); with puttu (page 80) or a rava or plain dosa (page 236).

Serves 4 as a side

1 tbsp coconut or vegetable oil

½ red onion, peeled and very
  finely sliced

20 fresh curry leaves

100g dried shrimp

2 tbsp chilli flakes

½ tsp salt, or to taste

1 lime

1. Heat the oil in a wok or frying pan over a medium-high heat. When the oil is shimmering, fry the onion for 5–6 minutes, until golden.

2. Add the curry leaves, stirring, and after 10 seconds add the dried shrimp. Cook for 3–4 minutes, stirring from time to time, until the shrimp is super-fragrant.

3. Add the chilli flakes and keep stir-frying for a further 1–2 minutes, just until the mixture has taken on some red colour and it smells spicy. Season with salt then remove from the heat and finish with a generous squeeze of lime.

Go And Get Fresh Curry Leaves

'I already told you, I can't cook without curry leaves or salt,' Mum was shouting, banging the cupboards in the kitchen as she made us all dinner. It was 1989, and it was a year of big changes. Mum got a perm, the Berlin Wall fell, and our household in England was to double in size. Piles of folded-up sheets and makeshift beds would fill the dining room and living room, the queue for the only bathroom would become an issue every day. We would all live like that for years, during which time I would complain about it regularly and noisily to Mum, to no avail. Mum was busy.

My mother doesn't ask for much, but there are a few lines in the sand you cannot cross. Get her the basics of salt and fresh curry leaves, and she will make you a delicious Sri Lankan dinner. She will require that all the food tastes great, because what is the point of cooking if it doesn't? Sure, I know sometimes you just need to eat something, but look, don't irritate Mum. She knows what she's on about, and your tastebuds will thank you.

Fresh curry leaves, or *karu-veppilai* in Tamil, have been used since at least 300 BCE. In tropical countries, curry leaf grows like mint, at an annoyingly fertile rate, and my aunties and uncles are constantly trying to stop them from overtaking their whole gardens and cannibalising their lovely flowers. Their other *rutacae* family members include bright citrus fruits like bergamot, kumquat, lime and calamansi; as well as delicious, numbing Sichuan peppercorns. Curry leaves taste wildly zesty and fragrant; they contain cinnamaldehyde, a cinnamon-y organic compound, and they're also fresh and herby, like mint or basil. The truth is, it's hard to explain exactly what they taste like because they are a kind of culinary axiom. Curry leaves taste like curry leaves is what I'm saying.

I think great taste is important to Mum because Mum comes from a family committed to fun. She grew up three miles down the road from our dad, in a completely parallel universe, with her own pet parrot, a dog called Duke, domestic help, and a car and driver to take her and her cousins to school. Her family loves to party, drink arrack and tell fart jokes, and they look great while they do it. When I was growing up, she would try to get me to take a bit more pride in my clothes, and say she'd been the first girl in her village to wear a miniskirt in the '60s. Mum loves

Bond movies and horror films, she'd paint our toenails and try to sneak us some fun while Dad was trying to get us to memorise poems and revise for exams.

When she married Dad and left Sri Lanka, Mum says she missed the warmth of home and the female company of her sisters. Dad was into politics and social justice, they had to live on a really tight budget, and Mum wasn't that confident with her English. I think, maybe, the shock of her new life was a real jolt, and it gave her a lifetime of anxiety. She'd get us to answer the phone for her because she was shy with strangers, and she'd get to the doctor's two hours early. Mum avoided stressful situations.

She packed her suitcase, filled the freezer full of curries, and got on a plane on her own, right into a warzone.

In 1989, Mum and Dad's tempers frayed more easily, and we noticed. They were getting worse and worse news from home. Sri Lanka was being torn apart by violence. The Tamil Tigers were fighting for a separate homeland; the Sri Lankan army were fighting them; a violent Indian Peace Keeping Force (IPKF) was fighting both; and Sinhala Marxists were leading bloody insurrections. By the end of 1989, almost every relative we had left in Northern Sri Lanka had finalised their plans to leave.

Everyone that is, except Ammamma. Somehow, our grandmother had gotten left behind. That August, the shelling got close to the old lady's house and Mum, her youngest child, was worried sick. 'Getting you to England seems impossible, Amma. I don't know how it can be done,' she wrote to explain on a pale blue aerogram. Ammamma replied in her childlike handwriting, that it was okay, to leave her in Jaffna. 'Let me die here,' she wrote in her neat Tamil letters.

With three young children at home and only two weeks of annual leave, Mum was determined to do something. She packed a suitcase, filled the freezer full of curries, and got on a plane, right into a warzone. She hadn't boarded a plane on her own before, finding the gates and check-in counters confusing. When she landed, Colombo was unfamiliar, erupting with checkpoints and violence. She made it to the British High Commission, she queued, and she waited. She explained her case over and over again, at appointment after appointment, across several days. The building was teeming with visa applicants, all trying to escape too. It wasn't looking good.

Then, at last, an understanding civil servant heard her out. He asked if she could write a handwritten letter to the British Home Secretary to explain what she had told him. So with a blue biro and a piece of paper, Mum sat down right there in the High Commission office, and she wrote it all out as best she could. Mum says she sat down in that chaotic room with a blank page in front of her, and she began to cry tears of frustration. Normally our dad would do this kind of thing, and she couldn't get hold of him, and she just had to write it right then and it wouldn't be good enough. She handed it over, and the Sri Lankan staff at the High Commission started to giggle and exchange glances when they read it. It was full of English mistakes. 'What, *Sithi*?' her nephew said when she came out. He'd gone to considerable lengths to get her an appointment. 'What have you been doing? Almost twenty years in England, you can't even write simple English?'

With the help of others – a magistrate who'd married her cousin, a guy who knew a guy – in that unfair way that Sri Lankan and British systems operate, while waiting and worrying and borrowing, Mum persevered, the Home Office said yes, and she and Ammamma got on a plane to the UK. And then two months after Ammamma arrived, one and then another of our young boy cousins, Ganesh Anna and Thambi, came to live with us, too. Teenage boys were a target those days for army intimidation or recruitment into the Tigers, and our aunties asked my parents to keep them safe.

So the two boys, my siblings, my parents, Ammamma and me were suddenly all of us living in our modest house in England. That humiliation over the Home Office letter meant that Mum had come back to the UK determined, and so at forty she started English classes after work on Thursdays and Fridays. She picked up romantic novels from the library, choosing them based on their covers: some Barbara Cartland, some Tolstoy. She went on to complete GCSEs, A Levels and trained as a teaching assistant, studying in her evenings and weekends. She did that alongside her full-time job in a factory, making chipboards with a soldering iron. And she did it while cooking for a family of eight, cleaning the house, doing all the laundry, carrying shopping home and getting five kids – two of whom weren't her own – to stop watching TV, finish their homework, shower, brush their teeth and arrive at school on time.

Last year I asked her if she'd had much help. She said with a smile, 'Sometimes your father washed his own plate.'

And sometimes, she had a meltdown.

Mum was always prepared to do it all for us, to watch *Top of the Pops* with us, and be silly with us, but she needed and still needs the food to taste good. Those days when she shouted for curry leaves, I think what she was really saying was: 'Hello? Can somebody help me?' Dad did a lot more than many men; he changed nappies, told us stories and bought the groceries. But when Dad heard her, I think it sounded to him like her

saying, 'I can shut this whole thing down, if you want.' And he definitely didn't want that. So he would put his coat on, go outside, return with fresh curry leaves and salt. And Mum would get the whole show back on the road again.

So he would put on his coat, go outside, return with fresh curry leaves and salt. And Mum would get the whole show back on the road again.

Mum's cooking style is full of shortcuts and innovations, guided by her fantastic taste for food, and it could not be further from her mother's style which was completely methodical and old school and consistent, every time. Once Ammamma was safely with us, she and Mum disagreed over many things, but they were united on the curry leaf issue. And if Mum was willing to let us all go hungry over it, with all that going on, I hope you are persuaded to track down fresh curry leaves (see page 18 for where). Like olive oil for Italian cooking, they are a fundamental pillar of Sri Lankan food, and, like our grandmother, they are irreplaceable.

Prawn curry with tamarind

Tamarind and prawns make a great couple. The acidic, tangy flavour of tamarind and the delicious sweetness in prawns just work like magic together. This spicy curry celebrates the match, hailing from the north of the island, with smoky roasted chillies in the spice mix and a little satininess from the coconut milk. In Sri Lanka it's made with the whole prawn – shells, heads and all – which then requires a little arm-wrestling and fiddling as you eat them. To make it easier for the eater, my recipe is made either with raw, shelled prawns, or prawns you have shelled yourself. If you have time and want the flavour bomb of the original, it's worth the effort to get shelling, and then to spend two minutes making a little spicy prawn oil with the shells and heads. It sounds like it could be a bit cheffy or oily, but it's super-easy and makes for a glossy, complex, glorious dish. Instructions for both methods are below.

Serves 2

500g raw prawns with shells on (300g without)

1 tbsp coconut or vegetable oil, plus 2 tbsp for the prawn oil

2 tsp SL curry powder (see page 21), plus 1 tsp for the prawn oil

1½ golf ball-sized pieces of tamarind block, soaked in 60ml warm water for 10 minutes

1 red onion, peeled and finely sliced

10 fresh curry leaves

1 garlic clove, peeled and finely sliced

2cm fresh root ginger, peeled and finely sliced

A pinch of salt

200ml coconut milk

½ lime

1. First, prepare the prawns. It may seem gross but it is actually very satisfying to clean prawns. You pull the head off each one, and then you slide a finger under the shell and peel it off like a jacket, leaving the tails on the prawns. Keep all the heads and shells in a separate bowl, but discard the 'vein' running down the back of the prawn if you want (I'm usually too lazy to devein them and the membrane isn't harmful, but if you want to: use a small, sharp knife to carefully cut a small line into each prawn by running it the length of the prawn's back, then with the tip of your knife, remove the black membrane and discard). Put the prawns back in the fridge.

2. If you're making the prawn oil, place a sieve over a heatproof bowl. Heat 2 tablespoons of oil in a wok or medium-sized pan over a high heat. When it's shimmering and hot, add the prawn heads and shells and 1 teaspoon of SL curry powder. Stir-fry vigorously for 7–8 minutes, until the shells are pink; give the heads a bit of a squeeze with the end of your spoon as you go, as they're full of sweet flavour. Switch off the heat, and pass the prawn oil through your sieve into the bowl, discarding any prawn shells left in the sieve.

3. To make the curry, squeeze the tamarind with your fingers, then discard the seeds and skin, leaving behind the pulpy water. Add 1 tablespoon of oil to your wok or pan over a medium-high heat. Fry the onion for 4–5 minutes, stirring occasionally, until soft. Add the curry leaves, garlic and ginger. Stir-fry for 30 seconds until the garlic is just getting fragrant, then stir in the tamarind water, 2 teaspoons of SL curry powder and the salt, and bring to a boil. Turn the heat down to a simmer and cook through for 2–3 minutes. Finally, add the prawns and coconut milk, and stir through. Bring back to a simmer and cook for 3–4 minutes – no more or the prawns will overcook. Switch off the heat and if you have it, pour the prawn oil into the curry and stir it in gently so that it is nice and glossy. Dish up, and finish with a generous squeeze of lime.

Jaffna crab curry

My Ammamma used to say that you were already aged two on your first birthday, that wearing a bra really showed a lack of decorum, and that Jaffna's famous crab curry should be cooked like meat. Look, we didn't agree about everything, but on crab, or *nandu*, and I know everyone says this about their own granny, there just isn't a greater authority. And of Sri Lanka's hundreds of lovely curry recipes, Jaffna crab curry is widely regarded as our best.

Luckily for you, this method is hers, no additions or subtractions, a century old, straight out of Karaveddy, and just as Ammamma said, cooked in a very similar way to a red beef or mutton curry. The key to Jaffna crab curry is a mix of sweet, salty, delicate crabmeat, spicy, smoky roasted curry liquid with plenty of coconut milk, curry leaves, fried onions and a little ginger, and then in the final seconds of cooking, a generous spice explosion of *eraichithool* or 'meat powder' spice mix, heavy on fennel, cardamom and nutmeg, making a layered flavour bomb. Unlike many Jaffna seafood recipes, the women in my family skip tamarind for crab and use fresh lime juice instead, which makes everything brighter and lighter. Traditionally, you stir through a light handful of bitter leaves of *murungai*, or moringa, which are wildly nutritious and slightly peppery. You can skip them altogether or if you can't get them, young mustard greens or rocket are a good substitute and also look very pretty.

I'm personally squeamish about cooking crab, so this is a beginner's guide – and I want to reassure you that if you want to brave it, it is actually very easy to make. It is a bit messy to eat, because you need to prise, crack and suck white flesh from crab's hard shell, but it turns out to be messy fun and I promise the rewards are worth it. Get the freshest, best crab you can, don't touch it too much as it cooks, and get ready for possibly the best recipe in the book, and the whole island.

Serves 4

1 large crab (approx. 1kg)

1 tbsp coconut or vegetable oil

1 red onion, peeled and finely sliced

2 garlic cloves, peeled and finely sliced

3cm fresh root ginger, peeled and finely sliced

20 fresh curry leaves

1 tsp salt, or to taste

1½ tbsp SL curry powder (see page 21)

1. If you get a live crab, put it in the freezer for 1 hour until it stops moving completely. Then, with your fingers, lift and twist off the triangular flap under the crab and throw it away. With your fingers, lift and remove the head of the crab, which you should keep for presentation. Discard any grey juice but keep the yellow liquid as it is full of flavour. Cut the crab in half like you were slicing through the spine of an open book (and if it's a big crab, into quarters too). Then pull off the claws and the legs. Crack the claws by tapping them with the back of a big knife to let the curry seep into the crab while cooking. Wash the crab pieces and set aside.

Continued overleaf

FISH, SEAFOOD & MEAT

Optional: 70g rocket leaves or
   mustard greens

100ml coconut milk

1 heaped tsp meat powder
   (see page 21)

½ lime

2. Heat the oil in a large saucepan over a medium heat. Fry the onion for 3–4 minutes, until soft. Add the garlic and ginger, and after about 1 minute when the garlic is starting to get fragrant, add the curry leaves, and cook for 30 seconds–1 minute, so the curry leaves are bright green. Add the salt, SL curry powder and the crab. Sauté for 3–4 minutes to give the crab a nice colour and fragrance. Pour over just enough water so the crab is about half submerged in liquid. Bring to a boil, then immediately turn the heat to a simmer and cook for 15–20 minutes. When it's ready, the crab should be pink and if you prise any flesh, it should not be slimy or raw.

3. Gently stir in the rocket leaves or mustard greens, if using, and coconut milk, and cook through for 3–5 minutes. Switch off the heat and stir through a generous teaspoon of meat powder. Dish up immediately onto a big sharing platter. Seconds before eating, finish with a squeeze of lime.

Crab fried rice

Fried rice is big in Sri Lanka; a hybrid Sri Lankan-Chinese food, and it tastes as brilliant as you'd expect from two powerhouse cuisines coming together. This recipe is inspired by my cousin's wife, Dharma, who made me some delicious fried rice for lunch one day when I went to visit her on her farm.

Dharma, her mum and her two teenage daughters grow peanuts and other vegetables on their efficient all-female farm in the north-east of the island, in a town called Viswamadu. Close to Mullaitivu, Dharma lives in a beautiful, glimmering arc of a white sandy bay with a lively fishing port for many incredible fish and sweet, small blue swimmer crabs. Like everyone else in the area, she and her family were among hundreds of thousands of Tamil civilians caught between government and rebel fighters at the end of the war, and the horrors of what happened have stuck around in their memory, like the shrapnel in her legs. That they managed to survive at all is a miracle. Now Dharma talks with a fast, acerbic wit, she is kind, she is unfeasibly practical, and she cooks, farms, makes sweets and does a million other things with the peanuts from the farm that keeps their family surviving.

Peanuts, rice and crab, I discovered that day, make a great trio; nutty and sweet and hearty. Like the busy working woman who taught me it, this recipe is intended to get you some of the highs of a Sri Lankan lunch as quickly as possible. This recipe is cooked fast, using cooked crabmeat (ideally the freshest you can get). You want the rice, on the other hand, to ideally be a day old, but I have included instructions if you need to cook it fresh. The rice grains should get a little crispy in the bottom of the pan, and they should soak up the hot, sweet curry liquid, which is made with tamarind, coconut milk and a mix of curry powders. Because crab curry is traditionally cooked in the north and east of Sri Lanka with *murungai-ilai* (moringa leaves), which have a slightly bitter taste, this recipe uses rocket to add some pep and freshness. Like Dharma, I love to add crunchy peanuts which take things up another gear, but if you're allergic you can skip them and still enjoy a nearly perfect dish.

Serves 2–3

350g leftover cooked rice (or 125g jasmine, basmati or short-grain uncooked rice)

1½ golf ball-sized pieces of tamarind block, soaked in 60ml warm water for 10 minutes

3 tbsp coconut or vegetable oil

½ red onion, peeled and very thinly sliced

15 fresh curry leaves

2 garlic cloves, peeled and finely sliced

Continued overleaf

1. If you need to cook your rice, pour the uncooked rice into a saucepan and rinse loosely under the tap. Drain well, then cover in 250ml water. Place over a medium-high heat, bring to a boil, then lower the heat to a simmer and cover with lid. Cook for 10–18 minutes depending on what kind of rice you're cooking, until the water is fully absorbed. Remove from the heat and let it sit for about 10 minutes, covered. Gently fluff the rice grains with a fork.

2. When you're ready to make fried rice, squeeze the tamarind with your fingers, then discard the seeds and skin, leaving behind the pulpy water. Add 2 tablespoons oil to a wok or large frying pan over a high heat. When the oil starts shimmering, add the about half the onion (which should sizzle), 5 curry leaves and all the garlic. Stir-fry for 2–3 minutes, until the onions are translucent, being careful not to burn the garlic.

1 tsp salt, or to taste

1 tsp SL curry powder
(see page 21)

2 handfuls of rocket leaves,
chopped

200ml coconut milk

150g picked, cooked crabmeat

1 large organic or free-range egg

1 tsp chilli flakes

1 tbsp mayonnaise (Kewpie,
if possible)

1 tsp meat powder
(see page 21)

2 spring onions, sliced
on the diagonal

Optional: 2 tbsp dry-roasted
peanuts, crushed

3. Lower the heat to medium-high, and add the tamarind water, salt, SL curry powder, rocket and coconut milk, and stir-fry for 2–3 minutes until it all bubbles a little bit. Add the cooked crabmeat, and let it soak up the curry for 2–3 minutes, stirring it once or twice to make sure the curry liquid touches all the crab. Spoon the crab curry mixture and all the liquid out into a bowl.

4. Back in the wok or frying pan, add the remaining 1 tablespoon of oil, turn the heat up to high and, when shimmering, add the rest of the curry leaves and red onion. Stir-fry until the onion is soft, then pull it over to one side and crack the egg into the middle of the pan. As the egg cooks, break it up with your spoon into pieces, to make small soft folds. After 30 seconds, add the chilli flakes and let them cook in the oil. About 30 seconds later, add the cooked rice, along with the mayonnaise. Stir-fry everything for 2–3 minutes until the rice is heated through thoroughly and some bits are getting a little crunchy. Return the curried crab to the pan, stir-fry for 30 seconds, switch off the heat and add the meat powder. Stir through, dish up and finish with sliced spring onions and peanuts, if using. Serve hot.

Shrimp and seafood kool stew

Kool is the seafood gumbo of Sri Lanka's Tamil communities: spicy and fishy and delicious all at the same time. Traditionally, it is thickened with *odiyal* flour, the pounded-up root of palmyrah trees – the beautiful spiky palms so emblematic of the north and east of the island – which give it a bitter taste. Because it is hard to come by, this one is thickened with ground rice or rice flour, which makes it less nutritious than the original, but makes for a velvety mouthfeel and gives it a nutty aroma.

My first kool experience was at Coventry Tamil hostess-with-the-mostess, Vathany Auntie's house. Vathany Auntie was the kind of mum that made all the other mums feel inadequate. She worked full-time, was doing a part-time PhD and she turned out insanely delicious food, all while raising her three over-achieving children. Annoyingly, she was also the kind of sweetheart who would drop round a curry just when you needed it, and everyone would like it better than yours. My father and all the other clueless uncles would beam effusively if Vathany Auntie was doing the cooking, and I'm ashamed to say, all us kids would too. Man, it was too good to pretend otherwise: those lovely soft rotis, that soft fried aubergine curry, that unfeasibly delicious dal, and her whirling around the kitchen like a smiley tornado. Our mum was less than thrilled by the endless praise these antics received but even she crumbled at a big pot of Vathany Auntie's kool. I remember her cooing 'oooooh' when she came across it. That's how I remember eating it: all the aunties and uncles fussing over a huge pot of seafood, fish, spices and rice, ladled out while Vathany Auntie probably did a solo cello performance.

Serves 4–6

3 golf ball-sized pieces of tamarind block, soaked in 240ml warm water for 10 minutes

125g white rice

300ml water

1 tbsp rice flour

350g monkfish tail

250g raw prawns, shrimp (peeled) or any other seafood (clams, mussels, crabmeat)

For the kool spice paste

7 dried red Kashmiri chillies

4 garlic cloves, peeled

1 tsp black peppercorns

2 tsp cumin seeds

1 tsp coriander seeds

3 or 4 cloves

½ tsp ground turmeric

1½ tsp salt, or to taste

1. Squeeze the tamarind with your fingers, then discard the seeds and skin, leaving behind the pulpy water.

2. To make the kool spice paste, put all the ingredients in a spice grinder and blitz until fine. Add a teaspoon or two of water and mix to a paste.

3. Pour the rice into a saucepan and rinse loosely under the tap, then drain well. Cover with 250ml water, then place over a medium heat and bring to a boil. Turn it down to a simmer, add the spice paste, cover and cook for 10 minutes. Cut the monkfish tail into 4–6 portions

4. Mix the rice flour with the remaining 50ml water in a small bowl to make a paste. Add to the pan, along with the tamarind water, monkfish and prawns (or seafood), stirring continuously, and cook for 3–5 minutes depending on the thickness of the monkfish tails. If necessary, add a little more water to loosen it; you want it to be more like a gumbo. To check if the fish is cooked, use a fork to gently flake a piece; it should be opaque all the way through and flake easily. Serve hot.

Lamb chops and mint sambol

We don't grill much in Sri Lanka, which is weird because most rural households go to all the trouble of making a fire with real firewood in a *dara lipa*. My parents used to dip chicken gizzards and little morsels of meat into Sri Lankan curry powder while they were cooking, and then hold them over a gas flame for us. It was probably very dangerous but it was the Eighties and no one wore a seatbelt either. It meant we all got a taste for spicy grilled meat from the time we were toddlers.

This easy, impressive-looking lamb dish is amazing cooked on the barbecue but if that's not an option, you can pan-fry then oven-cook it, as I have done here. It is basically a version of the red lamb curry (page 120), using all the same spices but with tender, juicy chops instead. It's perfect with some mint sambol, which is very traditional and is also magic with crab fried rice (page 112).

Serves 4

4 lamb chops (150–180g each)

1 tbsp coconut or vegetable oil

1 tsp meat powder (see page 21)

½ lime

For the marinade

200g thick coconut cream or Greek yoghurt

3 tsp SL curry powder (see page 21)

15 fresh curry leaves, very finely chopped

½ tbsp minced fresh ginger

½ tbsp minced fresh garlic

1 tsp salt, or to taste

For the mint sambol

50g mint leaves

50ml coconut milk

4 shallots, peeled

2 garlic cloves, peeled

2 green chillies, roughly chopped (deseeded if you prefer it less spicy!)

1 tsp salt, or to taste

Juice of 1 lime

120g freshly grated coconut (see page 175)

A grind or 2 of black pepper

1. To make the mint sambol, put all the sambol ingredients except the lime juice, grated coconut and black pepper in a food processor and blitz to a paste. Scoop out into a bowl, then use your hands to mix through the lime juice and grated coconut. Finish with a grind or two of black pepper, to taste.

2. For the lamb chops marinade, in a large bowl, mix together the coconut cream (or yoghurt), SL curry powder, curry leaves, ginger and garlic, and season with the salt. Put the lamb chops in the marinade and turn to coat thoroughly. Cover the bowl with a plate or lid, and leave at room temperature for 30 minutes–1 hour.

3. Preheat the oven to 220°C/Fan 200°C/Gas Mark 7. Heat the oil in an ovenproof large frying pan over a high heat. When the oil is hot, add the lamb chops and cook for about 3 minutes on each side until browned. Press the chops into the pan a little with tongs to get a nice colour.

4. Using oven gloves, place the pan in the preheated oven and let the chops roast to your desired doneness – about 10 minutes for medium-rare. The cooking time can vary a lot depending on the thickness of the chops and lots of other factors, so check back often. Transfer the lamb to a serving dish or platter, cover with kitchen foil, and let rest for 5 minutes. Finish with a pinch of meat powder and a squeeze of lime. Serve the chops with the mint sambol.

Slow-cooked lamb red curry

In 1992, my 18-year-old brother left home and my mother fell into a dark depression. There must be a whole chapter in the psychotherapy textbook for the sweet love that Sri Lankan mothers have for their sons. Treasured and exalted, they're often nicknamed 'king' while daughters sulk and do the dishes and their brothers watch TV. When Amu moved out, drunk with excitement, he taunted Mum's tear-stained face with 'Yes! At last! No more Sri Lankan food!', a quip designed to wound her deeply, a declaration of his independence.

But Amu, like the rest of his engineering buddies at Imperial College London, was a certified geek, seven days a week, and he soon found he couldn't do his laundry, or any other basic survival tasks beyond playing Street Fighter II. 'Mum,' he said, on his first pay-phone call home 'so how do you make lamb curry?' She was delighted. And so a ritual began of her cooking industrial-sized vats of delicious Jaffna-style lamb curry, portioning it into meal-sized freezer bags, and driving it to the King himself and the other princes of his corridor, every few weeks, for the entire four years he went to university and for several thereafter.

When you taste this lamb curry, you'll understand what was happening there.

Lamb – or for even better flavour, hogget or mutton – has the perfect luxurious, gamey, rich flavour for being cooked in the fragrant, fiery, smoky braising liquid of a roasted red curry, with just a little coconut milk. Killing a goat to cook it in this way is still a way we celebrate birthdays, successful visa applications and news of pregnancies in rural Jaffna, and I don't know a Sri Lankan man who doesn't get excited at the mere mention of the dish (even the vegetarians). I, too, like to cook it the old-fashioned way, using a lot of spice mix and a little coconut milk, and it works best with braising cuts like lamb shoulder, neck or leg, cooked over a low heat, until you can cut into the soft meat with a spoon. Please note: it looks very festive and dramatic as a whole shoulder on the bone, like in the picture opposite, but the spices really penetrate the meat best when cooked as cubes or as lamb shanks, as the recipe on the next page. If you'd still like to adapt it to cook as a whole bone-in shoulder, follow the instructions in the recipe, but use a deep, high-sided roasted tray in step 3, and after you add the water, cook covered with foil in the oven at 190°C/Fan 170°C/Gas Mark 5 for 3½–4 hours, until the meat is falling off the bone. I also like to throw in a few waxy potatoes, to soak up all the delicious curry liquor, and all the women in my family do the same.

I don't know what was going on with my brother in the Nineties, because despite its feasting reputation and how gorgeous it looks on a table, this is an easy dish to cook yourself. The thing that makes it sing is the *eraichithool* or meat powder spice mix you stir through at the end, after you have let it cook away while you were playing computer games for 2–3 hours. Meat powder adds a warm, wonderful anise-like taste that will transport you into your own experience of being an exalted Sri Lankan king. This is one of the spiciest curries in the book, and is not for the faint-hearted. To cool you down, make it alongside one of the yoghurt dishes on page 200 or 149.

Ingredients & method overleaf

Serves 5 or 6

300g potatoes, peeled and chopped into 2cm cubes

2 tbsp coconut or vegetable oil

2 red onions, peeled and finely sliced

30 fresh curry leaves

6 garlic cloves, peeled and halved

6cm fresh root ginger, peeled and sliced

5 or 6 bone-in lamb shanks (approx. 350g each) or approx.1.5kg boneless lamb shoulder, cubed

2 tsp salt, or to taste

2 heaped tbsp SL curry powder (see page 21)

500ml coconut milk

2 heaped tsp meat powder (see page 21)

1 lime

1. Put the potatoes in a large pan of cold water. Bring to the boil and par-boil for 4–5 minutes. They should still have a little resistance when you poke them with a knife. Drain and set aside.

2. To make the curry, heat the oil in a large saucepan over a medium heat. Fry the onions for 6–7 minutes, until starting to brown. Add the curry leaves, and after 30 seconds when they are bright green, add the garlic and ginger, and cook for a further 1–2 minutes until the garlic is beginning to brown.

3. Add the lamb, salt and SL curry powder. Pour in enough cold water to just cover the lamb, then cover with a lid slightly ajar. Bring to a simmer and cook for 1½–2 hours. It is cooked when the lamb is so soft you can cut through it with a spoon.

4. Get a small, clean saucepan ready. Using oven gloves, place the saucepan with the lamb on a heatproof surface on a table. Tilting the pan a little, use a ladle to scoop out the curry liquid and transfer it to the small saucepan. Add the potatoes and coconut milk to the curry liquid, and place over a medium-high heat. Let it bubble away for 10 minutes, to thicken the curry.

5. When the potatoes are very tender, switch off the heat, and stir through the meat powder.

6. Assemble the lamb curry by carefully transferring the lamb to a serving dish or platter. (It's very soft so it may be slippery!) Spoon over the curry liquid, and serve with a generous squeeze of lime.

Black pork belly curry

Black pork curry is one of Sri Lanka's most famous dishes. A few years ago, I ate my way through some of the island's reported best renditions. I have cooked in the kitchen, learning black pork curry with the chefs of the beautiful Barefoot Cafe; I have gorged it late-night at the venerable Dutch Burgher Union; I have guzzled it down in many homes. But none can hold a candle to the one my late cousin Sri Anna loved. Sri Anna was the kind of unrepentant gourmand who required many heart bypass surgeries and a cocktail of drugs to deal with his arteries, and who once woke up from an open-heart surgery asking for *kalu pol*, a wild boar, gamey – and at the time illegal – version of this curry.

My dear friend chef Harith Rajakaruna and I spent many hours cooking his style of black pork in his home kitchen in Colombo. Based on his ingenuity and his years of cooking with various of his aunties and friends, I found it is the closest to the way Sri Anna liked it. Harith's slow-cooked curry is simple to make but requires a bit of toasting and grinding in the prep stage, all in the service of giving the sweet, rich pork a smoky, toasty flavour. It is brightened up with vinegar and a little sugar, it uses an earthier spice mix and no coconut milk. It is absolutely delicious made with pork belly or another braising cut of pork, and it works well with something pickled (perhaps aubergine moju, page 198), yellow rice (page 206) and a cucumber mor yoghurt on page 200.

Serves 4

For the black spice mix

10 fresh curry leaves

Optional: 5cm piece of pandan leaf

1 stick of cinnamon

5 whole cardamom pods, lightly bashed in a pestle and mortar

1 tsp coriander seeds

1 tsp black peppercorns

1½ tsp mustard seeds

5 or 6 cloves

1 tsp cumin seeds

½ tsp fenugreek seeds

½ tsp fennel seeds

For the pork belly curry

25g rice (I use basmati or a short grain, whatever I have in the house)

1. First, make the black spice mix (which you can do as much as a few days ahead if you like). In a dry frying pan over a high heat, toast the curry leaves and pandan leaf, if using, for 2–3 minutes, stirring as you go, until they begin to turn brown. Turn the heat down a little to medium-high, and add the cinnamon, cardamom, coriander and peppercorns. Toast them all up, stirring every so often, for about a minute. Now add the more delicate spices that need less time: the mustard seeds, cloves, cumin, fenugreek and fennel. Keep toasting and stirring for a further 1–2 minutes, by which time everything should be smelling fragrant and toasty, but not burnt. Spoon it all into a bowl and leave to one side to cool. When cool, blitz in a spice grinder or mini food processor until fine. My advice is to then spoon it into a jar; any excess black spice mix can be kept in the fridge for a month.

2. Next, make the toasted rice coconut powder that will give the curry its dark colour and smoky, toasty flavour. In a clean frying pan over a medium heat, toast the rice, stirring it every few seconds so it toasts evenly. After 5 minutes, add the desiccated or freshly grated coconut. Keep stirring every so often for 8–10 minutes, until the coconut and rice grains are toasted and golden brown. You don't want anything fully black or burnt! Spoon into a bowl and leave to cool. When cool, blitz this as well.

Continued overleaf

25g desiccated coconut or
freshly grated coconut
(see page 175)

750g pork belly, skin on

Salt

2 tbsp coconut or vegetable oil

1 red onion, peeled and
finely sliced

4 green chillies, slit lengthways

8cm fresh root ginger, peeled
and sliced

1 lemongrass stalk, bruised

10 fresh curry leaves

Optional: 5cm piece of pandan
leaf

1½ tbsp black spice mix
(see previous page)

2 tbsp goroka paste if you can
get it, or 2 tbsp shop-bought
tamarind paste

1 tsp granulated sugar

350ml water

1 tbsp apple cider or
coconut vinegar

3. Finally, make the curry. Slice the pork into cubes, around 2–3cm thick, and toss a pinch or two of salt over them. Leave uncovered at room temperature while you get on with the rest of the curry.

4. Heat the oil in a large saucepan over a medium heat. When hot, add the onion and cook for 4–5 minutes, stirring occasionally so it doesn't stick to the pan. When translucent, add the green chillies, ginger, lemongrass, curry leaves and pandan leaf, if using. Stir-fry for 2–3 minutes, until the curry leaves are bright green.

5. Add the pork to the pan and cook for 3–4 minutes, stirring occasionally, to get a little bit of colour. Add the black spice mix, the goroka (or tamarind), sugar and water. Stir well to mix together and allow to come to a gentle boil. Lower the heat and leave to simmer for 2½ hours, with the lid slightly ajar. Around 30 minutes before the end of cooking, stir through the toasted rice and coconut powder, along with the vinegar. Turn off the heat and let the curry sit for 10 minutes before you serve.

Pickled pork curry

This gently spiced pork curry is an homage to an old Burgher recipe from housewives' favourite, the *Ceylon Daily News* cookbook. It is sweet and moreish. It works fantastically with pineapple sambol (page 180).

Serves 4

2 tbsp coconut or vegetable oil

2 onions, peeled and diced

20 fresh curry leaves

4cm fresh root ginger, peeled and sliced

2 garlic cloves, peeled and halved

450g pork ribs or pork shoulder, diced into 2–3cm chunks

2 tbsp pickled pork curry spice mix (see below)

125ml apple cider or white wine vinegar

1 tsp granulated sugar

2 lemongrass stalks

Optional: 5cm piece of pandan leaf

1 ½ tsp salt, or to taste

50ml coconut milk

For the pickled pork curry spice mix

2 tsp coriander seeds

1 tsp cumin seeds

5cm piece of cinnamon stick

⅓ tsp fenugreek seeds

½ tsp chilli powder

1. Make the spice mix by placing a small dry frying pan over a medium heat. Add all the spices and cook, stirring occasionally for 2–3 minutes, until fragrant. Transfer to a bowl to cool, then blitz in a spice grinder or mini food processor until fine.

2. Place a large saucepan or wok over a medium-high heat, add the oil and fry the diced onions for 4–5 minutes, until soft. Add the curry leaves, ginger and garlic. After 2–3 minutes, when the garlic is starting to brown, add the pork, 2 tablespoons of spice mix, the vinegar, sugar, lemongrass and pandan leaf, if using. Pour in enough water to just cover the pork, and sprinkle over the salt. Bring to a gentle boil and then turn the heat to low and leave to cook, partially covered with a lid, for 2–3 hours.

3. When the meat is very soft and you can slice a piece with a spoon, stir in the coconut milk and cook through for 3–4 minutes. Taste and if you think it needs it, add a teaspoon more vinegar.

Egg curry

This is a spicy, warming red curry which is very traditional in Sri Lanka, and makes for a delicious breakfast, although you can eat it at any time of day. I add a little more coconut milk in this one than other curries because I find it cools the roasted, smoky red curry liquor down and then you're not packing too much heat first thing in the morning. Using fenugreek in the temper will give it a slight bitterness and burnt sugar flavour. I let it cook a little longer than usual, so it gets glossy and thick and creamy, and then I can easily scoop it up with some quick little pol rotis (page 218) or crunchy buttered toast. The whole thing is finished off with a quick temper of crispy curry leaves and mustard seeds. I prefer the eggs with the yolks still soft inside, and if you have some seeni sambol (page 136) in the fridge, I recommend a spoonful on the side.

Serves 3–4

6 large organic or
free-range eggs

2 tbsp coconut or vegetable oil

½ red onion, peeled and
finely sliced

2 garlic cloves, peeled
and halved

2 medium tomatoes
(approx. 200g), roughly diced

Optional: 7.5cm piece of
pandan leaf

125ml water

2 tsp SL curry powder
(see page 21)

½ tsp ground turmeric

100ml coconut milk

1½ tsp salt, or to taste

For the temper

1 tbsp coconut or vegetable oil

6 or 7 fresh curry leaves

½ tsp mustard seeds

½ tsp fenugreek seeds

1 green chilli, sliced (and
deseeded if you like)

1. First, soft boil your eggs. Fill a large saucepan with water, and place over medium-high heat until it boils. You want a gentle rolling boil – big bubbles going at a regular pace, not really big noisy bubbles and not tiny bubbles either. Using a slotted spoon, carefully lower the eggs into the water one at a time. Using a timer, cook for 6½ minutes, maintaining a gentle boil as you go. Get a medium-sized bowl ready, filled about one-third full of cold water and 6 or 7 ice cubes. When the eggs are cooked, transfer them to the bowl of iced water. Wait 1–2 minutes for them to cool down a little, then gently crack and peel the eggs, starting from the wider end which contains the air pocket, then leave them in the iced water.

2. To make the curry, get a medium-sized frying pan or wok over a medium-high heat. Add the oil and onion, and fry for 3–4 minutes, until starting to become translucent. Add the garlic, tomatoes and pandan leaf, if using. Cook, stirring, for 1–2 minutes until the onion begins to brown, then add the water, SL curry powder and turmeric. Mix well and cook for 2–3 minutes, then stir in the coconut milk and bring almost to a boil. Dip a tablespoon into the liquid, and stir just the liquid lightly and rapidly as it simmers for 7–8 minutes (this helps stop the coconut milk from splitting as it thickens up). You want the consistency to be thick and glossy. Season with the salt then remove from the heat.

3. To make the temper, heat the oil in a small frying pan over a medium-high heat. Add the curry leaves which should sizzle up, the mustard seeds, fenugreek seeds and green chilli. Fry for 1–2 minutes until everything is really fragrant. Remove from the heat.

4. Finally, turn a medium-high heat under your curry and add the eggs, stirring carefully to coat them in the curry for just 1–2 minutes. Pour the whole temper, including the oil over the top, and serve.

Sri Lankan turmeric omelette

This is a favourite breakfast dish; one my mum cooks when she's taking orders for breakfast at the weekends from her grandson, Thierry, who may be only six but knows what's up. You can have it on its own with something fresh like a little dill, lime and watercress salad, perhaps with some soft white bread, too. It's very easy and quick: just softened onions, a little garlic, curry leaves, turmeric and green chillies. Don't skimp on seasoning, with plenty of salt, black pepper and cumin – an amazing mix called *milagai seeraham* in Tamil.

Serves 1–2

A pinch of cumin seeds

A pinch of black peppercorns

3 large organic or
free-range eggs

1 tsp salt, or to taste, plus more
to serve

¾ tsp ground turmeric

2 tbsp coconut or vegetable oil

½ red onion, peeled and finely
sliced (or a nice alternative
is 2–3 spring onions, chopped
into 2cm pieces)

1–2 green chillies, sliced

1 garlic clove, peeled and sliced

7 or 8 fresh curry leaves

1. For the pepper-cumin salt, toast the cumin seeds and peppercorns in a small dry frying pan over a medium heat for 1–2 minutes until fragrant. Transfer to a bowl to cool, then blitz in a spice grinder or mini food processor until fine, and keep aside for later.

2. In a bowl, whisk the eggs together with the salt and turmeric until frothy. Set aside.

3. Heat 1 tablespoon of oil in a frying pan around 20–25cm wide over a medium heat. Add the onion (or spring onions), green chillies, garlic and curry leaves. Allow to cook, stirring occasionally, for 4–5 minutes, so that the onion softens; don't allow it to crisp, and don't cook past the point that the chillies and curry leaves are still bright green.

4. Add the remaining tablespoon of oil to the pan, wait 30 seconds for the oil to get hot, and then pour in the eggs. Keep cooking over a medium heat and use a spatula to pull the edges in as they set, tilting the pan to spread the uncooked egg around. Continue this motion of pulling the edges in and tilting all around the pan, until the omelette is almost set, which will take around 2–3 minutes.

5. Fold in half and serve, dusting generously with pepper-cumin and a little extra salt.

Seeni sambol, egg and cheese sandwich

On our first few days in Colombo at the start of the holidays when we were children, we always wanted to eat all that we couldn't back in England: milk hoppers from that van guy at the Bambalapitya flats, sticky mangoes from Wellawatte market, crunchy fried falafels of shrimp *vadai* bought at the seaside at the Galle Face.

Our Colombo cousins were deeply, deeply unimpressed at this boring and earnest traditionalism, disappointed that we were so square that we could not bring even stories of burgers or pizza from home. I don't know who we thought we were kidding, but we sort of doubled down on our own hot air, and pretended that we thought the fast food joints that began opening in Colombo in the Nineties – KFC, Pizza Hut and, of course, McDonald's – were gross.

And so it wasn't until my twenties that I walked guiltily into a cool, air-conditioned McDonald's on Galle Road and inhaled that unmistakable whiff of French fries. Behind the smiling staff in hairnets, I eyed up the board and thought: 'Bloody hell. What *is* this menu?' Alongside the usual cheeseburgers and chicken nuggets was a list of local, Lankanised dishes, just as every regional McDonald's does to curry favour (sorry) with the locals. I ordered every Lankanised dish they had, and up first was a soft breakfast bun with seeni sambol, melted American cheese and a fried egg. It still is, without prejudice, the most delicious McDonald's dish I have tried in any McDonald's anywhere in the world. This recipe is an homage to that original.

Seeni means sugar, because you make the sambol by caramelising shallots or red onions, reducing and stirring until you get a jammy, sticky, molasses colour, adding sugar, cinnamon, tamarind for tanginess and a few other spices as you go. Seeni sambol is one of the big guns of the Sri Lankan sambol repertoire, a kind of magnificent, punchy, fiery shallot jam that you smear onto things, just as you would with a chutney or a salsa. It pairs very well with eggs, as the oozy richness of the yolks enjoy a mouth party with the tart, fragrant sweetness of the sambol – and so Sri Lankans are fond of eating this sambol with egg hoppers, egg rotis or in other egg sandwiches. This recipe makes enough to have sambol leftovers that you can store in a jar in the fridge for up to a month, so I wish you many fun adventures with seeni sambol. For this sandwich, any white bread will do (I use a potato sourdough from the Dusty Knuckle bakery in east London because my flatmate Sarah is mad for it and always has some in the house) and I think melted, strong Cheddar works better than Kraft, but see what you think when you make it yourself.

Ingredients & method overleaf

Serves 2

For the seeni sambol

2½ golf ball-sized pieces of tamarind block, soaked in 125ml warm water for 10 minutes

1½ tbsp coconut or vegetable oil

20 fresh curry leaves

2 x 5cm pieces of cinnamon stick

10 whole cardamom pods, lightly bashed in a pestle and mortar

6 cloves

4 green chillies, sliced into thirds

1 tsp salt, or to taste

6 red onions, peeled and finely sliced

1 tbsp apple cider vinegar

4 tbsp granulated or caster sugar

For the sandwich

Butter for spreading the bread, plus 3 knobs

4 slices of white bread (e.g. sourdough or white bloomer)

120g grated Cheddar or Gruyère

2 large organic or free-range eggs

Salt

1. For the seeni sambol, squeeze the tamarind with your fingers, then discard the seeds and skin, leaving behind the pulpy water.

2. Heat the oil in a large saucepan over a medium heat. Once hot, add the curry leaves, cinnamon, cardamom, cloves, chillies and salt. Cook for 2–3 minutes, stirring regularly, being careful not to burn the spices. Lower the heat to medium, add the onions and cover with a lid. Cook for 5 minutes, until they are soft. Take the lid off, reduce the heat to low, and cook for 25 minutes, stirring occasionally, until deep golden brown. If the onions look like they might dry out or burn, add a tablespoon or two of water at a time, and scrape up any browned bits that are stuck to the bottom of the pan. Once the onions are ready, deglaze the pan by adding the vinegar and scraping any browned bits that are stuck to the bottom, then cook for about 1 minute, until the liquid has evaporated. Add the tamarind water and sugar, and cook for a further 3–5 minutes, stirring regularly, until the mixture is dark brown. Remove from the heat, spoon into a clean jar with the lid off and let cool completely.

3. Butter your slices of white bread on one side. On a plate, place a slice of bread buttered-side down. Spread with a tablespoon schmear of seeni sambol, then top with some grated cheese and another slice of bread, buttered-side up. Repeat to make a second sandwich.

4. Set a large heavy-based frying pan over a low-medium heat and add a knob of butter. It should melt gently; if it sputters, turn the heat down a little. Place both sandwiches directly on the melted butter. Squish them down with a metal slice or a heavy pan, and fry for 3–4 minutes until golden brown, checking halfway through to make sure they are not burning. Once golden, take them out of the pan, add a second knob of butter and repeat the process on the other side of the sandwiches. Rest the sandwiches on a plate.

5. Add the final knob of butter to the pan. When melted, crack the eggs into the pan with a little distance between them so they don't bleed into each other. Season with a pinch of salt, and cook for about 2 minutes until the whites are nearly set on top and the yolks are still runny. Using a spatula, gently flip over the eggs one at a time, season with more salt, and let cook another 5–10 seconds. Transfer to a plate.

6. Take each toasted sandwich and split the two slices apart, add one egg and put the slices back together. Eat it piping hot.

Red chicken curry

This is the spicy Sri Lankan chicken curry you want when you go home to visit your parents even though you feel defensive about their perfectly sensible questions about how work is going or whether your boyfriend is serious. This is the curry so good that you eventually must face up to the spectre of your teenage bedroom and all those schoolbooks you still haven't thrown away. You give yourself up to your parents driving you crazy, be it because the remote control is still wrapped in clingfilm or because Mum appears to be rapping along to the radio. This curry will soothe you from your guilt and frustration about where you are in your life, because it is that delicious.

Like many other dishes in this book, this chicken curry is a Sri Lankan red braising curry, and it makes a soft, smoky, spicy, warming, everyday chicken dish. The coconut milk gives it a sweet lightness, and a couple of fresh tomatoes and a squeeze of fresh lime juice add an acidic brightness. I like it best with plain white rice and a couple of vegetable curries, the old-fashioned way Mum made it in the Nineties, but it is also a delicious partner for kiri bath (page 208) or spinach puttu (page 80). I like it with a little extra black pepper and a few whole cardamom pods, so these are both in the temper at the end of the dish, which I find makes for foolproof juiciness every time. This recipe uses my favourite flavoursome cut of chicken, thighs (either chopped into pieces or whole on the bone if you don't have time), but it's perfectly delicious if you prefer breast or leg.

Serves 2–4

2 tbsp coconut or vegetable oil

1 red onion, peeled and finely sliced

10 fresh curry leaves

1 tbsp sliced garlic

1 tbsp sliced fresh ginger

¾ tsp ground turmeric

2 medium tomatoes (approx. 200g), roughly chopped

1 heaped tbsp SL curry powder (see page 21)

1 tsp salt, or to taste

4 skinless chicken thighs

250ml water

150ml coconut milk

1 heaped tsp meat powder (see page 21)

½ lime

Continued overleaf

1. In a wok or medium-sized saucepan, heat the oil over a medium-high heat and fry the onion for 3–4 minutes, stirring occasionally, until soft. Add the curry leaves, garlic and ginger, and cook for 4–5 minutes, stirring occasionally, until the garlic is beginning to turn golden brown. Add a little splash of water if it starts to stick to the bottom of the pan.

2. Add the turmeric, chopped tomatoes, SL curry powder and salt. Slide the chicken thighs into the pot, and pour over the water. Let the liquid come up to a gentle bubble, and then turn the heat down to the slowest simmer, cover with a lid and cook for 45 minutes. To test if the chicken is cooked, fish out one of the thighs and pierce it with a skewer – if it is cooked, the juices will run clear; if the juices are still pink, the chicken needs to be cooked for longer.

3. When the chicken is cooked, transfer it to a plate. Then back in the pan, pour in the coconut milk, stir and turn the heat up to high to bring to a gentle bubble. Turn the heat back down and simmer for 3–4 minutes or until thickened.

For the temper

1 tbsp coconut or vegetable oil

10 fresh curry leaves

3 or 4 whole cardamom pods, lightly bashed in a pestle and mortar

A generous grind of black pepper

4. Turn off the heat, return the chicken to the pan and stir through the meat powder. Taste and adjust the salt if you think it needs a little more, then put the lid back on while you make the temper.

5. To make the temper, take a small frying pan and heat the oil over a medium-high heat. When the oil is shimmering and hot, add the curry leaves, cardamom and a couple of twists of black pepper, stirring a little so it doesn't burn. When the leaves are crispy, switch off the heat.

6. Dish up the chicken curry into a sharing bowl, and pour the hot temper and all its oil over the top. Finish with a generous squeeze of lime.

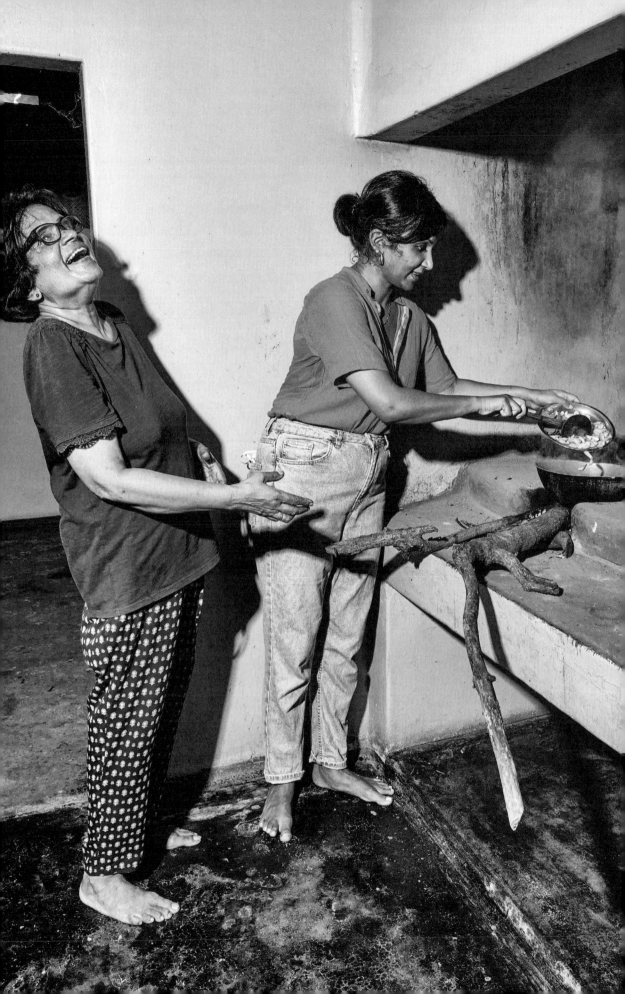

Chicken white sodhi curry

I have progressive hearing loss, and so does my mother and so did her mother. Because hearing aids didn't exist in 1930s Sri Lanka, my grandmother thought she was just deaf and so did everyone else. She didn't know it, but we all carry a gene called EPS8L2.

Ammamma was taken out of school when she was a pretty-faced thirteen-year-old and married to my grandfather, a gregarious guy with a flourishing series of grocery shops in the south of the island. Her blonde British headmistress got wind of the wedding and came to visit my grandmother's dad, a village chief. She pleaded with him to leave the girl in school, to do a little more of her education, and my great-grandfather nodded politely until she went home. The guy had eight daughters and in those days for every daughter you needed a dowry, a payment to the man who would marry her. So, when my grandfather offered to waive the dowry, Ammamma's dad ignored the white lady, and married off his daughter too young. Although she loved my grandfather very much, her married life was mostly spent in the kitchen, making food every day, unable to hear much.

When Ammamma moved to England in her seventies, my mum got her a hearing aid and she re-entered the world of sounds. When our parents yelled at us, we would sometimes dramatically march upstairs to our rooms and refuse to eat. (This is one of the sulkiest protests you can make to Sri Lankan parents who tend to get very stressed out about what you're eating.) After an hour or two, Ammamma would shuffle up the stairs and knock softly on the door, peering in to check we were okay, bringing something she had made for us. One of my favourite things she made was this comforting simple chicken *sodhi* curry.

Ammamma spoiled her kids and grandkids with food and stories for all the years I knew her, and a great many before. She was addicted to chewing tobacco, which is really carcinogenic, but she lived to the ripe old age of ninety, probably because she had had years of not having to listen to everyone's crap. The last time I saw her she took her solid gold earrings out of her ears to put them in mine, and made me swear not to tell anyone. I tried to tell her I had loads and I couldn't take them, but she was deaf to my protests. I wear them every day now. Anyway, she was a cool lady.

Ingredients & method overleaf

Serves 2

400g skinless chicken drumsticks

½ tsp cumin seeds

½ tsp coriander seeds

1 tsp salt, or to taste

½ tsp ground turmeric

3 garlic cloves, peeled
and halved

4cm fresh root ginger, peeled
and sliced

½ red onion, peeled and
finely sliced

4 green chillies, slit lengthways

10 fresh curry leaves

Optional: 5cm piece of
pandan leaf

200ml coconut milk

3 generous grinds of
black pepper

½ lime

1. Put the chicken, cumin, coriander, salt, turmeric, garlic and ginger in a large saucepan. Pour enough water into the pan so the chicken is just covered.

2. Place over a medium-high heat and bring to a gentle boil. Cover with a lid and turn the heat right down to a simmer. Cook gently for 30 minutes.

3. Add the onion, green chillies, curry leaves and pandan leaf, if using, and simmer for 10–15 minutes, until the meat is falling from the bone.

4. Stir in the coconut milk and bring it back to a gentle bubble with the lid off. Remove the chicken pieces and put them on a plate. Simmer the sauce for 10 minutes or until the sauce has reduced slightly and has thickened, then add the chicken back in.

5. Serve with about 3 generous grinds of black pepper and a squeeze of lime juice.

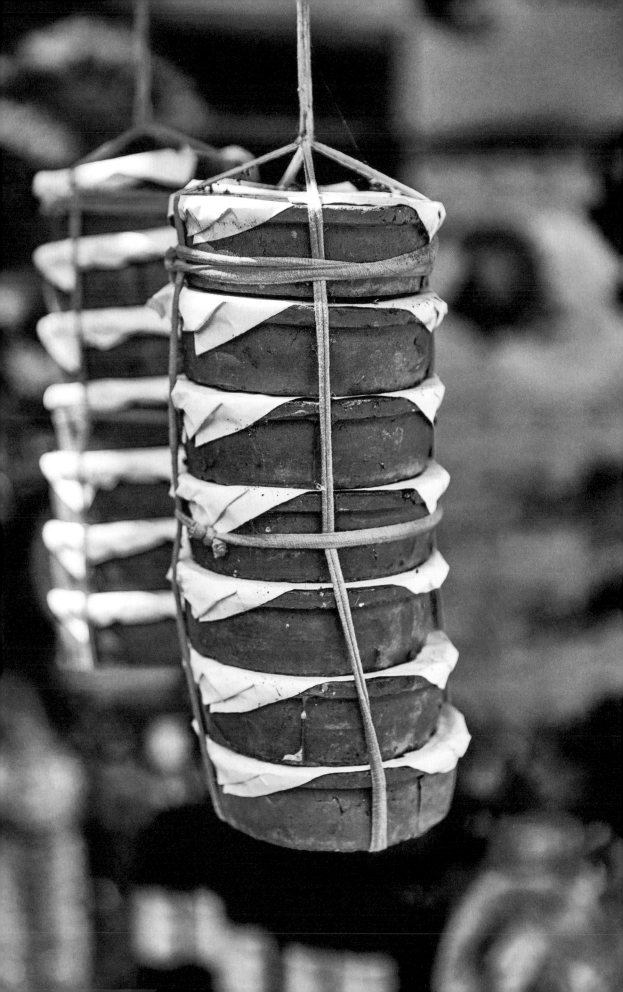

Lampra-ish with short-rib beef curry

All wrapped up in a banana leaf, a *lamprais* is a feast of rice, curries, crunchy things and pickles, and like much of the island's history its origins are both vague and hotly contested. To look at it, it is obviously the good-looking Sri Lankan cousin of the famous Malaysian breakfast dish, *nasi lemak*.

I like to imagine that it all began for *lamprais* (pronounced as it is spelled, 'lamp-rice' not 'lamp-ray', from the Dutch *lomprijst*, meaning rice packet) when an enterprising Sri Lankan cook one day about 300 years ago looked nosily over her shoulder at someone's *nasi lemak* breakfast. Eyeing up the delightful bundle (brought in by a Malay prince or perhaps it was a Javanese soldier), I like to think she thought to herself, '*hmm, looks good, but what if we switched it up a little bit?*' Plantain not peanuts, Sri Lankanised pickles, earthy, darkly roasted spices in the curry instead of *rendang*, a little of this, a little of that – and boom, Sri Lankan *lamprais* was born.

The best *lamprais* I've eaten was cooked by Mrs Warusawitharana in Colombo. *Lamprais* is the birthright of Sri Lanka's Burgher community, who have European ancestry and have been in Sri Lanka for over 300 years. Mrs W is among the best of the old Burgher aunties in Colombo, cooking up these hot, delicious parcels to order, and who gets booked out days in advance. If you are in town and you want a traditional and authentic one, I recommend hers or the Dutch Burgher Union's.

If not, this recipe is for you. It is <u>not</u> strictly traditional, and I am playing with fire here because Sri Lankans tend to go berserk if you mess with *lamprais*. Consider this, instead, a *lampra-ish*. Like my imaginary cook, I've made a few substitutions and adaptations. Instead of traditional *frikkadels*, which are fried meatballs, I have substituted panko-crusted soft-boiled eggs because they are easier and more fun to make (and because – yes, Sri Lankan readers – I am a philistine). I use yellow rice because I like it so much. You don't need a banana leaf, because baking parchment works very well. And I've substituted traditional plantain for a crunchy radish and cardamom yoghurt because I think it is light and cooling. Please be warned that although this recipe has been streamlined, it still requires a whopping six different elements. Think of it as one to make on a rainy day when friends are coming over later and you want to feel 'wow, I made so many things today', and everyone leaves well fed and madly grateful.

Ingredients & method overleaf

FISH, SEAFOOD & MEAT

Serves 4

Aubergine moju (page 198)

Yellow rice (page 206)

For the lamprais curry

4 tbsp coconut or vegetable oil

1½ red onions, peeled
   and sliced

20 fresh curry leaves

2 lemongrass stalks, bruised

6cm fresh root ginger, peeled
   and chopped

4 garlic cloves, peeled and
   halved

Optional: 2.5cm piece of
   pandan leaf

1 tsp ground turmeric

6 whole cardamom pods, lightly
   bashed in a pestle and mortar

½ tsp fenugreek seeds

1 tsp coriander seeds

1 tsp cumin seeds

6 cloves

1 stick of cinnamon

1 tsp chilli powder

2 meaty short-ribs of beef
   (approx. 1kg)

1 tsp salt, or to taste

4 tbsp apple cider or
   white wine vinegar

400ml coconut milk, plus
   8 tbsp to serve

For the panko eggs

5 large organic
   or free-range eggs

500ml vegetable oil,
   for deep-frying

4 tbsp panko breadcrumbs

For the lamprais curry

1. Heat the oil in a wok or saucepan over a medium-high heat. Fry the onions for 4–5 minutes, until starting to brown. Add the curry leaves, lemongrass, ginger, garlic and pandan leaf, if using. Cook for a further 30 seconds, until the curry leaves are bright green. Stir in all the spices and fry, stirring rapidly, for about 30 seconds until nice and fragrant. Take half of this onion-spice mixture out and keep aside for later.

2. Add the beef, salt and vinegar to the pan and top up with enough water to submerge the meat. Let the water come up to a low simmer with the lid on, then crack the lid slightly ajar and cook for 2–3 hours, until the meat is fork-tender. While the beef is cooking, make the panko eggs, radish yoghurt pachadi, prawn blacang, aubergine moju and yellow rice.

3. When the meat is tender, stir in the coconut milk and turn up the heat to medium-high so it bubbles gently. Add the remaining half of the onion-spice mixture and stir together. Turn the heat down and allow to simmer for 4–5 minutes.

For the panko eggs

1. Fill a medium-sized saucepan with water, and place over medium-high heat until it boils. You want a gentle rolling boil – that means big bubbles going at a regular pace, not really big noisy bubbles and not tiny bubbles either. Set a timer for 6½ minutes and gently lower 4 of the eggs into the water one at a time, using a slotted spoon. Get a medium-sized bowl ready, filled about one-third full of cold water and 6 or 7 ice cubes. When the eggs are cooked, transfer them to the bowl of iced water. Allow the eggs to completely cool (10–15 minutes). When cooled, gently crack and peel the eggs, starting from the wider end, which contains the air pocket.

2. Pour the oil into a large, heavy-based saucepan to a depth of about 4cm and set over a medium-high heat.

3. While the oil is heating up, beat the remaning egg in a bowl and put the panko breadcrumbs in a separate bowl. Dredge each soft-boiled egg in the beaten egg and then in the panko breadcrumbs, making sure they are well coated.

4. Place a wire rack over a roasting tin, next to your frying station. Drop a couple of breadcrumbs into the oil; if they sizzle, the oil is hot enough. Using a small stainless steel wire strainer (also called an Asian skimmer or spider strainer) or a slotted spoon, lower one egg into the hot oil. Gently turn the egg with the strainer to brown on all sides, which should take about 30 seconds. Drain the egg on the wire rack and repeat with the rest of the eggs.

For the radish yoghurt pachadi

2 bunches of radishes (approx. 300g), sliced into quarters

150g Greek yoghurt

A pinch of asofoetida

Salt, to taste

12–15 whole cardamom pods, seeds removed and crushed in a pestle and mortar

For the prawn blacang

1 golf ball-sized piece of tamarind block, soaked in 60ml warm water for 10 minutes

2 tbsp coconut or vegetable oil

½ red onion, peeled and finely sliced

10 fresh curry leaves

2 garlic cloves, peeled and roughly chopped

½ lemongrass stalk, bruised

3 tbsp dried shrimp

1 tsp ground cinnamon

100ml coconut milk

1 tsp granulated sugar

For the radish yoghurt pachadi

1. To make the pachadi, mix everything together in small bowl, except half the cardamom. Sprinkle over the rest of the cardamom.

For the prawn blacang

1. Squeeze the tamarind with your fingers, then discard the seeds and skin, leaving behind the pulpy water.

2. Heat the oil in a wok or saucepan set over a medium-high heat. Fry the onion for 4–5 minutes, until browned. Add the curry leaves, garlic and lemongrass, and stir-fry for a further 30 seconds or so until the leaves are bright green.

3. Stir in the dried shrimp, tamarind water, cinnamon and coconut milk, and let it cook for 3–4 minutes with the lid off. Reduce to a low simmer and cook for 10–15 minutes, until the consistency is thick and jammy. Stir in the sugar 2–3 minutes before serving.

To assemble and serve

1. Preheat the oven 200°C/Fan 180°C/Gas Mark 6. Get a couple of baking trays ready and tear off 4 big rectangles of baking parchment, each about 50cm long.

2. In the middle of each piece of parchment, place a quarter of the yellow rice, topped with 2 tablespoons of lamprais curry liquid, 2 teaspoons of aubergine moju and 1 teaspoon of prawn blacang. Pour 2 tablespoons of coconut milk over the rice.

3. Fold over the parchment to make neat little parcels and place on two baking trays. Cook the lamprais for 10–15 minutes, until fragrant. Remove from the oven and set aside to cool.

4. To serve, slide each parcel onto a plate, and open them up slightly to place a shortrib on top, a panko fried egg and some radish yoghurt on the side.

The King Of Sambols

In Sri Lanka, sambols are the unpickled condiments and side dishes on the table at every mealtime, and they each deliver a hit of concentrated flavour in their own unique way. A Javanese loan word, Sri Lankan sambols are distinct from an Indonesian *sambal oelek* or any chutney in South India, coming in a confusing array of avatars. Sometimes a sambol is a salad (like carrot sambol on page 182), sometimes it's like a relish to be spread onto your hoppers or rice (like jammy caramelised shallot seeni sambol on page 136), sometimes it's a dip (like burnt aubergine sambol on page 162). Whatever's going on with Sri Lankan sambols, they are all delicious and highly prized, and you can – and should – have many sambols going on at the same time at the same table. Some sambols are considered best with certain dishes, and on the next page there is list of all the sambols in the book and my recommended pairings.

Of all Sri Lanka's sambols though, pol sambol is the undisputed king. It is as ubiquitous and essential on the table as is ketchup at a greasy spoon, and sometimes just referred to as 'sambol' as if it were the only one that really mattered.

Smashed up in a heavy pestle and mortar or (for inferior results) an electric grinder, pol sambol combines the sweet velvetiness of freshly grated coconut, the dry heat of Kashmiri red chillies, the zing of fresh curry leaves and freshly squeezed limes, with saltiness and the unmistakable punch on the nose that is Maldive fish.

As a kid, I always thought Mum and the aunties were saying 'mouldy fish', which sounded gross, and when I grew up and finally cooked with the stuff, I realised that, in a way, they were. Like Japan and most of South East Asia, Sri Lanka has an ancient and formidable tradition of drying and smoking fish, which we call *karavaadu*. The most common type is smoked, dried tuna flakes, called Maldive fish, or you can use bonito or katsuoboshi flakes from Japanese or Asian supermarkets, which are essentially the same thing – but there are lots of other varieties, like mackerel, bream, jackfish, shrimp and even (illegally) shark. Maldive fish or bonito are completely legal, however, and don't be afraid, just a tiny pinch of the stuff levels up your pol sambol. The result won't taste fishy but will transform the ingredients in the bowl into an unapologetic umami bomb. In this version of pol sambol, there's also a little grated ginger and cumin for deliciousness (which I straight-up copied from our Jaffna neighbours, Dani and her mum).

Soft white bread makes the perfect vehicle for pol sambol because the sambol itself is such a megastar and so heavyweight in flavour, and the pillowy soft, clean flavour of a white slice allows it to sing. As a result, white 'roast paan' bread and pol sambol are a kind of Sri Lankan fast food and eaten all over the island. I once sat down to eat this classic Sri Lankan sandwich after a hairy, hot, nine-hour car journey from the airport on the west coast in Katunayake, all the way up to the top of the country to the northernmost tip in Nelliady, Jaffna, where my parents grew up and retired. I parked up, unloaded my bags, splashed some cold water on my face, and sank my teeth into a pol sambol sandwich and cool fizzy drink combo Dad dished up for me, with all the grateful joy and relief I wish you when you make this yourself.

A GUIDE TO SAMBOLS

In Hindu mythology, all the gods have a little animal friend they sit on for transportation and companionship. The young, gleaming God of War, Lord Murugan, has a brilliant peacock, the cerebral Goddess of Music, Saraswati, has a regal swan, Lord Ganesha, who is rotund and an avid dancer, has a naughty-looking mouse, and the formidable Goddess of Destruction, Shakti, has a roaring tiger. In short, there is the perfect vehicle for everyone. Here are the perfect vehicles for some of the island's biggest sambols.

Mint sambol, page 118
Fragrant, refreshing, paste-like sambol.
Great with crab fried rice, buriani, lamb chops.

Seeni sambol, page 136
Spicy, cinnamon-heavy caramelised onion. Jammy texture.
Great with eggs, sandwiches, hoppers, puttu.

Pol sambol, page 156
King of sambols: coconut, dried red chillies, spices.
Great with everything, especially puttu, all curries, rice.

Burnt aubergine sambol with coconut milk, page 162
A dip with Sri Lankan baba ganoush energy.
Great with crudités, poppadoms, smeared onto toast.

Daikon, mint, carrot and kohlrabi sambol aka *slambol*, page 164
Crunchy, light, raw salad. Bright and refreshing.
Great to accompany barbecue or rich curries (e.g. black pork or cashew nut).

Parsley and fresh lime sambol, page 176
Like a Sri Lankan tabbouleh or green salad.
Great with all curries, especially prawn curry, all the fish curries.

Green mango sambol, page 178

Almost like a Sri Lankan som tam salad, citrusy and salad-like.
Great with all the seafood and fish recipes, also any veg curries.

Fresh pineapple sambol, page 180

A sweet, light salsa-like sambol.
Great with all the pork dishes, and with many rice dishes.

Raw carrot sambol salad, page 182

A crunchy, clean-tasting, fresh side.
Great with red lamb, chicken or fish curries.

Cucumber sambol with salted spiced mor yoghurt, page 200

A yoghurt-dipped cucumber sambol.
Great with grilled meats or rotis.

Black sesame sambol, page 184

A concrete-coloured, nutty, creamy dip.
Great with dosas and doughnut vadai.

Tomato thokku sambol, page 236

A spicy tomato relish.
Perfect with plain dosas or rava dosas.

Dill sambol, page 270

A herby dip.
Great with all the fish recipes.

Pol sambol and fried chicken sandwich

Pol sambol itself requires no cooking and is simple and fun to make. But for this sandwich recipe I've added cardamom fried chicken, in homage to a food memory of respite after a long, sweaty marathon. When we were kids in Coventry, Dad, who was usually a strict junk-food-and-homework disciplinarian, would let up on one day each year. On the day we sat our last summer exams, my brother and sister and I would be rewarded with a family bucket of fried chicken. Like most things, we'd eat it up with pol sambol, and so should you.

Serves 4

8 slices of thick, soft white bread, crusts trimmed

Optional: A bunch of lemon sorrel or mustard greens

For the fried chicken

6 whole cardamom pods, lightly bashed in a pestle and mortar

200ml buttermilk

2 skinless, boneless chicken thighs

75g polenta

100g rice flour

1 tsp salt, or to taste

500ml vegetable oil, for deep-frying

For the pol sambol

4 dried red Kashmiri chillies (or mild dried red chillies)

3cm fresh root ginger, peeled

1 tsp cumin seeds

1 tsp salt, or to taste

10 fresh curry leaves

Juice of ½ lime

Optional: 1 tsp Maldive fish flakes, bonito flakes or katsuoboshi

100g freshly grated coconut (see page 175)

1. Take a small dry frying pan and place over a medium heat. Add the cardamom and toast, stirring occasionally, for about 2 minutes. Tip into a bowl and when cool, blitz in a spice grinder or mini food processor until fine. Tip into a medium-sized bowl, pour in the buttermilk and stir well. Add the chicken thighs and coat all over with the marinade. Cover to make airtight and refrigerate for 30 minutes.

2. Meanwhile, in a mini food processor, blitz all the pol sambol ingredients except the coconut. Using a stone pestle and mortar for best results (or failing that, your hands), mix the fluffy grated coconut into the pol sambol mix.

3. In a small bowl, mix together the polenta, rice flour and salt. Take the chicken out of the fridge.

4. Set a wire rack over a roasting tin, next to where you'll be frying the chicken. Pour enough vegetable oil into a heavy-bottomed pan so it comes about one-third up the side of the pan, and set over a medium-high heat. To test it is hot enough, a cube of bread dropped in should brown almost immediately.

5. When the oil is hot enough, dredge the chicken thighs thoroughly in the polenta mixture, turning to coat them all over and get the flour mix right into the crevices.

6. Lower the chicken thighs, flat, gently into the hot oil and fry for 5–8 minutes until deep golden brown, adjusting the heat if necessary so that they don't burn. Transfer to the wire rack set over the roasting tin.

7. To assemble the sandwiches, cover one slice of bread with a tablespoon or two of pol sambol, and top with 3 or 4 lemon sorrel leaves or a few greens, if you're using them. Place a fried chicken thigh on top, then the final slice of bread. Slice in half with a sharp knife.

COOL, RAW & PICKLED DISHES

Burnt aubergine sambol with coconut milk

This is a very quick and ancient sambol dip, which is fun to eat with bread or roti, scooped up with a poppadom, or with toast. It's kind of a Sri Lankan version of a Middle Eastern baba ganoush, where traditionally you would blacken the aubergines over a flame. It is just as delicious and requires much less standing around since you put whole aubergines under the grill. You then let them cool, strip the skins and mash the smoky soft aubergine insides with green chillies, curry leaves, coconut milk, salt and a squeeze of lime juice – the result is a smoky, creamy sambol with plenty of zing and aromatics.

Serves 2–4

2 medium aubergines
  (approx. 500g)

2 tbsp coconut or vegetable oil

200ml coconut milk

3 green chillies, finely sliced

10 fresh curry leaves, very
  finely diced

A generous grind of black
  pepper

1 tsp salt, or to taste

Juice of 1 lime

1. Preheat the grill as high as it will go. Prick the aubergines a few times all over with a fork and rub with a little oil to grease. Place on a foil-lined baking tray under the hot grill, turning the aubergines regularly, for 30–45 minutes or until blackened all over and starting to collapse. Don't worry if the aubergines look burnt: the charred skins will produce the intense smokiness we're looking for. Carefully transfer to a plate using oven gloves, and then leave aside to cool.

2. When cool enough to handle, cut a long slit in each aubergine and scoop out the insides into a bowl.

3. Using the back of a fork, mash up the aubergine with the coconut milk, green chillies, curry leaves, cracked black pepper, salt and lime juice. You can leave it slightly chunky if you like, but I prefer it a bit more mashed.

Daikon, mint, carrot and kohlrabi sambol aka slambol

This fresh, citrusy, summery sambol was invented by my dear friend and chef, Katja Tausig, who came to Sri Lanka with me on holiday and got stuck in cooking with Mum and the aunties. Daikon is that long white, carrot-shaped radish you might not have cooked before, but seen in Asian or African shops. It has a peppery, fresh taste, which is delicious in this bright, crunchy sambol. If you can't get hold of daikon, any radishes will do. Instead of a traditional single-ingredient sambol like carrot or green mango, Katja bought some kohlrabi, daikon and carrot in our local market in Nelliady and made a slaw-inspired sambol (which she's calling 'slambol') with some garden mint and plenty of lime. The aunties were impressed, and it's become a favourite to remake. It's nice to cut the vegetables into little sticks so they have some crunch and bite.

Serves 2–4

8 shallots

8 fresh curry leaves

A handful of fresh mint leaves

½ daikon

1 carrot

½ kohlrabi

2 limes

Optional: 1 tsp Maldive fish flakes, bonito flakes or katsuoboshi

½ tsp salt, or to taste

1. Peel and finely slice the shallots. Shred the curry leaves and mint as finely as you can. Peel and then chop the daikon, carrot and kohlrabi into little sticks. Zest and juice the limes.

2. Mix everything together, including the Maldive fish, if using, in a bowl, and season with salt. Be generous with the lime zest and juice.

Puff Up Your Coconuts With Pride

Freshly grated coconut is a thing of wonder. The little shavings are somehow both airy and juicy. Like soft, puffy clouds, they are called 'coconut blossom' in Tamil, and share the lovely delicate quality of tiny white jasmine petals. Each strand is full of coconut milk: light and clean and sweet all at the same time.

If you soak and then squeeze grated coconut hard with a clenched fist, it produces a trickle of fresh coconut milk, which is used in cooking curries. The initial squeeze delivers the creamier, whole milk of coconut milk, called the 'first press'. It's added to curries at the end of cooking to make them emulsify, so they get glossy and thick. Then there's the 'second press' when you squeeze the same handful for a second time, to get a skinnier, skimmier milk. It is used to braise or boil whatever it is you're cooking, before you add the first press, maybe a temper and perhaps some lime to finish it off. For the recipes in this book, I'd recommend you skip hand-pressing your own coconut milk and buy a high-quality tinned or powdered version instead. I say this both because the good store-bought stuff is excellent and because, look, I too want to hurry up with dinner and watch Netflix.

But for freshly grated coconut, the substitutions are trickier. I'm sorry to say it, but you categorically *cannot* substitute desiccated for fresh coconut. Not ever – other than with the one exception of making black curry (pork page 124 or pineapple page 44), which requires toasting the coconut. Desiccated, from the French 'sec', means dry, and the crispy contents of a packet of the stuff are little mummified coconut bodies of dryness. Just as a raisin cannot again become a grape, you cannot soak some dried-out coconut and hope that it puffs up in water. *Frozen* grated coconut is actually a great substitute for fresh, but is very hard to come by. So, for the short list of recipes that require it, I promise it's worth the trouble to buy a £5 grater, whip it out, crack open a coconut and lacerate its insides. I am pleased to also report that smacking open a whole coconut takes all of two minutes, requires very little skill, and is highly fun.

When you have grated your own, you can mix your fresh coconut into raw vegetables and herbs for fresh, salad-like sambols like green mango (page 178), parsley (page 176), pineapple (page 180) or carrot (page 182).

You can stir it through fried chickpeas (page 186) or grilled corn (page 188) for Sri Lankan Tamil *sundals* – a kind of delicious, zippy, fresh snack or side. You can sprinkle it into dry curries, called *varais* or *mallungs*, like the sweet roasted beetroot (page 54) or burnt cabbage (page 56) versions in this book. And you can mash it up (with your hands or with a pestle and mortar) for soft, spreadable sambols that you can schmear onto bread or rice, like the all-time king of sambols, pol sambol (page 156) or mint sambol (page 118). The result is to add lightness, softness and a little flavoursome fattiness to each dish.

You probably think I grew up knowing how to break down coconuts, that I started cracking them open in my babygro. But when I left home and first moved to London, I used to avoid the intimidating piles of them, stacked up in front of the Turkish, Indian and African shops near me in Dalston and Bethnal Green. How much were they? No idea. What would I do with them? Injure myself probably. Don't you need a machete to open coconuts? I don't want to be a wimp, but I'm scared of machetes, and, okay, I was scared of coconuts, too. So they remained where they were; scary, hairy, brown balls of mystery all huddled together, and I would breeze past them to buy some Sesame Snaps to munch on the bus home.

You probably think I grew up knowing how to break down coconuts, that I started cracking them open in my babygro.

My fear of coconuts felt for a while like some kind of joke of the gods. 'Coconut!' means being completely out of touch with your culture, brown only on the outside but a white person on the inside, and an offensive term my friends and cousins used to tease me and my brother and sister with, because we spoke incoherent Tamil and made bad fashion choices.

These developments had not been an accident. Our parents are not coconuts. They are Sri Lankan all the way through. In fact, Dad is something of a coconut opening pro. He's the uncle who always gets asked to crack open a dozen coconuts at a Hindu wedding, and he does so with ease. He never taught us, though. Because Dad knows how important it is to assimilate.

When we visited Sri Lanka as children, sometimes we'd go to a cafe in Kandy or Gampola for lunch, washed down with a cup of Ceylon tea. Those days, a tea boy would pop up, around nine or ten years old, eyes big and dark from the kind of life he was living, skinny from surviving on the tiny wages hill country Tamils tend to earn. He would pour a sweet, milky brew for us from steel tumbler to tumbler, making it froth like a cappuccino. Dad would ask, 'Hey, *thambi?* Little brother, why aren't you in school?' And the kid would frown, or maybe smile a boy's big-toothed smile in a drawn, adult face, and say something like, 'School, no point sir,' looking around to see if he was being overheard. Dad would reply with abandon, 'I used to be a shop boy like you and then I went to school and now I don't work in a shop anymore.' The boy would look confused and disbelieving at this British dude in his Nineties polyester trousers – so long out of Sri Lanka he was sweating under a fan, his bratty kids with English accents trying to figure out their cameras – then he'd scuttle back into the kitchen to receive more orders.

Back in Ceylon, he was at last somebody; no longer just a poor drunk's son, no longer labouring in the tobacco fields, no longer a shop boy.

Dad had been the kind of poor kid who got the cane at school for not being able to afford his 1p school fees; and the kind of clever kid who other kids paid to do their homework for them. One of seven children to his struggling parents, he, his hard-drinking dad and his hardworking brothers used to farm their tobacco fields before school. When Dad was twelve, he was taken out of the school he had won all the prizes in, and was sent away to work as a shop boy, in plantation country, hundreds of miles from his family. He did not come home until he was fourteen. Like so many child labourers, he was terribly beaten and brutally treated by his adult co-workers in those two years. The experiences stayed with him and he would cry sometimes as he told us about them.

By the time of his A Levels, Dad had become the only kid from his batch at Nelliady Central who had made it into the University of Ceylon, in Peradeniya. When he graduated from his Combined Science degree, he was offered a prestigious job as a lecturer. But instead of staying on, he applied for that golden ticket – a British Ministry of Labour voucher scheme for science graduates from former colonies. And he got one. So, with some borrowed money, he bought a plane ticket and headed to England, where he lodged for free with an old uni friend. Photos from that time show a young man in a hurry, with his high, thick and wiry Tamil hair and big moustache, his new flared suit and his shiny degree. Back in Ceylon, he was at last somebody; no longer just a poor drunk's son, no longer labouring in the tobacco fields, no longer a shop boy.

When Dad first arrived in London, it was the cold spring of 1968. It would be the year Enoch Powell would make his big speech about the Rivers of Blood, and the year Dr King would get shot. Students protested racial injustices all over the world, Nixon got elected and James Brown released *Say It Loud – I'm Black and I'm Proud*. Someone made a weird trippy animation of *Yellow Submarine*, and Dad still sings 'we all live in a yellow submarine' happily while he's waiting for the kettle to boil, probably from that first landing. By the autumn, the first Race Relations Act was passed into British law, making it technically illegal to refuse anyone employment or housing on the grounds of race.

As he remembers it, the reality was different. Dad began going to job interviews that he found himself rejected from, one after the other, after the other. Dad's science degree was laughable, they said, and although he was born into the British Empire and had studied in English, his accent was apparently too difficult to understand. They didn't say they had a problem with his race, but when, finally, a pharmacist gave him his first job, his employers asked him not to use the same toilet as them. In time, he got a better job, as a maths supply teacher. In his first few weeks, he sent a student out of the room for not doing their homework. When Dad walked back in the next day, he found WOGS GO HOME scrawled on his blackboard in big chalk letters. Right there, he made a decision: he wouldn't reprimand his students again.

The disciplinarian in him didn't die overnight. Dad did his time, tutored kids in the evenings to make ends meet, and won a scholarship to MIT to do a PhD. But he decided he couldn't afford to go to America, instead taking a job in Coventry at the Polytechnic. With a new British Master's degree he found British colleagues who gave him a chance and became lifelong friends. He was a stickler about money, sending it home to his family, a large brood so on the brink of poverty and war that he did everything he could to help them get out of the country for good. His mission was to protect us all from the precipice. And so his ambitions, his discipline, his focus, shone like a hard light on us. Dad is the kind of proud Tamil who tried to teach us about the island and our history, who drove us to Tamil school every weekend, who cares about what is happening in Sri Lanka very deeply. But he never spoke Tamil to us at home, because he was so stressed out about whether we would do well in our exams. The most important thing of all was whether my sister and brother and I were getting As in school. It felt like we were killing him if we didn't.

————

Once, I almost killed him with *Aladdin*.

It was my eleventh birthday, and my father was focused on figuring out which secondary school I would go to. Coventry had more than its fair share of sink schools and we couldn't afford to live in the areas of town with better ones. Dad's hopes of pretending I was Catholic so that I could get into a good Catholic school had died when I crumbled under questioning. Now my whole future was riding on my entrance exam to a private school. And so that's what I had to prepare for, after school and at weekends.

Mum had other ideas. She wanted to take me to see the new Disney movie. It had just come out and it looked so funny and *A Whole New World* was playing on the radio nonstop. She wanted to buy me some birthday popcorn and forget the pressure for a few hours. But the exams were just a month away and I guess Dad felt I was like a finely tuned athlete. *Aladdin*, he said with desperation, would ruin my life.

I listened as they shouted at each other and I said to Mum, 'It's okay, I don't need to see it!' But Mum insisted, and so we went: me and her, in the pouring rain, popcorn and pic-n-mix and Happy Birthday To Me, under a dark cloud of my father sulking. Neither Mum nor I could shake a heavy feeling when we were in that small cinema, giggling at the Genie.

After forty years of holding yourself so tight that nothing will go wrong, you don't want your kids to fuck it up with Aladdin and cracking coconuts.

They say to make it out of poverty, you need a run of twenty years where nothing goes wrong. I guess Dad had to do that twice, once in Sri Lanka and once in the UK. And I guess after forty years of holding yourself so tight that nothing will go wrong, you don't want your kids to fuck it up with *Aladdin* and cracking coconuts.

Our dad is the kind of feminist who thinks his daughters can do anything. But when Dad had said 'anything', he hadn't meant Sri Lankan cooking. When I started becoming interested in food, I could see his disappointment. It was taking me away from a career with stability, one that paid well. He thought it was a waste.

For a long time, it felt like I cooked from a tightrope. One side was a kind of crazy perfectionism, a focus on getting it all right, making no mistakes. And the other side, I had assimilated too far, so I didn't belong in Sri Lanka anymore, with a lot of deep shame about being crap at the Sri Lankan things I should *just know*. But one day I thought: I don't have to give up all the skills of our ancestors just because I don't already know them. I'm going to watch a *YouTube* video on cracking coconuts, and I'm going to get over it. Because first of all, I really fancy a sambol, and you know what, you can just learn. I'm now learning beginner's Tamil as an adult on Zoom lessons; it's not the neatest handiwork but I can tie my own sari these days, and look, I don't want to blow my own trumpet, but I can really crack a coconut with the best of them.

A Beginner's Guide To Freshly Grating Coconut

If I can do it, anyone can, so here is your own guide. If it's a little tricky at first, don't worry, it was the same for me too. Just try another one.

1. Buy a coconut that isn't too light when you pick it up – that will mean that it isn't too young and should have a lot of coconut meat. When you shake it close to your ear, you should be able to hear plenty of water sloshing around inside – that means it's not too old either. Use it in the first couple of days when you get it home.

2. To get set up you'll need:
- a big knife or meat cleaver, around 3mm thick, or a rolling pin
- a large bowl to collect the coconut water

3. If it's really hairy, start by ripping off a little of the thick brown hair from the coconut over a bin and discarding it. It doesn't need to be completely bald, but you want it not to moult too much if you tap it. This should mean that when you grate the coconut you won't get too many fibrous brown hairs messing up your perfect white shavings.

4. Now to get cracking: if you're right-handed, pick up the coconut with your left hand. You want to cup it with your palm, so that the end with the three little eyes is to the left; and the pointed end is to the right. Keep your left thumb low and out of the way!

5. Hold the coconut over the bowl. Look for one of the thick ridges that go from the pointy end of the coconut to the end with the eyes. There will be three such ridges. When you find one, use your right hand to hit it hard – once – with the **blunt** side of your knife or the rolling pin.

6. Rotate the coconut a bit by tossing it up in the air a tiny bit and catching it with your left hand, so that you can smack another side of the coconut's equator. Hit it again.

7. Keep tossing and smacking, going around the meridian of the coconut until it cracks, and then prise the two sides apart. Drink the water or discard it. Now you're ready to grate!

8. Attach your coconut grater to a solid tabletop, with a clean bowl underneath to catch the shavings. Use the palm of your hand to hold the coconut shell to the rotary, and use your other hand to turn the handle. Keep going, moving the shell round every so often, until you've grated the whole shell, and repeat with the other.

9. Freeze any excess coconut in an airtight container. Use up what you don't freeze on the same day.

Parsley and fresh lime sambol

Parsley doesn't grow very well in hot, humid Sri Lanka but *gotukola* or pennywort does, and I find it has a very similar, peppery taste. This quick, easy sambol is very common all over the island, packed with iron and nutrients and it will furnish your meal with a refreshing brightness, almost like a Sri Lankan tabbouleh. Use flat-leaf parsley and slice it carefully with a sharp knife just once; you don't want it to bruise.

Serves 2–4

2 large handfuls of parsley

1 small red onion

1 green chilli

½ freshly grated coconut (approx. 100g) (see page 175)

1 tsp salt, or to taste

Optional: 1 tsp Maldive fish flakes, bonito flakes or katsuoboshi

Zest and juice of 2 limes

1. Roughly chop the parsley, peel and very finely dice the red onion, and finely slice the chilli.

2. Mix all the ingredients except the lime juice in a bowl, then finish with lime juice.

Green mango sambol

Some days you walk into the supermarket and come across the hardest looking lump of unripe fruit you have ever seen, and you just buy it anyway because sue me, you fancied a mango. Maybe you hoped that en route to your house it would magically morph into a sweet, juicy fruit? Also, the alternative was to buy an intimidating box of twenty honey mangoes from the Pakistani cornershop which, although delicious, *is it* a good idea to eat twenty mangoes? If this happened today, here is something completely delicious to make with your stubbornly unripe or, to say it another way, your green mango.

Sri Lankans feel that green mango is not an unripe mango; it is a wonderful entity in its own right, called *mangai* in Tamil (which is where the English word mango comes from). This is one of my favourites of all sambols: super-bright and fragrant and sharp with the green mangoes, curry leaves and lime juice. Try this sambol with grilled fish or one of the other dishes in the fish and seafood section of this book, it makes a natural friend to them; or with a richer, sweeter dish that might like a little freshness on the side, like the black short-rib curry, or the cashew nut or dal curries (pages 146, 74 or 40).

Serves 2–4

2 green (unripe) mangoes

1–2 small green chillies, sliced

½ small red onion or 1 shallot, peeled and very finely sliced

1 tsp salt, or to taste

½ freshly grated coconut (approx. 100g) (see page 175)

10 fresh curry leaves, finely chopped

4 or 5 mint leaves, finely sliced

Zest and juice of 1–2 limes, to taste

Optional: ½ tsp chilli flakes

Optional: A pinch of Maldive fish flakes, bonito flakes or katsuoboshi

1. Peel the green mangoes with a potato peeler or a knife, then slice them into the thinnest slivers you can. You can use a large-size grater, or like they do in Sri Lanka, you can shred it using only a knife, making long cuts in the flesh, then thinly slicing off the top layer into a bowl, continuing until most of the mango is shredded into thin wedges. Put the mango into a bowl.

2. Add the chillies, red onion, salt, freshly grated coconut, curry leaves, mint leaves and lime zest and juice. Mix together, then sprinkle with the chilli flakes and Maldive fish, if using.

Fresh pineapple sambol

Fresh and light, in Sri Lanka this is frequently an accompaniment to something rich like fried rice. I like it as a tart, sweet salad sambol that is a perfect pairing with pork, beef or potato. Warning: pineapple numbs. Your tongue bounces back quickly enough, but I find the sensation dangerous and exciting: pleasure and punishment in equal measure. The feeling comes from an enzyme called bromelain that breaks down the proteins on the surface of your lips and tongue, leaving a sort of gentle fizzing sensation. This sambol really lets that quality sing, combining fresh, juicy pineapple with freshly grated coconut, raw shallot or red onion for sharpness, generous lime juice, curry leaves and chilli flakes.

Serves 2–4

1 medium-sized fresh pineapple (approx. 500g)

3–4 shallots or 1 medium red onion

10 fresh curry leaves

50g freshly grated coconut (see page 175)

Juice of 1 lime

2 tsp chilli flakes

1 tsp salt, or to taste

Optional: A generous pinch of Maldive fish flakes, bonito flakes or katsuoboshi

1. Peel and slice the pineapple into chunks, discarding the core. Peel and finely slice the shallots or red onion. Very finely slice the curry leaves.

2. Just before serving, mix together all the ingredients in a bowl.

Raw carrot sambol salad

Fresh, light and bracingly citrusy, think of carrot sambol as the Sri Lankan answer to a Thai som tam salad. Rather than adding fish sauce or other flavours to the raw ingredients, this sambol at its most basic is just grated carrots, lime and salt. There are a whole set of other sambols in this category made in basically the same way: green mango, cucumber, green papaya, radish, daikon and kohlrabi, sometimes adding finely sliced onion, bonito or Maldive fish, fresh curry leaves, chilli flakes or, optionally, grated coconut.

In my version, I've added a handful of lentils, soaked for an hour while I'm doing something else, to give it a kind of clean, nutty flavour, like South Indians do when they make carrot *kosambari*. I also add the zest of the lime to amp up the flavour (to try to recreate the power of mad flavoursome little Sri Lankan limes). And I've included Mum's invention, which is to add some chopped coriander (because she saw Jamie Oliver make a nice-looking Vietnamese salad with carrot and coriander once on TV so there we are). This is just a great, quick way to eat carrots, with simple grilled fish or at a summer barbecue. It is also the perfect accompaniment to rich vegetable curries like cashew nut or roast pumpkin (pages 74 or 30), and meaty dishes like lamb curry or grilled beef, or with any of the fish dishes in this book because it's so fresh.

Serves 2

1 carrot

1 or 2 small green chillies, sliced

½ small red onion or 1 shallot, peeled and very finely sliced

1 tsp salt, or to taste

10 fresh curry leaves, finely chopped

A small handful of coriander leaves, roughly chopped

Optional: 1 tbsp freshly grated coconut (see page 175)

Optional: A handful of split mung beans or urad dal, rinsed, soaked in water for 1 hour, then drained

Zest and juice of 1 lime

1. Peel then grate the carrot into a bowl. Add the chillies, onion, salt, curry leaves and coriander leaves. Mix together with the freshly grated coconut and soaked mung beans, if using.

2. Finish with the lime zest and juice.

Black sesame sambol

Sesame is a very ancient and beloved ingredient of the Tamil community, and is said to have many medicinal benefits. It's just delicious in this sambol, a wet, cement-grey mix of spices, tahini and black sesame, which makes for a nutty, moreish dip. Try it with dosas (page 236), with a little bread, or as an accompaniment to your rice and curry, or with some poppadoms to scoop it up. It looks striking and tastes even better.

Serves 2

For the sambol

1 golf ball-sized piece of tamarind block, soaked in 60ml warm water for 10 minutes

200g black sesame seeds

1 tbsp groundnut or rapeseed oil

20g split yellow dal, rinsed

2 dried red Kashmiri chillies

50g freshly grated coconut (see page 175)

50g tahini

1½ tsp salt, or to taste

For the temper

1 tbsp coconut or vegetable oil

1 tsp mustard seeds

20g split yellow dal

2 dried red Kashmiri chillies

1. Squeeze the tamarind with your fingers, then discard the seeds and skin, leaving behind the pulpy water.

2. Place a dry frying pan or wok over a medium heat, and roast the sesame seeds, stirring occasionally, until they start popping. Remove from the heat and tip into a small bowl to cool.

3. Pour the oil into the same pan. Add the split yellow dal and red chillies. Fry over a medium heat for 1–2 minutes, until the dal is fragrant and has changed colour but not gone brown. Tip into the same bowl as the sesame seeds to cool.

4. When cool, in a mini food processor, blitz the coconut, roasted sesame seeds, tamarind water, tahini and salt. Add a little water if necessary, and keep blitzing until you get to a grainy paste consistency.

5. Finally, make a temper. Heat the oil in a small frying pan. Add the mustard seeds, split yellow dal and dried chillies. Fry for about 1 minute until the seeds are golden. Pour the temper and its oil over the sambol and serve.

Fried chickpea and yoghurt sundal

This recipe is a variant on the popular street snack *kadala* which you may purchase in Sri Lanka at the beach or on a train from a person helpfully shouting *kadala kadala kadala kadalaiiiiiii*. There, you will be handed a small newspaper wrapping of salty chickpeas, stir-fried lightly in mustard seeds, red chillies and curry leaves, and mixed up with freshly grated coconut. This mix is very delicious, made from either black or white chickpeas. My chickpea *sundal* recipe adds a thick cumin yoghurt, and shallow-fries the chickpeas so that they are crunchy on the outside. I find the combination to be creamy, crispy and fragrant.

Serves 2 as a side

400g tinned chickpeas

3 tbsp vegetable oil

50g freshly grated coconut
(see page 175)

½ red onion, peeled and very
finely sliced

½ tsp coarsely ground
salt or salt flakes

For the temper

2 tbsp coconut or vegetable oil

7 or 8 fresh curry leaves

2 dried red Kashmiri chillies

2 tsp mustard seeds

1 tsp cumin seeds

For the cumin yoghurt

1 tsp ground cumin

200g Greek yoghurt

1 tsp salt, or to taste

A pinch of asofoetida

1. First, mix together the cumin, yoghurt, salt and asofoetida in a small bowl. Set aside.

2. Next, fry the chickpeas. To stop the oil spitting as you cook the chickpeas, rinse and drain them really well. Heat the oil in a large, heavy-based saucepan over a medium-high heat. Add the chickpeas and leave them to cook for 3–4 minutes, stirring occasionally, until golden. Fish them out with the slotted spoon and put them in a bowl lined with kitchen roll to absorb any excess oil.

3. Then make a temper. In a small pan, heat the oil over a medium-high heat. When hot, add the curry leaves, which should sizzle and crisp up. Then add the chillies, mustard seeds and cumin seeds. After 1–2 minutes, remove from the heat. Remove the kitchen roll from the chickpeas, then pour the temper over the chickpeas along with the grated coconut and red onion, and stir through.

4. To assemble, spoon the yoghurt into a bowl. Pile the chickpeas on top and finish with a sprinkle of sea salt.

Corn sundal salad with lime, coconut and curry leaves

There was once a great self-taught Tamil mathematician called Ramanujan, who by aged eleven was creating proofs from scratch in his bedroom. Living in a remote village in extreme poverty, Ramanujan's family discovered the child was a genius, and credited his gifts to the gods. Specifically, he said Namagiri, the Hindu Goddess of creativity, came to him in different visions, sometimes writing out whole equations and proofs in his dreams. Together, they invented entirely new mathematical ideas as she wafted in and out.

What Ramanujan and his family didn't know was that many of his early mathematical discoveries had already been worked out by Pythagoras and the other Greeks 2,000 years before him. I console myself with this thought when I try to come up with new recipes. 'One day I'll be a kitchen Ramanujan,' I think, as I discover another thing I thought I invented has already been done.

This is one of them, a delicious bright, Tamil *sundal*. Whoever invented it, it is very lovely – grilled corn and coriander work beautifully together, and the coconut and lime make it very light and refreshing. A *sundal* is a kind of Tamil salad, which can be made with legumes or wholegrains. They're all made fragrant with curry leaves and tempered spices. It's a perfect summer salad for a Sri Lankan barbecue – perhaps with grilled lamb chops (page 118), grilled fish (page 96) and some pol rotis (page 218).

Serves 2–4

3 corns on the cob

1 tbsp coconut or vegetable oil, plus extra for brushing the corn

10 fresh curry leaves

1 tsp mustard seeds

½ tsp cumin seeds

40g fresh coriander leaves, roughly chopped

½ coconut, freshly grated (approx. 100g) (see page 175)

1 lime

1. Either preheat the grill to high or put a griddle pan over a high heat. Lightly brush the corn cobs with a little oil and then grill or griddle them for about 10 minutes, turning over throughout so the corn chars evenly; you want slightly blackened corn in parts.

2. Remove from the heat and let the corn cool slightly. Hold each cob upright, preferably in a wide shallow bowl or on a chopping board, and use a sharp knife to slice off the kernels vertically downwards, letting the kernels fall into the bowl or onto the board.

3. Heat the oil in small frying pan over a medium heat. When hot, add the curry leaves and fry for 1–2 minutes, until crispy and green. Add the mustard seeds and cumin seeds, and let them sizzle for a minute or so before taking off heat.

4. In a bowl, mix together the corn, coriander leaves, freshly grated coconut and the contents of the pan, and finish with generous squeeze of lime.

Eat Fruit With Salt And Chilli

Back in the early Eighties, England didn't have any of our other family in it. It was just Mum and Dad, my brother and sister. Home was predictable. We hung out in our bedrooms or in the living room, we rode our bikes. We did our schoolwork, watched TV. After dinner, Mum would peel apples and cut them into quarters for us; cool and crunchy and good for you. We would munch them until the nine o'clock news, which was our curfew. The next day would be like today.

My parents had tried to make local substitutions for the gorgeous crowds they'd left behind; the thirty-seven immediate family between them, the many hundreds of extended. Dad kept his eyes peeled for anyone with trademark dark brown skin and very dark brown eyes in the queue at Sainsbury's, or looking for carrots in the Pakistani corner shop. Beginning with a '*Tamil-a*? You're Tamil?' and immediately escalating to 'would you like to come for dinner?' his pickup technique didn't only result in some embarrassing run-ins with Somalis and West Indians, it created a kind of people salad, a pot-luck of curios, companions only in exile. There was the incurable romantic, Mahes Auntie. She served us M&S crisps and homemade fruitcake. There was Thillai Uncle, who looked like Sam the Eagle from *The Muppet Show*. He'd bark things at his wife, Sagoo Auntie, and she'd giggle madly and pour us milky tea. The community they'd made was precious to my parents, but it seemed weird to me. Because I was the youngest, I had to traipse around to these offbeat house visits while my siblings mumbled 'homework'.

So when in the summer we could return to Sri Lanka – at last amid the battalions of our family – it felt like a glorious power. Mum and Dad walked taller and talked louder. We were back in the squad and the squad gave us swagger.

In a Tamil dictionary next to the reductive English idea that is 'uncle', you have a choice of at least seven Tamil words and there are many, many more in common use. There is specificity in the words for family: was it your dad's little brother or your mum's middle one? Did his mum find him cute ('*kooty maama*' or – one of my favourites – '*baby maama*')? Did he have major flaws ('*kattai maama*', he's a short-ass, or worse, '*koothu maama*' which means he, er, stabbed someone)? Was he a stone-cold sweetheart ('*asaimaama*'), did he live far away ('*Trinco-maama*'), did he have any distinguishing features (a fancy Toyota '*car-maama*' or favourite food '*puttu-maama*'). Every person,

including me, including if you have never met them before, immediately has many names, many avatars. And each name asks and answers who is this guy to you, how are you tied together – the love and rancour and guilt of family all woven tightly into the very words.

My favourite uncle was my dad's little brother, who we called Athappa, from my brother's toddler lisp for '*asaiappa*' or 'sweet guy, younger, on your dad's side'. He was like a skinny, funny version of our dad, happy to lie to his big brother to protect us: 'Oh yeah they're asleep already,' or 'No, no she didn't eat any sweets, she must have got food poisoning,' as I puked up peanut *aluwa* noisily in the bathroom. He drove us in his ragged old Jeep up and down the brilliant green hill country where he was stationed as an engineer, explaining hydroelectricity and kidding around. His eyes fired up when discussing all the injustice of the tea plantations, how to be careful of leeches, how the Kotmale Dam he was helping to build held back water, how the force of the waterfalls could become electricity.

One day, Athappa put a small, hairy, red and yellow fruit into my hands from a brown paper bag and told me to crack it open. A rambutan.

One day, Athappa put a small, hairy, red and yellow fruit into my hands from a brown paper bag and told me to crack it open. A rambutan. I dug my nails into the crisp, spiky shell and prised out a translucent orb, a meaty scented jelly, all sugar and perfume and a faint sourness at the same time. I had another and another. We looked at each other with excitement. The next bag over had mangosteens, dark indigo, powdery balls, which stained your fingers as you scooped out juicy white, wet cloves of intense deliciousness that tasted of ripe peaches, lychees and roses. Then a huge spiky green monster of a fruit, cut down from Athappa's tree, which he peeled back to reveal masses of sticky, sweet, orange fibrous segments with almost a bubblegum flavour. So this was jackfruit! I should have guessed from the glint in their eyes when Athappa and Dad handed me my first little *nelli* gooseberry saying, 'it's very sweet,' but I had to spit its mouth-suckingly sour remains out, as they collapsed into uncontrollable laughter.

Lankan fruits, like family, come in abundance. They come thick in sheets like, oh my god, what do we do with them all? A banana tree in the back garden would suddenly have forty-six bananas that were going to go off in two days, so we ate and we ate together.

There seemed to be so much family then, in so many places I didn't know – Dehiwala, Hambantota, Kotmale, Nelliady, Batticaloa, Matara – that I couldn't remember who was who or what was where. Back then, I didn't know that the squad would die, that the swagger would leave us.

At the end of those summers, when it was time to go back to England, Athappa would load us up with a gut-destroying freight of homemade snacks, of fruits that would rarely survive the journey. He would drive us to the airport, grinning his big, skinny grin and waving and running alongside as we moved through all the departure checks. We'd try to hold back our tears, fighting them until we burst, electric tears streaming down our faces. Every time we looked back, he was still there, waving to us through the brown-tinted Perspex, lifting our baby cousin onto his shoulders, waving all the way until we were gone through security, gone from Sri Lanka, gone forever until the next time.

Then one year, he was just gone forever – first Canada and then cancer. And suddenly it wasn't just that person that was gone, but that Sri Lanka that was gone. As if the homeland that existed in our mind, bound to us at birth, had become a heavy moon in our orbit, stretching out its ties to us like tightly strung tendons. And one by one, each of those bonds snapped as our family fled Sri Lanka's different dangers, as the family who stayed grew old, died. We hadn't known it when he was alive, but Athappa was the strongest heartstring we had to Sri Lanka, and when he was gone, we felt a hard whiplash in our necks and in our spines. For me, he died twice, first when I heard he was gone, and then again when I returned to Sri Lanka, to an airport where he wasn't smiling and waiting in arrivals, to an empty Colombo flat without his singing in it.

What happens to a homeland when no one is left to take you to the airport? When no one is there to cry real tears when it's time to fly home? Are you even Sri Lankan anymore if there are no old friends or family left to tease you about your silly new hairdo? Is the country anything more to you now than familiar fruits and smells? Or the building Mum said was the school she went to? Where she was a ghost, where we were a ghost's children?

One April after the end of the war in 2009, I got on a flight back to Sri Lanka for the first time after a long absence. Ammamma had died, and I was going to her funeral. I was in a funk, not really able to process what was happening, going to the wrong departure gate at Heathrow. The air stewards looked at me funny, I realised my face was wet with tears, my mind mixing some reverb onto the tannoy announcements.

I emerged at last to the familiar waving palms at Katunayake, and there it all was again, that smell of kerosene and tarmac, the humidity sticking to your skin. There it was, and there it wasn't: each time it seemed so different, each time I seemed so different too.

The funeral was unlike any I had been to. Everyone was chatting and drinking Nescafe in the sunlight in front of a white stucco Colombo 7 house in a fancy part of town, while my grandmother decomposed on a bed of flowers inside. 'Hi Ammamma,' I thought. Another heartstring gone. It didn't look like her. She was dressed in a pink-and-gold sari, but she only really liked to wear her widow's white, down to her neat little shoes. Distant relations said, 'Cynthia! Nice to see you'; people who wouldn't recognise me in the street, nor I them. I tried to get a cab back to our flat by myself, my Tamil hopeless, my Sinhalese non-existent. The guy drove off. I didn't belong here, this wasn't home. The country had become a strange moonscape I didn't know.

A cherished auntie was at the funeral, but not her estranged daughter. I heard the girl had married a lovely, well-educated Muslim boy and, in shame, my auntie had cut her off. I noticed my auntie was ignored by lots of other family at the gathering. When I asked Mum about it, she explained she herself had been estranged from her parents because she had left her cheating husband. Story after story came tumbling out during those few sad days of the funeral, of generations of pointless, petty blood feuds, many of them decades if not centuries old. I heard an uncle say something vile, and looked up to meet Mum and Dad's eyes. They agreed with me, but we were all silent, hearing the trash talk about a divorced great-aunt, a gay cousin, a Muslim son-in-law, the 'low-caste' neighbours; hearing the same kind of grotesque everyday hatred that had been directed at Tamil people for so long. This, too, was in our Sri Lankan family, all of that harshness, a difficult police force bearing down on who you were, who you could love, who you could be.

I had lost one story of home and in that losing, I had been given the freedom to make another.

That year, I began to make my own friends in Colombo and Jaffna, and saved a few cab numbers in my phone. I felt awkward at first, too old to be trying to bond with new people, but in time, I met a group of lovely, warm souls, with characteristic Sri Lankan generosity and bawdy humour. I realised I could make my own chosen family, that I had been doing that all these years, in London and now in Sri Lanka, too. I had lost one story of home and in that losing, I had been given the freedom to make another.

Nothing you can eat, no matter how delicious, can ever make up for the heartbreak of losing your family, and the place they call home. But for me, those glorious seasons of Sri Lankan summer are loaded up with meaning now. All that family, all that fruit, the abundance of it all. And just like you can't really bring a fruit on a plane to England (because it won't be the same and it will damage the environment) you can't really go back to the people that have been lost. But you can preserve the memories, with all the bittersweet feeling they have now. I think Sri Lanka's fruit pickles are a bit like that. They're a way to hold on to the fruits of different seasons; they're salty and powerful and sweet at the same time.

Apple acharu

Fruit pickles are eaten all over the island, with mangoes, pineapple, veralu, and more. Try this technique with apples, oranges, plums or gooseberries when you're next cooking for family, chosen or not. It makes a great little snack or starter.

Serves 2

420g apples

1 tsp crushed black pepper

1 tsp chilli powder

1 tsp salt, or to taste

For the pickling liquor

380ml water

50g caster sugar

2 tsp salt

1 tsp black peppercorns

2 tsp coarsegrain mustard

250ml apple cider vinegar

1. First, make the pickling liquor. Put all the ingredients apart from the vinegar into a saucepan. Bring to the boil, then simmer gently for 5 minutes. Remove from the heat and leave to cool for at least 20 minutes to room temperature. Stir in the vinegar.

2. Peel and chop your apples into 2cm chunks. Place in a clean snug container, like a jar. Pour over the cooled pickling liquor.

3. Cover tightly and refrigerate for 30 minutes–1 hour.

4. Serve, scattered with a little crushed black pepper, chilli powder and salt.

Fried aubergine vinegar moju

Mojus are a kind of pickle, a wildly flavourful combination of sweet and sour, with cloves, cardamom, cinnamon, lemongrass, curry leaves and, if you can get it, pandan leaf. Aubergine moju is made of soft, caramelised deep-fried aubergine, red onion that turns pink in vinegar, and Turkish green peppers – those long, light green capsicums. You can eat it warm, or you can stash it in a jar and eat it at room temperature the next day, when all the flavours will have had time to get intimate with each other and perform their magic. Traditionally, it is made with fried sticks of aubergine or little baby ones, but I like a slice, so you get some gooey-ness in the middle and a bit of crispiness on the outside. Try it with yellow rice (page 206) or alongside any curries or sambols you like.

Serves 2–4

2 medium aubergines, sliced into 2cm-thick slices

1½ tsp salt

3 red onions, peeled and finely sliced

100ml apple cider or coconut vinegar

400ml vegetable oil, for deep-frying

4 light green Turkish peppers, or yellow banana peppers, sliced into 1cm strips

3½ tsp granulated sugar

For the spice paste

2.5cm fresh root ginger, peeled and roughly chopped

4 garlic cloves, peeled and roughly chopped

1½ tsp SL curry powder (see page 21)

5 cloves

5 whole cardamom pods, lightly bashed in a pestle and mortar

2.5cm piece of cinnamon stick

2 tsp mustard seeds

1 lemongrass stalk, roughly chopped

10–12 fresh curry leaves

Optional: 10cm piece of pandan leaf, roughly chopped

1. First make the spice paste. Blitz everything together in a spice grinder or mini food processor to form a paste. Keep in an airtight container and set aside while you cook the aubergines.

2. In a large bowl, mix the aubergine slices with 1 teaspoon of salt. Leave them aside for a few minutes. Put one of the finely sliced red onions in a small bowl with 60ml vinegar and the rest of the salt. Let it pickle slightly and turn pink while you get on with everything else.

3. Set a wire rack over a roasting tin, next to where you'll be frying the aubergine. Pour the oil into a medium-sized heavy-bottomed saucepan no more than 4cm up the side of the pan, and set over a medium-high heat. To test it is hot enough, gently lower a little piece of aubergine into the oil; it should start to bubble and cook immediately. Turn the heat down if it bubbles too ferociously. Gently lower 4 or 5 slices of aubergine into the pan with a slotted spoon. Fry for about 4 minutes, then turn them over and fry for a further 4 minutes, until golden on both sides. Transfer to your wire rack to drain off excess oil. Repeat with the rest of the aubergine.

4. When you've fried all the aubergine, fry the rest of the onions in the hot oil for 4–5 minutes, turning once, until golden brown, then add them to the aubergines to drain.

5. Fry the Turkish green peppers in the same way for 5 minutes, until the edges begin to brown. Add to the aubergines and onions.

6. Drain off all but 2 tablespoons of oil from the pan into a bowl to discard when cool. Place the pan over a medium-high heat, cook the spice paste for 2–3 minutes, until it begins to colour. Add all of the vegetables, along with the rest of the vinegar, a splash of water and the sugar. Stir gently to coat in the mixture and simmer for 5–6 minutes, until most of the liquid has bubbled away and the aubergine is shiny. Scatter over the pink pickled onions and serve warm or at room temperature. Allow the oil to cool completely before you discard it.

Cucumber sambol with salted spiced mor yoghurt

This isn't completely traditional, but is my thick version of *mor*, the cooling ancient Tamil drink traditionally made with salted buttermilk, water, spices and herbs. Sri Lankan food, especially in the north of the island, can be paralysingly spicy, and I have always found *mor* a welcome relief, particularly in the hot months of April and May. Rather than a drink, this is a crunchy, summery salad version of all the same ingredients. Straining the yoghurt – for the same tangy flavour as buttermilk – through a muslin sounds like a fuss but it is very easy and will make for a much creamier, more luxurious feel. If you can get your hands on *mor milagai*, lucky you, but if not, skip them and the dish works anyway.

Mor milagai are really special. Made in Sri Lanka, they are buttermilk-soaked chillies that are then laid out to dry in the sun, and that crisp up when you chuck them in hot oil. You end up with chillies that are salty, tart, smoky and fiery all in one.

Serves 2–4

500g full-fat Greek yoghurt

1–2 tsp salt (it seems a lot but it should be salty)

Optional: 5 or 6 mor milagai (buttermilk-soaked chillies from a Sri Lankan food shop)

2 tbsp coconut or vegetable oil (if you are using mor milagai)

1 cucumber, cut into 4cm wedges

Zest and juice of 1 lime

1cm fresh root ginger, peeled and crushed

A handful of dill leaves, roughly chopped

For the temper

1 tbsp coconut or vegetable oil

10 fresh curry leaves

1 green chilli, finely sliced

1 tsp cumin seeds

1 tsp mustard seeds

1. Place a piece of cheesecloth, muslin or a clean tea towel over a colander set inside a bowl. Pour the yoghurt and salt onto the cloth. Tie the ends of the cloth together, and put a couple of tins or another bowl on top of the cloth to weight it down. Then put the whole lot in the fridge overnight.

2. The next day, squeeze out any excess liquid, and mix the yoghurt well. Set aside.

3. If you have mor milagai, heat the oil in a medium-sized frying pan or wok set over a medium heat. When the oil shimmers, gently lower the mor milagai into the oil. Fry for 3 minutes, then turn over and cook for another minute or so. Use a slotted spoon to transfer them to a plate lined with kitchen roll to drain off excess oil. When cool, break and crush them lightly with your fingers.

4. In a bowl, mix the cucumber with the lime zest and juice, ginger and dill.

5. To make the temper, place a clean small frying pan over a high heat, and add the oil. When the oil is shimmering, add the curry leaves, green chilli, cumin seeds and mustard seeds. Stir rapidly to avoid burning for 1–2 minutes until fragrant. Switch off the heat.

To assemble, spread the strained yoghurt onto a bowl or plate. Top with the cucumber. Pour the tempered spices and hot oil over the cucumber. Finish with crunchy mor milagai, if using.

RICE, ROTI, HOPPERS & DOSAS

Yellow rice

Metropolitan, mixed race, English speaking: Sri Lanka's Burgher community has been the source of many delicious dishes, and yellow rice is one. Burghers come in two types – those with Portuguese heritage, and those with Dutch heritage, each with different specialities.

If you are in Colombo, call up the Dutch Burgher Union before 11 a.m. and ask them to put aside a yellow rice packet for you. When you pick it up, your parcel will contain a boiled egg, pickled onions, a fish cutlet, some sambols, some other things, and honestly who cares, because you will get this glorious yellow mountain of sticky, delicious rice.

If you aren't, it's easy to cook yourself. Yellow rice is cooked in a 2:1 ratio of chicken stock to coconut milk, after being fried in a little butter, delicious spices and fragrant pandan and curry leaves. It is a little sweet, a little sticky and completely addictive, and you will find yourself craving it with all kinds of curries and sambols for dinner, just with a crunchy pickle and a dollop of yoghurt for lunch, or perhaps with a simple fried egg for your breakfast.

Serves 4

200g short-grain rice

1½ tbsp butter

½ red onion, peeled and very thinly sliced

6 whole cardamom pods, lightly bashed in a pestle and mortar

6 cloves

10 black peppercorns

1 tsp ground turmeric

10 fresh curry leaves

Optional: 3cm piece of pandan leaf

300ml chicken stock

150ml coconut milk

1 tsp salt, or to taste

1. Pour the rice into a bowl and rinse loosely under the tap, then drain well.

2. Take a medium-sized saucepan, add the butter to it and set it over a medium-high heat. When it has completely melted but is not yet brown, add the onion and fry for 5–6 minutes, stirring occasionally until it is past translucent, and going slightly brown. Then add all of the spices, the curry leaves, pandan leaf, if using, and the rice. Fry for 2–3 minutes, stirring constantly to ensure as many rice grains as possible have been coated in the spicy butter.

3. Pour in the chicken stock and coconut milk, add the salt and bring to a boil. Turn down to a low simmer, cover with a lid and cook for 11–12 minutes, until the rice is cooked. You'll know when it is ready, because the spices will emerge on the top. When that happens, switch off the heat, remove any whole spices you don't want to find in your rice, fluff the rice up gently with a fork and serve.

Coconut rice kiri bath with lunu miris

On one long flight to Sri Lanka as a child, a smiling air hostess wearing a turquoise sari that looked like a peacock came over to offer me breakfast. Feeling fragile from the flight and little sleep, I chose a flaccid 'omelette' and regretted it. Dad was way ahead of me. 'Ohh yes! Kiri bath for me!' he said with cheer, leaving me to fend for myself. He peeled back the foil to reveal warm, tender grains of rice, sweet and plump with coconut milk, served with a variety of sambols. I had learned to always eat the Sri Lankan option when flying Sri Lankan Airlines, and that kiri bath was creamy, thick-set coconut rice, usually combined with very savoury curries and the spiciest of Sri Lankan sambols.

I had never eaten kiri bath before because Sri Lanka is fairly split on coconut rice. At Sri Lankan new year in mid-April, Tamil families cook pongal, a delicious and ancient rich and creamy coconut porridge, which has many incarnations, including a sweet jaggery and cashew-nut version; and a savoury version like the one on page 210. And Sinhalese families cook kiri bath, thicker than pongal as the coconut milk is reduced for longer, cleaner and simpler in flavour, with just four ingredients: rice, cinnamon, salt and coconut milk. It's usually eaten for breakfast, but it makes a delicious dinner or lunch too. Try it with either a spicy fish curry (page 94) or coconut dal (page 40) and, perhaps, a sambol like lunu miris, below.

Serves 4

For the kiri bath

200g short-grain or jasmine rice

200ml water

1 tsp salt, or to taste

1 stick of cinnamon (about 8cm)

400ml coconut milk

For the lunu miris

Zest and juice of 1 lime

1 tsp salt, or to taste

1 tsp ground turmeric

4 dried red Kashmiri chillies or 2 tsp chilli flakes

Optional: 1 tsp Maldive fish flakes, bonito flakes or katsuoboshi

1 red onion, peeled and very finely diced

1. First, make the lunu minis. Put the lime zest and juice, salt, turmeric, dried chillies and Maldive fish, if using, in a pestle and mortar or mini food processor and blitz to a thick pulp. Transfer to a bowl, mix in the red onion and set aside.

2. Pour the rice into a large saucepan and rinse loosely under the tap then drain well.

3. Add the water, salt and cinnamon and bring to a boil. Turn the heat right down to low and simmer with a lid on for 15 minutes. Stir in the coconut milk then cook over a low heat for 10–15 minutes, stirring gently, until the rice is creamy and very thick – so that if you run your spoon or spatula through it, the rice moves back to fill the space very, very slowly.

4. To shape the kiri bath, spoon the hot coconut rice onto a baking tray or large plate. Put a sheet of baking parchment on top, then spread the rice out using a spatula so it is 2–3cm tall, in a rough square. Cool for 5–7 minutes, to set. Take off the parchment and cut into diamonds, about 6cm long. Serve with a little lunu miris spooned over each one.

Turmeric rice pongal with eggs and beetroot acharu pickle

The rice dish pongal is very dear to Tamil people, and is as ancient a food as you can get. This combination isn't traditional, but the thing is, pongal is just fantastic with bright Sri Lankan pickles and a soft-boiled egg. I make them together for breakfast in homage to the delicious dish *tamago kake gohan*, a classic Japanese breakfast of rice, pickles and an egg. I first ate it in Tokyo with my dear old Sri Lankan friend from school, Nathalia, when we went backpacking around the country on bullet trains, aged nineteen. I like to tell myself that Sri Lanka is among the most creative cuisines in the world, and so it's actually traditional to break with traditions sometimes and we shouldn't have to live in a mausoleum. On this one, my mother disagrees however, so feel free to make the rice just on its own, or the pickle on its own, to enjoy with some curries if you prefer.

Pongal is so important to the Tamil community that there are not one but two festivals dedicated to it, and by all accounts they have been going for more than 2,000 years. The word 'pongal' comes from the verb 'pongu' which means to bubble up, fizz, to protest. Pongal is considered cooked when the little grains commit a political act right there in the pot. In some places, people shout 'pongalo pongal!' joyously when they do, which kind of means 'let the pongal rise up!' You can get lots of different varieties of pongal in this world, but I only had space for one in this book, so I chose my favourite. This one is known as *venn* or 'hot' pongal, and the turmeric, black pepper, fresh ginger and asofoetida make it earthy, warming and lovely. Should you get to Sri Lanka or to a pongal-lover's house, I hope you get to try other varieties, like the sweet jaggery-infused *sakkarai* pongal studded with sultanas, cashews and cardamom that is widely made at harvest time. I also hope you get to taste a fragrant spicy chicken *kozhi* pongal, a vegetable feast called *sanyasi* pongal or a bright green pongal, like the one I had once at Taste of Asia in Colombo, made with peppery, parsley-like *gotukola*, coconut milk and black pepper.

You can make the accompanying bright, fragrant pickle in this recipe with any hard vegetables that can be eaten raw, like carrots, red cabbage or cucumbers. Wait for the pickling liquor to cool down before adding it to the vegetables or else they'll start to cook and soften. You want them nice and tart and crunchy against the spiced, luxe-y feeling rice and the richness of an oozy egg.

Ingredients & method overleaf

Serves 4

For the beetroot acharu pickle

200ml apple cider vinegar

1 tbsp yellow mustard seeds

100g granulated or caster sugar

1 tsp salt

1 stick of cinnamon

4 or 5 cloves

2 beetroot (red, candy or golden would all work well), peeled and finely sliced

3–4 green chillies, slit lengthways

1 red onion, peeled and finely sliced

For the pongal

75g yellow or split mung dal

1 tbsp butter

150g arborio rice, rinsed and drained

1 tsp salt, or to taste

300ml water

300ml coconut milk

½ tsp asafoetida

2cm fresh root ginger, peeled and crushed or grated

1½ tsp ground turmeric

For the soft-boiled eggs

2 large organic or free-range eggs

For the temper

2 tbsp butter

½ tsp cumin seeds

½ tsp black peppercorns

8–10 fresh curry leaves

1 tsp asafoetida

1. To make the pickle, pour the vinegar into a small saucepan set over a high heat. Add the mustard seeds, sugar, salt, cinnamon and cloves and bring to a gentle boil. Reduce the heat and simmer for 3–5 minutes. Remove from the heat and leave to cool completely. When cool, pour over the beetroot, green chillies and onion in a bowl (don't use a metal one because it can react with the vinegar). Transfer to a clean airtight jar and let it pickle for about 30 minutes before using. It will keep for up to a week in the fridge.

2. To make the pongal, pour the dal into a saucepan and rinse loosely under the tap, then drain well. Add the butter and cook over a low-medium heat for 5–7 minutes, stirring often, until it begins to smell toasted and aromatic, but hasn't yet gone brown. Add the rice, salt and water, and turn up the heat to bring to a boil, then lower the heat to a simmer. Cover with a lid and forget about it for 15 minutes.

3. Take off the lid, add the coconut milk, asafoetida, ginger and turmeric, and keep stirring as it cooks on the same heat for a few minutes until it achieves a creamy rice pudding consistency. If you find it a bit too thick, add a tablespoon or two of water, and stir for a couple of minutes to loosen it up, until you get the consistency you like. When the rice is cooked, remove from the heat and cover to keep warm.

4. To cook the eggs, fill a medium-sized saucepan with water, and place over medium-high heat until it gets to a gentle rolling boil. Set a timer for 6½ minutes, then gently lower the eggs into the water using a slotted spoon. Get a medium-sized bowl ready, filled about one-third full of cold water and 6 or 7 ice cubes. When the eggs are cooked, transfer them to the bowl of iced water. Allow the eggs to cool completely (about 10 or 15 minutes). When cooled, gently crack and peel the eggs, starting from the wider end, which contains the air pocket.

5. Finally, make a temper. Heat the butter in a small frying pan over a medium heat. When hot, add the cumin seeds and peppercorns. When the cumin seeds splutter, add the curry leaves and asofeotida. Fry for about 30 seconds–1 minute until aromatic and the curry leaves are crisp. Pour half the temper including the butter, into the pongal and stir through.

6. To plate up, spoon a generous dollop of pongal into bowls or onto plates. Pour the remaining temper on top, and serve with a soft-boiled egg and some of pickle on the side.

Sticky chicken buriani

Sri Lankan biriyani – or more correctly, *buriani* – has been cooked island-style since at least 1923, when it was on the menu at the Kamal Pasha Hotel of Maradana. My friend, the food historian Asiff Hussein, says that Sri Lankan buriani is best made from a delicious, pearl-shaped short-grain rice called samba, cooked in ghee with either chicken or beef and potatoes, spiced, and then scented with rosewater.

I find rosewater a little overpowering, so for this buriani dish, I skip it. Instead, I use a spice mix my grandmother wrote down for Mum for a kind of sticky coconut chicken dish, which is fragrant, light and cooked in coconut milk. The resulting buriani is a flavourful, comforting feast, covered in crispy shallots and streaked in golden saffron water. I recommend it with a mint sambol (page 118).

Serves 4

800g combination of chicken legs and breasts, skin removed

2 heaped tbsp buriani spice mix (see below)

150ml coconut milk

300g white, basmati or jasmine rice

600ml water

Salt

1 stick of cinnamon

2 lemongrass stalks, bruised

3 tbsp coconut or vegetable oil

125g shallots, peeled and finely sliced

6 whole cardamom pods, lightly bashed in a pestle and mortar

2 tbsp raw cashew nuts

A pinch of saffron threads

2 tbsp hot water

For the buriani spice mix

15 dried red chillies

1 tbsp coriander seeds

1 tsp fennel seeds

5 whole cardamom pods, lightly bashed in a pestle and mortar

4cm piece of cinnamon stick

5 or 6 cloves

½ tsp poppy seeds

1. Make the buriani spice mix by dry-frying all the ingredients in a small pan set over a medium heat for a few minutes, until it smells very fragrant. Transfer to a bowl to cool, then blitz in a spice grinder or mini food processor until fine.

2. Put the chicken pieces in a bowl and add the 2 heaped tablespoons of spice mix (if you have any excess, it will keep in an airtight container for up to a month) and the coconut milk. Mix to coat the chicken then leave to marinate for 30 minutes at room temperature, or overnight in the fridge.

3. When ready to cook, pour the rice into a saucepan and rinse loosely under the tap, then drain well. Add the water, a pinch of salt, the cinnamon and lemongrass. Bring to the boil and cook for 6–8 minutes until al dente, then drain well. Keep aside.

4. In a separate pan, heat the oil over a medium heat, and fry the shallots for 5 minutes. Add the cardamom and cashew nuts, and continue to stir-fry for 5 minutes, until the shallots are brown. Set aside, along with all the oil. Place the saffron in the hot water.

5. Preheat the oven to 190°C/Fan 170°C/Gas Mark 5. Put all the chicken pieces in a heavy-bottomed casserole or ovenproof pan and pour over enough water to come a quarter of the way up the chicken. Place the casserole in the oven, covered, for 20 minutes.

6. Bring the dish out of the oven and spoon half the rice over the top. Layer in half the fried shallots and cashews and some of the oil in which they were fried. Sprinkle in a pinch of salt, then cover with the remaining rice. Return to the oven and cook, covered, for 30 minutes.

7. Finally, to serve, drizzle over the saffron water and spoon over then the remaining shallots, cashews and oil.

Flaky paratha

These flaky, crispy parathas are kind of like the all-butter croissants of rotis. Made from delicious layers of dough, they are great fun to try. You first drip the dough with oil, roll it out so it gets nice and thin, coil it up into snail-shaped spirals and then roll it. They're not usually made at home, this is more of a cafe or takeaway treat.

Makes 4–6

240g plain white flour

½ tsp salt, or to taste

½ tsp granulated sugar

80ml vegetable oil, plus more for oiling and frying

70ml water

1. Put the flour, salt, sugar, 80ml vegetable oil and water in a mixing bowl. Using your hands, bring it together to form a dough and then knead it thoroughly for 5 minutes in the bowl or on an oiled surface. It should feel smooth and a little sticky, but it shouldn't be stiff or crumbly – if it is too crumbly, add a tablespoon of oil and a tablespoon of water, and work that in. Leave the dough in the bowl covered with a damp clean tea towel to rest at room temperature for 2 hours.

2. Divide and shape the dough into 4–6 balls and rest the dough balls for a further 5 minutes under the damp tea towel.

3. To roll them out, drip a little oil onto a rolling pin, and lightly oil your work surface. Roll out each dough ball into a little disc, 12–15cm in diameter. Sprinkle with a little more oil.

4. Use your fingers to lift and gently stretch out the dough until it is 1mm or so thin. When it's very thin (don't worry if you get a few holes), pinch together a corner between one thumb and index finger, and an opposite corner in your other hand, and pull the two ends into a single line, so you get a kind of pleated effect. Then curl the line of dough round to make a snail or pain au raisin shape. Repeat with all the dough discs. Rest the snails for 5 minutes on a baking tray, covered in a damp clean tea towel.

5. When you're ready to cook, roll out the dough snails with a rolling pin to make roughly 15cm circles. Oil up a frying pan with a little drizzle of oil, and place over a high heat. When hot, cook each paratha for about 1 minute on each side until nice and golden. Then turn the heat right down and cook for 1 minute on each side on a low heat.

6. Puff up the paratha a little by gently clapping its sides, then serve.

Coconut and onion pol roti

I always felt like pol roti was the sort of poor relation of glorious flaky paratha (page 216) or a stuffed, crispy roti, and then one day I was driving through the jungle in Sri Lanka's 'coconut triangle' as the sun was going down. There, by the roadside, were small, soft, hot rotis, cooked over a wood fire, covered in wonderfully pungent sambol, like this Maldive fish sambol in the photo. After that, pol roti became a quick, no-knead favourite, sweetened with fresh coconut and amped up usually with green chillies and red onion, although I've also used spring onions, shallots, calçots and other delicious members of the onion family. It's not traditional, but I add yoghurt to the dough, for a slightly softer, spongier roti.

Makes 10 small rotis

300g plain white flour

200g freshly grated coconut
(see page 175)

½ red onion, peeled and diced

1 green chilli, finely sliced

½ tsp bicarbonate of soda

1 tsp caster sugar

2 tbsp coconut or vegetable oil,
plus more for greasing the
work surface

60g Greek yoghurt

120ml water

1. Put the flour, coconut, onion, chilli, bicarbonate of soda and sugar in a medium-sized mixing bowl. Add 1 tablespoon of oil, the yoghurt and a splash of the water. Mix well, adding the water a little bit at a time until you have a dough. If the dough is too soggy and sticks to your fingers, add more flour; if it is too dry, add a little more water. The perfect dough should roll easily into a large ball without cracking. You don't need to knead it; it just needs to be well mixed together. Portion the dough into 10 equal balls.

2. On a well-oiled surface, flatten and stretch out each ball of dough to a round shape, about 0.5cm thick. You can use a rolling pin or tortilla press if you have one. I like mine about 20cm or just under in diameter.

3. Oil up a frying pan with a little drizzle of oil and spread it over the base of the pan with a piece of kitchen roll. Get it over a medium heat and when hot, place a roti on the pan and cook for 2 minutes, then flip it over and let it cook through for another 2 minutes, or until it is lightly charred and has golden brown spots covering both sides. Repeat with the rest of the roti. Keep the warm cooked rotis wrapped in a clean tea towel.

Thin godamba roti

Godamba means wheat, and this handkerchief-thin roti is made with it in the form of plain flour. Nice and simple, they can be eaten on their own with a variety of curries (perhaps cashew curry, page 74, or beef curry, page 146). They are also the basis for stuffed rotis (page 258), the laminated crispy flaky paratha (page 216) or rolled, sliced and refried in kothu roti (page 228). It's okay if it has a few holes in it, it is meant to be a homely, forgiving flatbread.

Makes 12

250g plain white flour, plus more for dusting

1 tsp salt, or to taste

3 tbsp vegetable oil, plus more for greasing and cooking

100ml warm water (you might need a little more)

1. Sift the flour and salt into a bowl. Add the oil and a tablespoon or so of warm water. Using the handle of a wooden spoon to stir, add the rest of the water little by little, until it's all in. Then use your hands to mix everything together until it comes together into a soft, pliable dough.

2. Turn out onto a lightly floured work surface and knead for about 10 minutes until smooth and elastic. Drop the dough into a clean, lightly oiled bowl and seal it tightly. Leave to rest for at least 1 hour and up to 3 hours.

3. Divide the dough into 12 even-sized pieces.

4. Working with one piece at a time, keep the rest covered with clingfilm or a damp clean tea towel so they don't dry out. Roll out the first dough ball on a lightly oiled surface. When it gets to about 4mm thick, start using your fingers to lift the edges of the dough to stretch it out – you want it 1–2mm thick, like thick card. Don't worry if you get a few holes, that's part of the charm.

5. Heat a flat griddle or heavy-based frying pan over a medium heat. Cook the roti for about 30 seconds until you see it starting to bubble up, then turn it over and cook for 1 minute, until crisp and golden on the outside with brown spots. Wrap it in a clean tea towel to keep it warm. Roll out the next roti while you're waiting for the last one to cook. Repeat with the rest of the rotis.

Sri Lankan Muslim Street Food

In that refuge for drunk kids and insomniacs that is the Hotel de Pilawoos in Colombo, you can order a cheese dolphin kothu twenty-four hours a day. Sure, Pilawoos isn't a hotel and the kothu doesn't have any dolphins in it, but when the food is this good, who cares? When the chef receives your order, they will commence a rhythmic and largely unnecessary *dang-a-dang-dang-a-da-dang* of clanging as the ingredients are stir-fried together with hot metal cooking utensils. Finally, a crispy, piquant wonder of melted cheese, curried minced beef, fresh herbs and fried roti will arrive at your table. You will feel like a spicy Sri Lankan cheeseburger has been detonated happily onto your plate.

Like so many of the world's greatest street foods – kebabs, falafels, biriyani, satay – kothu roti was invented by Muslim cooks. A stroke of Seventies genius, it was born near the Kattankudy mosques near the eastern city of Batticaloa, sometime in the dawn of the decade. The dish is basically a hot remix of yesterday's leftovers in a single cheap, filling plate. Mum and Dad say that, like disco, when they left Sri Lanka kothu didn't exist. Then one year when they returned, both kothu and *Daddy Cool* were everywhere, and the island was changed forever.

It may be young compared to ancient Lankan dishes like kiri bath or puttu (pages 208 and 80), but kothu has fast become a Sri Lankan essential. It's now a kind of basic human right for the hungover or too-tired-to-cook, and easily the national favourite of the island's beloved street foods. Almost a Sri Lankan chilaquiles or panzanella, the main ingredient in kothu is fried bread – specifically chopped (or 'kothu'd') godamba roti (page 220). Godamba roti is a thin sheet of plain flour dough, fired over a hot plate. For kothu, it is then rolled up, shredded into little pieces and fried, so the edges get nice and oily and crispy. The refried roti pieces are mixed up with a spicy, dry-ish curry of your choice, to a loud drumming of metal spoons and hotplates, designed to draw the hungry in, a kind of street food siren. Originally, back in the streets around the Kattankudy mosques, it was made with soft, smokily spiced curried beef, but nowadays frequently it is made with red lamb curry, spicy chicken, potatoes studded with leeks and spices, or, my favourite, seafood, where the sweetness of a little salty squid

or crunchy curried prawns marries brilliantly with roti. Finely sliced red onions are added for sharpness, plenty of curry leaves for aroma, a squeeze of lime and a couple of fried eggs, and *dang-a-dang-dang* that's your lot.

I'd never been to Batticaloa until this year. But I first tried Muslim cooking in the lunchboxes of my friends at school when we were about six. Our neighbourhood then was mostly white and Pakistani, with a few with heritage in other places. 'Fatty' and Tas were sharp and funny and really good dancers. From them I learned you fasted all day and ate all night during something called Ramadan, you got wicked henna patterns on your hands at something called Eid, and although it was a close call, these guys rivalled even us for the strictest parents of any kids in the playground. They spoke fluent Urdu and English, which meant they could have a joke when buying 2p sweets at the corner shop with the shopkeepers. My siblings and I didn't speak Urdu but the corner shop guys were very friendly with us anyway and, in the season, they sold honey mangoes, which Mum would buy by the box.

At the time, I didn't really know that we were any religion at all. I would later find out that my parents come from observant Hindu Tamil families, but Dad wanted to try beef curry when he went to uni, so wanted to bring us up with the freedom to choose.

If you grow up outside of your country of origin, you can only see fragments of the place your family calls home, and this means you can only see fragments of yourself.

Our school was run by the kind of nice white hippies who got us to celebrate all of each other's festivals, and sing Bob Dylan songs in assembly. It was from them, not Mum and Dad, that I learned the Diwali story, and together our whole class painted clay *diya* candleholders for the festival of light. For Chinese New Year, we made papier mâché animal masks and ran around trying to be the first to cross a tissue paper river. When we learned about Mecca, we made little cardboard model *kaabahs* with felt tip and glitter. The places of worship were differently shaped and they had different songs, that much I knew. I didn't know that anyone would have anything to fear from each other.

If you grow up outside of your country of origin, you can only see fragments of the place your family calls home, and this means you can only see fragments of yourself. Neither I, nor our Pakistani friends, nor any of the other children of immigrants learned anything about our own countries at school. Mum, and especially Dad, tried to plug the gaps, to teach us some Sri Lankan facts after work and between household chores, but they were only human. Sometimes they'd get irritated at our stupid questions. I remember Dad telling me his mother would really appreciate the toast crusts I didn't want, and me replying 'well why don't you send them to her?' which got me into *big* trouble. Sometimes we'd glaze over and watch *Neighbours*. And so I'd missed huge chunks of the story of Sri Lanka. One story it took me a long time to learn was the story of Sri Lanka's Muslim food. I didn't actually even know that the Sri Lankan Muslim community existed at all, nor that they had faced all sorts of persecution. And I definitely didn't know about 1990.

It wasn't until I was about nineteen, and Mum and Dad had a few friends round for tea and fish cutlets, that that changed. One of the aunties began reminiscing about cake. 'You remember, that perfect butter cake in that Muslim bakery that used to be there, no? Before they got chased out?' she said to the others. Everyone nodded. It was the offhand way people say things like 'after what Thatcher did to the unions' or 'well before they let Black performers on MTV'. The kind of passing sentence that would make you think, wait *what*? And you're suddenly aware of a big gaping ignorance, a need to Wikipedia something as soon as you get home.

I read the internet for whatever I could find. I learned that on a very hot day in the summer of 1990, a group of men and little boys were kneeling down in four different mosques in Kattankudy for Friday evening prayers. Without warning, around thirty armed Tamil Tigers came into the mosques just after 8 p.m. and opened fire onto the crowds. The bullets hit the bodies of the unarmed faithful, wounding them in their backs and their sides, scarring the mosque walls. It was one of a number of organised massacres of Muslim men, women and children by Tamil Tigers that took place within a single stretch of thirty-two days. By the end of that period, the death toll was near 400, most of whom were from Kattankudy.

By October of the same year, the centuries-old Muslim communities in the north of the country had been ripped apart. The Tigers announced over loudspeakers and at gatherings in mosques all across the north of Sri Lanka that Muslims had to vacate their homes, giving them just forty-eight hours to leave. In what would become known as The Expulsion, whole Muslim communities and families were uprooted from their land and homes. Called informants, traitors, slandered in various different ways, they were not allowed to take property deeds or money or belongings. Over 90,000 people were made homeless. More than thirty years later, many are still dreaming of their return home.

The stories I read that day have stayed with me. I was already old enough to know this already, but it was a kind of deep realisation that there was a lot of hate and horribleness in humanity. Maybe it was in everyone, in every community; maybe it was in me too. And I felt how much the darkness of hate often starts with lies. Even if it's something small, like an

omission about who dreamed up that delicious fried kothu you're eating, or who created the buriani masterpiece on your plate.

There is no way that Sri Lanka's wonderful food would exist without centuries of Sri Lankan Muslim culinary ingenuity. Sri Lankan Muslim cooking tells a story of survival and creativity, of melding influences together. The island community is a diverse one, made up of Sri Lankan Malays (from Indonesian Sumatra and Malaysia), those with Indian and Pakistani roots (the centuries-old Bohra and Memonite communities), and then the largest group, the Moors, including the Galle Fort community, those in the north, in the east, in the central region and in the south. Each region and community has its own traditions and dishes, drawing on Arabic, Malay, Javanese, Mughal and Persian influences.

As a non-Muslim, I could never begin to tell the whole story of the cuisine. But it has been a joy to cook and eat the Sri Lankan Muslim dishes I know, and to honour them in the recipes in this book. The island's favourite pudding, the coconut, cardamom and jaggery-infused custard that is *watalappan* (for which the tart on page 298 is named) is Muslim. Many of the island's delicious sweets have Arabic or Persian roots: falooda (page 304), *dodol*, a thick black jelly of coconut, rice and jaggery syrup, and love cake (page 288). As is often the case, Sri Lankan Muslims make the island's most succulent barbecue, specifically with grilled skewers of peanut-heavy *sathe* (a Lankanised Malay satay), and skewers of grilled beef called *sutta erachi*, a speciality of the east coast. But perhaps finest of all is Sri Lanka's Muslim street food: kothu, in all its glorious forms (page 228), Sri Lankan fried rice (page 112), Sri Lankan buriani (page 214), fried chicken (page 156), *isso vadai* (page 264) and many of the island's patties or *pasthols* (page 272), all made as night falls, and the roadside shops and stalls begin to hum.

Today, if you visit, the streets of Kattankudy are still alive with the sound of the kothu drumbeat. Kothu there, and all over Sri Lanka, is now made in many variations: with the long strands of rice noodles we call string hoppers, with the puttu (page 80), so beloved of the Tamil and Muslim communities, with yoghurt, in a dish called *palandi*, with cheese, with fried chicken, with offal, with big pieces of roti (bafflingly called 'dolphin'), with tiny pieces, and more. I ate a delicious *babath* or tripe kothu on my visit there and it was just absolutely banging. I wondered if there could be a dish more symbolic of modern Sri Lanka. A true melting pot, a remix of the remains of yesterday, brimming with deliciousness and creativity.

Cheeseburger kothu roti

The key to great kothu technique is not too much curry liquid – too much and it will congeal and become heavy. You want just enough to flavour the roti and to give it some colour, but not all pieces of the roti need to be soaked in it.

Makes 4–6

For the beef curry

1 tbsp coconut or vegetable oil

1 red onion, peeled and sliced

2.5cm fresh root ginger, peeled and sliced

3 garlic cloves, peeled and sliced

10 fresh curry leaves

500g minced beef

2 lemongrass stalks, bruised

5cm piece of cinnamon stick

1½ tsp salt, or to taste

2 tsp SL curry powder (see page 21)

75ml coconut milk

1 tbsp meat powder (see page 21)

For the kothu roti

250g godamba rotis (see page 220) or white tortilla wraps

2½ tbsp vegetable oil

1 red onion, peeled and diced

10 fresh curry leaves

2.5cm fresh root ginger, peeled and finely sliced

Optional: 2.5cm piece of pandan leaf

¼ white cabbage or spring greens, very finely shredded

2 carrots, peeled and grated

2 large organic or free-range eggs, lightly beaten

80g grated Cheddar

½ tsp salt, or to taste

4 spring onions, finely sliced

1 lime

1. First, make a quick beef curry. You can do this a day or two ahead. Heat the oil in a large saucepan set over a medium-high heat. When hot, cook the onion for 8–10 minutes, until translucent. Add the ginger, garlic and curry leaves, and cook, stirring every so often, for 2–3 minutes until the curry leaves are bright green.

2. Add the beef, lemongrass, cinnamon, salt and SL curry powder. Cook, stirring occasionally and breaking up any large pieces of mince with your spoon, for 2–3 minutes until starting to brown. Just cover with water, turn the heat down to a low simmer, and cook with the lid slightly ajar for 35 minutes. Add the coconut milk, bring to a simmer, and stir occasionally for 3–4 minutes. Remove from the heat and stir through the meat powder. Keep aside for the kothu roti.

3. Shred the rotis or tortilla wraps: take a whole stack and roll them all up together as if you were rolling up a rug. Slice them diagonally into ribbons, about 1.5cm wide. Then slice them all in the opposite direction, so you are making small diamonds or rough rectangles, about 3cm long. You don't need to be too precious about this; kothu is a street dish and it can be a bit messy.

4. Heat 2 tablespoons of oil in a wok over a high heat. When the oil is shimmering hot, add the onion, curry leaves, ginger and pandan leaf, if using. After 30 seconds or so, when nice and fragrant, stir in the cabbage and carrots, and cook for 1–2 minutes, stirring until everything is slightly softened.

5. Add the shredded roti and stir-fry for 3–5 minutes, until it has absorbed most of the oil and has started to get crispy at the edges. Push the mixture to one side of your wok and add the remaining ½ tablespoon of oil to the bottom of the wok. Add the beaten eggs; they should hiss and start to cook quickly, so use your spatula or wooden spoon to scramble them, stirring fast to break up the egg folds. When the eggs seem like they've just formed into little shapes, mix back in the roti-vegetable mix.

6. Add the beef curry, and at most 1–2 tablespoons of the curry liquid. Stir-fry to make sure everything is well coated, and add the cheese. If you feel it looks a bit dry, add a tablespoon or two more of the curry liquid, and keep stir-frying. After 2–3 minutes, test some meat to see if it is hot all the way through. Remove from the heat, season with salt and scatter with the spring onions. Dish up and finish with a generous squeeze of lime.

Hoppers

All lace-like edges and fluffy pads of crumpet in the cups, think of hoppers as the racy underwear of Sri Lankan food. To me, my mum and many of our fellow Sri Lankans, hoppers have remained exciting for a lifetime. Never – in over a thousand years – have they gone out of fashion.

The word 'hopper' is an Anglicisation of 'aapa' in Sinhala, or the Tamil 'appam'. It means a bowl-shaped pancake, made from a fermented batter of rice flour and coconut milk. They're also made in Tamil Nadu, and in the neighbouring Indian state of Kerala, but in my (biased) opinion, there is no contest. Sri Lankan hoppers are the crispiest, milkiest, most delicious incarnation of this lovely dish you can eat anywhere. As the sun begins to go down each night at around 5 p.m. in the island, you will find people starting to queue for hoppers from the best street vendors and kiosks. They are cooked to order, as many as six or eight at a time, usually by just one guy who makes it all look easy. Then they get piled up into the bags of happy customers for a light takeaway dinner. Hoppers are also cooked at home, often for a filling and delicious breakfast. Once you get the hang of it, they're very fun to make.

Making the perfect hopper requires good technique as well as the perfect batter. In the earliest reference to hoppers I could find – a vivid 782-line poem called *Maduraikanchi* from 300 CE – the narrator gives many delightful descriptions of food from ancient times. Walking around the city of Madurai in Tamil Nadu, he writes: 'at nightfall, the sounds of conch shells cease, and shops are shut, their screens pulled down. Vendors, who sell delicate hoppers that are like honeycombs. . . go to sleep.' This millennia-old cooking note still holds: you're looking for a delicate, honeycomb consistency at the crispy top of a hopper. That means swirling it round the pan with your wrist fast enough that the edges are nice and thin, and so that you can see light through the little holes.

To make your own, you'll need three things: a hopper pan, a gas stove and a little time – the fermentation takes a few hours and getting the knack of it will take a few tries. When you do, you can make plain hoppers, egg hoppers (where you break an egg into one, sunny side up) or milk hoppers with coconut milk and perhaps muscovado sugar or jaggery dropped into it. I've included recipes for all three, and hope you use them to scoop and mop up whatever other sambols and curries you have going on at the table: perhaps seeni sambol (page 136), turmeric fish curry (page 92) or cucumber curry (page 64).

Ingredients & method overleaf

Serves 3–4 (makes about 10–12 hoppers)

300g white rice flour

40g caster sugar

1 large organic or free-range egg, beaten

175ml warm water, plus 50ml for the yeast

10g dried fast-action yeast

400ml coconut milk

½ tsp baking powder

½ tsp salt

1 tbsp vegetable oil

For egg hoppers

1 large organic or free-range egg per hopper

Salt and black pepper

For milk hoppers

1 tbsp coconut milk

1 tsp jaggery or dark muscavado sugar

1. In a large bowl, use a wooden spoon to mix together the rice flour, all but 1 teaspoon of the sugar, the beaten egg and 175ml warm water to make a firm dough. Get your hands into the bowl and knead it until if you press the dough with a finger, it leaves a little indentation. Cover the bowl with a clean tea towel and leave it in a warm place to ferment for about 2 hours (or up to overnight).

2. When you're ready to make your hoppers, pour the 50ml warm water into a small bowl with the yeast and the remaining teaspoon of sugar, and set aside.

3. Add the coconut milk and the baking powder to the bowl with the hopper dough. Massage and swirl the mixture with your hands until it has the consistency of double cream. If you dip a spoon into the mixture and draw a line on the back of the spoon with your finger, the line should stay there. Add a little more warm water if necessary.

4. When the yeast has doubled in size, add it to the rest of the hopper mixture along with the salt and mix well with a whisk. Keep whisking until you see small bubbles.

5. Get a hopper pan over a medium heat, and grease it lightly with a little kitchen roll dipped in vegetable oil. When the pan is hot, pour a small ladle of the batter into the centre of the pan, and quickly swirl it all around just once in a circular motion, to cover the sides of the pan in a thin layer, while the rest sinks to the bottom of the pan. Cover with a lid and cook for 2–3 minutes. You want to be able to prise the edges away easily with a spatula. Lift the pan off the heat, carefully dishing the hopper up to whoever is first in line. Don't worry if the first one is a little odd; the first hopper never works. If it wasn't crispy enough, crank up the heat a notch or two and try again.

For egg hoppers

In step 5 above, 30 seconds after you have covered it with a lid, crack an egg into the centre of the hopper. Allow to cook for 2½ minutes more with the lid on. Season with salt and pepper.

For milk hoppers

In step 5 above, 1 minute after you have covered it with a lid, add the coconut milk. Allow to cook with the lid on for 2 minutes more. Serve sprinkled with jaggery or sugar.

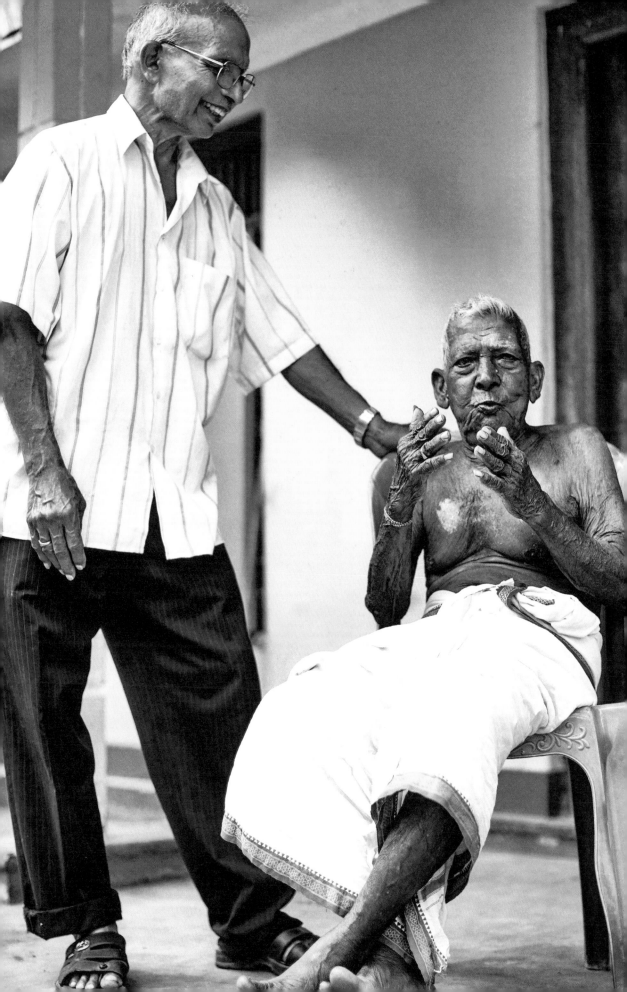

Curry leaf rava dosa

Rava or semolina dosas are nature's instant dosas, requiring no fermentation and making a stiff, crispy, lacy pancake. These ones are made with crushed-up fried curry leaves, which add fragrance to the dish. It's delicious to eat with tempered tiny dried shrimp or kunisso (page 98), but would also be lovely with lamb curry (page 120), sambar (page 58) or black sesame sambol (page 184).

Makes 8–10

2–3 tbsp groundnut or rapeseed oil

20 fresh curry leaves

100g fine semolina

100g rice flour

50g plain white flour

1 tsp cumin seeds

1 tsp salt, or to taste

1 tbsp Greek yoghurt

500ml water

1. Heat 1 tablespoon of oil in a frying pan over a high heat. When the oil shimmers, add the curry leaves; they should sizzle and crisp up within about 30 seconds. Turn off the heat and fish out your crispy curry leaves, placing them in a bowl for later.

2. To make the dosa batter, put the semolina, rice flour and plain flour in a large mixing bowl with the cumin and salt, and stir together. Shape this mixture into a kind of flour mountain. Make a well in the centre with a spoon and dollop the yoghurt into it. Add about a quarter of the water into it too, and mix it all well using a spoon, making sure there are no lumps. Keep adding the water, little by little, mixing until all the water has been incorporated. You want a thin batter with a watery consistency – like thin buttermilk. Cover the bowl with a clean tea towel and leave it to rest at room temperature for about 20 minutes. When you return to the batter, mix it well. Crush the crispy curry leaves with your fingers, sprinkle them into the batter, then stir through.

3. To make your dosas, pour a little oil into a small bowl. Fold up a sheet of kitchen roll ready to dip into the oil to grease the pan between cooking each dosa.

4. Set a large frying pan or flat griddle pan over a high heat. Grease the pan with kitchen roll, being careful not to burn your fingers. Using a small cup, drip the batter onto the pan from a height of about 8–10cm, in a zig-zag motion to form a rough square or circle. Lower the flame to medium and cook until one side of the dosa turns golden and crisp (you don't flip rava dosas as they're so thin and crispy).

5. Using a palette knife or spatula, fold the dosa over, and dish up. Serve while they're hot. Cook the rest of the dosas in the same way, making sure to mix the batter first, as the semolina soon sinks to the bottom.

Plain dosas and tomato thokku sambol

My cousin Sobi who lives in Toronto is a fantastic cook. We have around thirty cousins and all get very overjoyed to see each other because we spent many summers together as kids. That means the first cousin night together is always a really big night. One trip, when we had all flown out for a wedding, Sobi woke up early after our first night together to host many hungover grownup cousins and cranky little kids. The windows of her house fogged up as we trudged through the snow into her house. We could smell the food before we were inside: crispy hot, sour dosas and this tangy, sweet tomato sambol. Because Sobi is basically a chef, she had also made an option of a stack of hot, thick American pancakes and maple syrup. That stack didn't get touched because this is mad delicious. Any leftover tomato sambol will keep in the fridge for a week.

Serves 2 (makes 8–10 dosas)

For the dosas

70g urad dal (split black gram)

2 tbsp chana dal

1½ tbsp fenugreek seeds

250g uncooked basmati rice

½ tsp salt, or to taste

2–3 tbsp groundnut or rapeseed oil

For the tomato thokku sambol

1 golf ball-sized piece of tamarind block, soaked in 60ml warm water for 10 minutes

2 green chillies

2 garlic cloves, peeled

12 medium tomatoes, roughly chopped

2 tbsp coconut or vegetable oil

10 fresh curry leaves, chopped

1 tsp fenugreek seeds

2 red chillies

1 tsp asafoetida

1 tsp salt, or to taste

1 tsp sugar

Continued overleaf

1. To make the dosa batter, pour the urad dal, chana dal and fenugreek seeds into a large bowl. Rinse loosely under the tap, then drain well. Into another bowl, pour the rice. Rinse the rice in the same way as the dal mixture. Pour enough cold water into both bowls to cover the dal and rice by about 4cm. Leave to soak uncovered for 4–5 hours.

2. Keeping the liquid, drain the water from the dal completely. Spoon the drained dal into a food processor. Add a few tablespoons of the drained water and the salt. Blitz until the mixture is smooth and frothy, adding more liquid if you need to. Pour the batter into a clean metal or ceramic bowl.

3. Preheat the oven to a low heat around 60°C. Drain the rice, leaving a few tablespoons of liquid. Blitz the drained rice until it is smooth, adding a little more drained dal liquid if you need it. Pour the rice batter into the dal batter and mix well with a wooden spoon. Put in the oven and leave for at least 6 hours and up to overnight. The batter is now ready, and you can keep it in the fridge, covered, for up to 5 days until you're ready to make your dosa pancakes.

4. To make the sambol, squeeze the tamarind with your fingers, then discard the seeds and skin, leaving behind the pulpy water. Put the green chillies, garlic, tamarind water and the tomatoes in a food processor. Blitz a few times to form a purée but not a juice. In a medium-sized frying pan over medium-high heat, heat the oil. After a minute or two when the oil is hot, add the chopped curry leaves, fenugreek seeds and whole red chillies, and cook for 30 seconds until the curry leaves start to go bright green. Add the tomato mixture and asafoetida, and stir well. Add the salt and sugar, then turn the heat down to low and simmer for 30 minutes. The tomatoes should darken and everything should be very fragrant. Pour into a small serving bowl.

For the temper

2 tbsp coconut or vegetable oil

10 fresh curry leaves

1 tsp mustard seeds

5. To make the temper, heat the oil in a small frying pan over a medium heat and fry the curry leaves for 30 seconds until they go bright green. Add the mustard seeds, stirring until they start to pop, and the curry leaves crisp up. Pour over the tomato sambol, to serve.

6. When you're ready to make your dosas, place a frying pan over a medium heat and drizzle some oil into it. After 1–2 minutes, when the pan is nice and hot, get a ladle and stir the batter. Pour a ladle of batter into the centre of the frying pan, then use the back of the ladle to spread it around in a circular motion, starting from the centre until you have made a circle.

7. Drip a couple of drops of oil on top of the dosa while it is cooking. After about 1–1½ minutes, when it is cooked, no longer wet and the bottom is golden and crispy, transfer to a plate. Ideally, let it be eaten immediately with a dollop of sambol. Repeat until you've made all the dosas.

DRINKING SNACKS & SHORTEATS
DRINKING SNACKS & SHORTEATS
DRINKING SNACKS & SHORTEATS
DRINKING SNACKS & SHORTEATS
DRINKING SNACKS & SHORTEATS
DRINKING SNACKS & SHORTEATS

Shorteats Are Portable Snacks

If you're at my kind of Sri Lankan party, naughty drunk uncles will shout rude jokes at each other, laughing uproariously. They will get into hot political fights with their mates and receive ice-cold glares from their wives. The music will be so insanely loud you will get tinnitus, and you will oscillate between thinking 'this music is nuts' and tapping your toes involuntarily, itching to dance. Your sequinned sari will get stained with someone else's wine, and in the loos some nice auntie who is a total stranger will fix it. You will do her eyeliner. What began as some gawky kids jumping up and down in their ra-ra skirts on the dance floor will give way to, wait is that *Mum*? And all her friends will be dancing too, shimmying to silly lyrics like '*hey girl, I brought you a fish*!', a twanging kazoo and Sri Lanka's African-Portuguese calypso, *baila*.

And where there's a Sri Lankan party, there are Sri Lankan party snacks. Before dinner, before the main event, before people start asking you 'did you eat *payasam*?' (a stodgy tapioca dessert you've never wanted to be honest, especially not now) – there will be snacks. There will be long tables groaning with piles of breaded spicy fish croquettes ('cutlets') (page 270), flaky, golden patties of curried meat (page 272) or spicy potatoes. Good-looking young men and women will have been emotionally blackmailed into carrying around whole trays of puff pastries with hot fillings, mountains of spicy chicken wings or beef samosas. You might get breaded curried mutton or vegetable rolls (page 266), perhaps you'll get rotis – a pliable, thin godamba roti – folded around potato (page 220), studded with whole spices and grilled to crispiness on a hotplate. If it's a daytime party, there might be buns.

Malu buns (page 252) are perhaps the quintessential Sri Lankan shorteat: fluffy little triangular parcels of enriched, pale yellow dough, stuffed with spicy fish and tempered potatoes with green chillies, herbs, turmeric and plenty of black pepper. Similar soft buns can also be filled with fiery shallot jam, seeni sambol (page 136), or curried beef or chicken. Or they can be wizened into a crocodile shape and covered in sugar for *kimbula* buns. Nothing compares to *malu* though. Like other shorteats, because of their shape and size and overall portability, they're also great for long journeys; fuel to get you through a trek or long train ride. Or, perhaps, a war.

In the summer of 2003, in the first island-wide ceasefire since 1983, I was back on holiday in Sri Lanka for my sister's wedding. After the celebrations in Colombo, for the first time since I was a toddler, I travelled up into the north. Dad and I had to move slowly through the areas that had been neglected and obliterated by fighting, past the tall spiky palmyra trees and buildings riddled with bullet holes. We travelled all the way from Fort Station in Colombo, through the country to Vanni – at that time controlled by the rebel Tamil Tigers – and on to Dad's old house in rural Jaffna, then controlled by the government.

You could smell the pure fear in the air, the tight discipline of the Tiger administration.

We were told to change our clocks by thirty minutes when we stepped into Vanni. It was indeed another country, another planet. Here, at twenty-one, was my first through-the-looking glass experience of Tamil police, Tamil judges, a Tamil administration, Tamil everything. I had never seen anyone like me routinely in positions of authority or control. Tiger songs blared over the loudspeakers in the streets. Women wore their long hair folded and braided high on their heads, cycling around looking strong and independent. Were they fighters? I wondered. Or was it fashion? A nice, chatty elderly man at the post office said to us that Vanni was completely safe, free of crime. When Dad replied, to make conversation, 'Oh yes?' the old man replied, 'Yes, because here it will be a Tiger policeman to arrest you.' That was a conclusion in its own right, I realised. You could smell the pure fear in the air, the tight discipline of the Tiger administration.

We stopped in a fantastically orderly, spotlessly clean cafe called Cheran in Vanni's capital city, Kilinochichi, where Tamil Tigers in hairnets and brilliant white uniforms served tea and dinner and shorteats to various visiting NGO and UN personnel. Dad and I got talking to a neighbouring table of friendly students from Canada. They were studying economics at Waterloo University, and they were cute. For the first time in my life, Dad seemed fine with me talking to attractive boys I wasn't related to. I was an economics student, too, at Cambridge University, which seemed to impress everyone, and so they asked if I'd like to help them draft some ideas for a strategy document for the United Nations Development Programme on regenerating the area. I leapt at the chance, and got a tour of some immaculate Tiger facilities, where they grew pineapples, reared chickens, and where a big mad machine churned out perfectly triangular, neatly stuffed and extremely tasty *malu* buns.

'What are they for?' I asked, biting into one, and finding it spicy and utterly delicious, sour and fragrant with lots of curry leaves. 'This recipe can last for months in the jungle,' they said. 'Oh okay, why do you need them though?' They looked at me inscrutably. 'Is the fighting going to continue?' I kept going. Their eyes looked unreadable. There was a lot I didn't understand.

––––––––––

Tamil parties are about many things: pelvic-explosive dancing, reckless flirting while the snitches are definitely watching you. It is about that cheesy song you don't even like but that can voodoo your feet right into a jostle of warm dancing bodies. It is about snacks. It is about the intense feeling of performing, producing and consuming joy. And to understand the joy of a Tamil party, I think you have to understand the pain.

There isn't a memory I have of Sri Lanka that isn't touched by the brutal suffering of Tamil people. For all the years of riots, curfews, bus bombings, checkpoints and heavy military presence in Colombo and other areas of the south, nowhere suffered more than the north and the east. I first went to Sri Lanka as an eight-month-old baby in the summer of 1982, the year after the biggest collection of ancient Tamil manuscripts in the world, the Jaffna Library, was burned down; 90,000 books destroyed by government thugs. It was the year before the country's watershed race riots in 1983. There had been anti-Tamil riots in 1956, 1958, 1977 and 1981, which had left hundreds dead. But 1983's Black July was Sri Lanka's Kristallnacht, in which thousands of Tamil families and civilians were brutally murdered, burned alive and their businesses and houses systematically destroyed by marauding state-sponsored Sinhala mobs. Our family and our friends were full of stories of those who had been hidden by Sinhala friends, and had managed to escape the bloodshed; 150,000 Tamil people became homeless. That year, an armed Tamil uprising began, and the fighting would last thirty years. In government massacres and bombings, an estimated 47,000 ordinary Tamil people like me and my family were killed before 2009; and then an estimated 70,000 more in the final year of the war.

I had seen my cousins shaking with fear when stopped by the police, routinely suspected and frequently harassed, which was better than the alternatives of being detained, beaten or most macabre of all, 'disappeared'. I had seen friendly faces change when they realised I was Tamil, sometimes when I was least expecting it – a lovely Sinhalese waitress in a nice hotel or the cheeky ticket guy wearing too much aftershave at the Sri Lankan Airlines office. When I was eight or nine, in Hambantota, in southern Sri Lanka, Dad pulled us aside to warn us not to say anything in Tamil because it was late at night, it was a notoriously racially tense bit of the country, and because we'd missed the last bus, we were about to clamber into a wagon full of drunks and lost souls. I understood what he said, but minutes later I wondered aloud about someone chewing tobacco that 'smells like Ammamma'. I didn't really know that the word we used

for grandmother was Tamil, but Dad looked at me with pure and almighty fury. I had endangered not just me, but my sister and him. I had betrayed us all by revealing we were not Malaysian tourists, we weren't Keralan Indians, we were nothing but ordinary Sri Lankan Tamils. I felt sick all the rest of the journey. Although nothing came of my big mistake, I have never forgotten it.

I've also never forgotten the feeling that for no reason other than Dad being good at maths and someone loaning him some money for a flight to Heathrow Airport, we got to be in the safety of watching *The Fresh Prince of Bel Air* while our Sri Lankan family became acclimatised to an everyday life of violence. Mum's cousin, her beloved Parka Anna, was shot dead by the Sri Lankan Army near her house because he broke a curfew one night to take some food to his geriatric parents: six bullet holes in his back, the tin of food still by his bicycle. Parka Anna was deaf. He hadn't heard their warning. I watched from the landing as she sat on the stairs by the phone and sobbed all night. Our stammering, shy, thirteen-year-old cousin – so bright he was on a scholarship to the best school in the whole province, so nerdy his glasses were thick like milk bottles, the smallest kid in his class who sang sad soulful songs in temple – was detained, tortured and interned in a camp by the army on the grounds that this weak kid might grow up to become a rebel fighter. He was left with debilitating PTSD he would never recover from.

And then there was our neighbour, Devi.

The Sri Lankan army began an occupation of Jaffna in 1995. Sometimes young, bored soldiers would stop Tamil people in the street, sometimes they would knock at the door, ask questions, point guns. One day, four soldiers came to Devi's door and they asked where her remarkably beautiful fifteen-year-old daughter was. They searched the house. The girl was sleeping over at her aunties', so the soldiers left. They said they would be back 'to see her' the next day.

Her eldest son ran away to join the Tamil rebels that night. He was just eighteen years old. In the morning, already nauseated with worry about her daughter, Devi found her boy gone, his white school uniform folded, his textbooks and pencil case still in his bag.

As the weeks turned into years, she found ways to hide and protect her daughter, but she received no news of her son. And the chances he remained alive began to fade like the grinning photos of him she had in her drawer. News of bloodshed and body counts fizzed from the radio night and day, but about him she received only silence. No small, neat telegram saying he had been killed in combat. No call. She wouldn't ever know if her first baby was really gone, whether it had happened long ago when he was young and inexperienced, whether he had become senior and commanding. Had he been frightened when he'd died, had he bitten upon the cyanide capsule all Tamil Tigers wore around their necks, had he been captured, tortured, thrashed, blown up, butchered by explosives, limbs dismembered, whatever it had been? There was no feeling his cold and hard body with all the life gone out of it, no screaming her grieving cries onto a casket, no funeral, no goodbye. And that not knowing left her with an open wound of hope. Even ten years after the end of the civil war in Sri Lanka, when there was really no chance at all that he could yet be among the living, she told me that she still heard his voice sometimes. When the wind would blow a certain way, she would think she heard him at the gate, a forty-five-year-old man she wouldn't recognise, greying by now, she could hear him calling 'Amma,' saying he was home.

Every one of us was a survivor.
To even get to a party meant that we were alive.
It meant we had survived.

I don't know I ever thought about it at the time, but those parties had this desperate energy. Every one of us was a survivor. To even get to party meant that we were alive. It meant that we had survived. In grief, like Tennyson says, you make music as before, but vaster.

There used to be a weird privacy to this experience, one only other Sri Lankans knew. You'd meet a mate's nice English dad who was into cricket, and he'd say kindly, 'It's so sad about what's happening in Sri Lanka,' and you'd nod blankly, unsure how to turn it into an anecdote. Then one day, one album, one person changed that forever. When I was just out of uni, like all my other friends I bought a yellow album covered in graphic art, with a black-and-white picture of a woman on the cover. It was called *Arular*, and it *banged*. The singer was M.I.A. and she became the biggest Sri Lankan artist in the world. When we listened to it, it felt like she had printed out Tamil party invites and was belting them out on the radio. Here she was, a kind of party leader; Tamil pain and joy wrapped up in her music and functioning like a release valve for our own. An M.I.A. track came on one night out in London and the crowd was shouting 'BOYZ THERE! HOW MANY?! BOYZ THERE!' My friends, white, Black and Indian were shouting it too, making me feel like the whole world knew what we knew and were singing along. All of us singing 'ta-na-na-na-na-na-na' like all the old folk singers, every heart pulsating to the same irresistible ancient *koothu* Tamil drum beat. When I'm making shorteats, getting my dancing shoes on, it feels like that now, like we can all go to a great big Lankan party, thankful to be alive. A whisky, a mutton roll, we'll remember forever, we'll dance tonight.

Malu buns

I owe this recipe to my dad's littlest sister, who we call Cinnauntie. She is the kind of shy, gruff lady who I sometimes had dinner with in complete silence when I was a teenager, and who would spend a whole day making me buns if she heard I liked them. My dad's family is full of this sort of quiet, unstoppable sweetness, and as I got older I learned that it was easier to do practical things with these guys than to try too much chit-chat. So I got her to teach me these buns. This recipe is Cinnauntie's punchy, delicious, tinned fish filling and her method of folding up the buns, but using a slightly different dough. These days I make *malu* buns with an easy, sweet brioche, made with a quick *tangzhong*, a Japanese baking technique to make the buns softer and last longer. The filling is very easy, with no bones or cooking fish. Try them as a lunchbox treat to take to work, or for a rainy afternoon tea.

Makes about 16

For the dough

500g plain white flour, plus more for dusting

120ml milk, at room temperature

1 tbsp dried fast-action yeast

5 large organic or free-range eggs, at room temperature

50g caster sugar

1½ tsp salt

250g butter, softened

A little coconut or vegetable oil, for greasing

1 large organic or free-range egg, beaten with 1 tsp milk, to glaze

Optional: 2 tsp sesame seeds, for decoration

For the filling

200g nice waxy potatoes (e.g. charlotte or new potatoes), peeled and halved

1 tsp ground turmeric, plus a pinch

1 tsp salt, plus a pinch

2 tbsp coconut or vegetable oil, plus a little more for greasing

1. To make the dough for the buns, start by making a *tangzhong*. Put 100g plain flour in a medium saucepan. Add the milk and whisk to form a smooth slurry. Place the pan over a medium heat and continue to whisk vigorously until the consistency is between thick custard and creamy mashed potatoes; it will take 2–3 minutes. Switch off the heat, scrape the slurry into a large bowl or dough mixer, and allow to cool.

2. When cool, add the remaining flour, yeast, eggs and sugar to the bowl with the slurry and mix well. If you're using a dough mixer, this should take 7–10 minutes on the slowest setting; and if by hand, bring together into a rough dough, then dust a clean surface lightly with flour and knead for 10 minutes.

3. Add the salt and the softened butter, a little at a time. Keep mixing and when it is well incorporated and kneaded, add more butter until you have added all the butter. Keep kneading until when you stretch out a piece of the dough between your thumb and first finger, you can see some light through it without it breaking. Don't feel disheartened if your dough feels very wet, it will get better! Just keep kneading.

4. Shape the dough into a large smooth ball. Line a bowl with a little oil, and place the dough in it. Put the bowl, covered, in the fridge to rest for at least 2 hours or up to overnight.

5. While the dough is proving, make the filling. Put the potatoes in a large pan of water along with a pinch of turmeric and a pinch of salt. Bring to the boil and cook for 6–7 minutes, then drain and allow to cool.

Continued overleaf

1 red onion, peeled and
finely sliced

10 fresh curry leaves,
finely sliced

1 lemongrass stick, bruised

400g tinned fish, e.g. sustainably
caught mackerel, sardines or
tuna, drained

4 or 5 green chillies, deseeded
and finely sliced

2 garlic cloves, peeled
and minced

4cm fresh root ginger, peeled
and minced

1 tsp caster or granulated
sugar

2 tsp ground black pepper

2 tsp cumin seeds

2 tsp mustard seeds

Juice of 2 limes

6. Heat the oil in a saucepan over a medium heat and when hot,
fry the onion, stirring occasionally, until golden. Add the curry
leaves, and after 30 seconds, stir in the 1 teaspoon turmeric and
1 teaspoon of salt. After 2 minutes, add the rest of the filling
ingredients and stir well, cooking for 4–5 minutes over a medium
heat so the fish takes on all the flavour. Remove from the heat and
allow to cool.

7. Smash the cooled potatoes using your hand. You don't want
them to be too fine! Stir the smashed potatoes into your fish mix.

8. Grease a baking tray with a little oil. Divide the dough into
about 16 balls, each weighing roughly 75g. Squidge a ball of dough
between your hands so it's about 10cm in diameter, and fill it with
1–2 tablespoons of the filling. Fold it over and tuck in the ends.
Shape them however you like – I like triangles as that's how they
are made in Sri Lanka, but you could make them into circles if
you prefer. Repeat to use up all the dough and filling.

9. Place all the buns on the greased baking tray, leaving about 10cm
between them as they will grow in the oven. Cover with a clean tea
towel and let it sit at room temperature for 30 minutes. Preheat the
oven to 190°C/Fan 170°C/Gas Mark 5.

10. Once they've rested, brush them with egg wash and, if using,
scatter sesame seeds over the buns. Bake for about 20 minutes until
golden, rotating the tray after 10 minutes for an even bake.

Devilled party cashew nuts

If you're having a party, you need party nuts and nothing says party like some spicy cashews. Devilled cashews are on every bar menu in Colombo, to be lobbed into your mouth like popcorn as you are knocking back an arrack sour or a Lion beer, feeling the sauna of summer heat open your very pores to spice and crunchiness. The crispy mix of curry leaves, sweet plantain chips and nuts, all thoroughly doused in spices and salt, is so moreish that you will struggle to leave enough room for your meal, so proceed with caution.

According to my dear friend Jon Spiteri, one of the founders of the restaurant St John in London (that temple of British food and history), in British terminology, 'to devil' something, culinarily speaking, is to put the devil into it, to make it hot and spicy – like devilled eggs or devilled kidneys. I'm pretty sure that means you take an ingredient from its original, chaste purity of virtue and thrust it into the devil's own hell of chillies, spices, sex and sin, which is problematic as all fuck isn't it? Then again, the devil's party does sound like the better one to go to, so if you'd like to come too, please make these devilled hot party nuts. They take ten minutes and they will transport you immediately to a rowdy afternoon bar in Colombo.

Serves 4

3 tbsp coconut or vegetable oil

8–10 fresh curry leaves

250g raw cashew nuts

1 tbsp SL curry powder
(see page 21)

200g plantain chips

Salt

1. Heat the oil in a frying pan over a high heat. Add the curry leaves and let them sizzle and crisp up for 2 minutes, then remove them from the oil and put them on a plate.

2. Turn the heat down to medium and add the cashew nuts to the oil. Cook, stirring occasionally, for about 10 minutes, until the cashews are golden on both sides.

3. Add the SL curry powder and stir-fry until the nuts are fully coated in the spices. Stir in the plantain chips and the crispy curry leaves, season with salt and serve.

Potato and leek spicy stuffed roti

Stuffed Sri Lankan rotis probably have origins in Sri Lankan Malay and Sri Lankan Muslim food traditions. They closely resemble Indonesian and Malay *murtabak*, a wonderful stuffed, fried roti that made its way all the way from Yemen – from the Arabic for 'folded' – and that are eaten all over the Middle East and South East Asia, with many fantastic local variations.

Sri Lanka's ones are spicy, packed with vegetables or meat and often have a little sweetness from cinnamon. You can find stuffed rotis in roadside kades and brightly lit bakeries up and down the country, like at Perera & Sons. I also like to pop round the corner from Bhama Auntie's house in Wellawatte in Colombo to purchase a few from the brilliant Taste of Asia for the plane home, perhaps pausing to eat one while it's still hot, with a ginger tea. You get lots of variants like beef, fish, even egg, but I think there's nothing like a potato and leek roti.

Makes 12

1 x quantity godamba roti
  dough (see page 220)

For the filling

400g potatoes, peeled
  and quartered

2 tsp ground turmeric

2–3 tsp salt, or to taste

2 tbsp vegetable oil, plus more
  for greasing

1 medium onion, peeled and
  very finely sliced

20 fresh curry leaves

Optional: 5cm piece of
  pandan leaf

1 tsp cumin seeds

1 tsp mustard seeds

1 tsp caster sugar

1 carrot, peeled and grated

1 medium leek, finely sliced

2 tsp SL curry powder
  (see page 21)

½ tsp ground cardamom

Optional: 1 tsp Maldive fish flakes,
  bonito flakes or katsuoboshi

½ tsp freshly ground
  black pepper

1. Make the godamba roti dough and leave aside in a bowl for about 30 minutes.

2. Meanwhile, make the filling. Put the potatoes in a saucepan and just cover with water. Add ½ teaspoon of turmeric and 1 teaspoon of salt. Bring to the boil over a medium-high heat, then simmer for about 8 minutes until tender. Drain and let the potatoes cool. When they're cool enough to handle, mash them with your hands so they're broken up but are still nice and chunky.

3. Heat 2 tablespoons of oil in a saucepan or wok over a medium heat. When the oil is hot and begins to shimmer, fry the onion until translucent, stirring occasionally. Add the curry leaves and pandan leaf, if using. After 30 seconds, stir in the cumin seeds, mustard seeds and sugar. After another 30 seconds add the grated carrot, and stir-fry for 1–2 minutes until the carrot is tender.

4. Add the cooked potato, leek, SL curry powder, cardamon, remaining 1½ teaspoons of turmeric, 1 teaspoon of salt and the Maldive fish, if using. Stir-fry for 3–5 minutes, until the leek is tender and everything is well coated and fragrant. Remove from the heat, stir through the black pepper and adjust the salt to taste. Set aside to cool.

5. To assemble the rotis, grease two dinner plates with a little oil. Pour a little more oil onto your hands, and divide the roti dough into 12 equal balls, each one weighing roughly 50g. (Any excess dough can be frozen, if you like.) Cover each ball in oil and place them all on one of the dinner plates.

Continued overleaf

6. Place one of the dough balls in the middle of the other greased dinner plate. Using your fingers, smooth and stretch it out until it is 2–3mm thick. Place 2 tablespoons of the potato mixture into the centre. Carefully fold the stretched dough around it, until you have a rough tube shape, and place back on the greased plate with the remaining balls. Repeat for all the rotis.

7. Set a flat griddle pan or frying pan over a medium heat. Using a piece of kitchen roll, smear a little oil over the base of the pan and leave it for 1–2 minutes to get hot. Place 2 or 3 of the rotis in the pan, and cook for about 30 seconds until golden brown, which will also create a flat side to each roti. Rotate the roti 90 degrees, and cook for 30 seconds on this side, until golden brown. Keep rotating the roti until each one is a long box shape, and all the sides and the ends are golden. Place on a cooling rack and repeat with the remaining rotis.

Vadai doughnuts

These crowd-pleasing fritters have a fluffy consistency and come in a round doughnut shape, studded with onions and spices. There's a Tamil nursery rhyme about a crow stealing these golden, pillowy vadais with glee right out of the shop, and snaffling them off to a tree to gobble up, and when you taste them you'll see why. They're made with urad dal, which is a cheap lentil to buy in most Asian shops and often, these days, supermarkets. You have to soak the lentils for at least thirty minutes, which is the perfect opportunity to get on with a nice dipping sambol or chutney to go with them – perhaps the black sesame sambol on page 184 or the tomato thokku sambol on page 236.

Makes 10–12

250g urad dal

½ tsp salt, or to taste

1 tbsp white rice flour

50ml ice-cold water

3 green chillies,
  very finely sliced

20 fresh curry leaves,
  very finely diced

½ medium red onion, peeled
  and very finely diced

A few generous grinds
  of black pepper

1 tsp cumin seeds

A pinch of asafoetida

500ml vegetable oil,
  for deep-frying

1. Pour the urad dal into a bowl and rinse loosely under the tap, then drain well. Cover with fresh water and soak for at least 30 minutes and ideally 1–2 hours (a longer soak gets a spongier, springier fritter).

2. Rinse the lentils again and drain well. Put them in a food processor with the salt, rice flour and 2 tablespoons of ice-cold water. You want to achieve a fluffy batter and you do this by adding the ice-cold water a little at a time to make sure everything stays nice and cold. The batter is sensitive to temperature and will start to cook and get weird if the food processor gets warm. So blitz for about 30 seconds, then scrape down the sides of the food processer using a spatula and add another 2 tablespoons of ice-cold water and blend for a further 30 seconds. Repeat until you've added all the water, and the batter is completely blended, thick, fluffy and aerated. It might need an extra 2–3 tablespoons of water, but don't add more than that or it won't puff up properly. It should be white, not yellow, when you're good to go. Transfer the mix to a bowl and gently fold in the green chillies, curry leaves, onion, black pepper, cumin seeds and asafoetida, until they're mixed through.

3. Now, get your stations ready for cooking the vadai doughnuts. Put some water in a small bowl and get a plate lined with a couple of sheets of kitchen roll on standby. Pour the oil into a large heavy-based saucepan to a depth of 4cm, and set it over a medium heat.

4. Dip your hands and the spatula into the water. With one hand, place a dollop of about 10% of your vadai batter onto the wet spatula. Pat it and shape it into a round doughnut shape, using your finger to make a hole in the centre. Take the spatula close to the hot oil, and carefully drop in the vadai. Fry in batches of two or three, for 2–3 minutes, then flip them over so they get golden all over. Drain on the kitchen roll, while you fry the rest. Serve immediately with a dipping sambol.

Prawn fritters isso vadai

These little prawn fritters are sold on the streets all over Sri Lanka, most famously of all on Colombo's Galle Face Green, that lovely stretch of families, flying kites and hot food vendors on the seafront at the top of the Galle Road. There are different kinds of *raal* or *isso vadai*: those flat, crunchy hard discs called *Point Pedro vadai*, and those more puffy, softer *kadala vadais* which are made with soaked dal. These ones are like a lovechild of Cantonese prawn toast and a Yemeni falafel: prawny, crunchy, and fluffy, with some cumin, green chillies and sesame seeds for flavour.

Galle Face Green lies opposite the Galle Face Hotel, a beautiful old hotel, where Clark Gable once stayed, and my sister once got married (though not at the same time). I spent the entire wedding navigating a scary lady with a clipboard, who insisted our sound system, chairs and even flowers were moved from the wedding hall to the ballroom. We had, apparently, to accommodate the other major event of the day, the Mrs Sri Lanka beauty pageant for wives, an event notorious for its assaults, arrests and small-time divas. Luckily, I was that day also a scary lady with a clipboard turned small-time diva, and thanks to an almighty fight behind the curtains, my sister and her husband got dibs on the full-pelt sound system with which to dance the night away. After the wedding we walked around outside, past all the *isso vadai* sellers, feeling the warm sea breeze and smelling the freshly cooked treats. When you eat these *vadais* I wish you the smug satisfaction I had of seeing my sister on the happiest day of her life, prawn *vadai* in hand, and knowing you were 1-0 up against Mrs Sri Lanka.

Makes 9

190g chana dal

1 dried red chilli

2.5cm fresh root ginger, peeled and roughly chopped

3 green chillies (or to taste), chopped

2 tsp sesame seeds

1 tsp cumin seeds

10–12 fresh curry leaves, chopped

100g gram flour

1 tsp salt, or to taste

500ml vegetable oil, for deep-frying

250g medium-sized prawns, shells removed

1. Pour the lentils into a bowl and rinse loosely under the tap, then drain well. Cover by about 4cm of water and soak for 2–3 hours.

2. Drain the lentils, keeping the liquid. In a food processor, blitz the drained lentils, dried red chill and ginger with 2–3 tablespoons of the lentil water, until it has a coarse consistency, adding more liquid a tablespoon at a time if you need it. Transfer the mixture to a bowl and add everything except the oil and prawns. Mix well until just combined.

3. Pour the oil into a deep-sided, heavy-based saucepan, leaving at least 4cm at the top of the pan. Set over a medium-high heat. While the oil is heating up, roll the lentil mixture into 9 small balls. Press one or two prawns into each ball and flatten into the patties, so they get nestled firmly into the vadais.

4. Test if the oil is hot enough by adding a pinch of the isso vadai mixture or a small cube of bread; if it sizzles it is ready. Use a slotted spoon to gently slip 2 patties into the hot oil. Deep-fry for 3–5 minutes until crisp and golden brown. Remove with the slotted spoon and drain on a plate lined with kitchen roll. Repeat with the remaining mixture. Serve hot or at room temperature.

Mutton rolls

In the Hotel Nippon, a Wes Anderson-like old hotel in downtown Colombo, you can pop in for a crispy 'roll', widely regarded as the city's best. In Sri Lanka, a 'roll' doesn't refer to a type of bread or a dance move, it refers specifically to a tube-shaped shorteat, made ideally from a hot red beef or mutton curry that is wrapped up in a Chinese pancake, breaded and then fried into a piping hot snack. These ones are made with lamb, but you can use mutton or hogget, which have more flavour – the recipe cooks very slowly so the meat is soft and delicious.

Downtown Colombo is a mix of fancy hotels and street eats, which makes for my kind of night out. Hotel Nippon is in an area called Slave Island, and I was introduced to the area and the rolls by my friend, Firi Rahman, who that night showed me the beautiful murals he had painted in and around the area. One hot night he and his fellow artist, Vicky Shajehan, walked me around the street vendors and century-old cafes nearby in Malay Street, a centrepiece of the island's 40,000 strong Sri Lankan Malay community, as I braved eating deep-fried cow's lung and *barbath*, a delicious tripe curry. We drank hot spiced tea and talked about their home. Slave Island, they told me, is often caricatured by Colomboites as dangerous, but their work was telling a story of place, where people lived in close communion with each other, where, without gated communities or security dogs, you could be safe with modest means, where Vicky – who is trans – felt more protected than in any fancy part of town, where several old and distinct communities had made their home for a hundred years, where history was thick in the buildings, where a brave community of artists and activists were working hard to defend their home from developers and destruction.

My favourite thing I ate that night were those rolls. This recipe is my best attempt to recreate them. They are a fantastic little snack, and probably the No. 1 shorteat if you ask a Sri Lankan friend what treat they want when come home from work, or with a beer on a night out. Serve them with hot sauce, ketchup or Sriracha, and imagine you are at Hotel Nippon about to walk around into a beautiful maze of streets, to try things you have never eaten before, a side of Sri Lanka which may not be long for this world.

Makes 8

For the filling

2 tbsp coconut or vegetable oil

1 red onion, peeled and finely diced

10 fresh curry leaves

1 garlic clove, peeled and finely chopped

2cm fresh root ginger, peeled and finely chopped

300g lamb or mutton, trimmed of fat and diced into 2cm cubes (shoulder or leg is best)

1. To make the filling, heat the oil in a large saucepan over a medium heat. Fry the onion, stirring occasionally, until translucent. Add the curry leaves, garlic and ginger and cook for 1 minute or so, until the garlic is beginning to brown.

2. Add the lamb, cinnamon, sugar, salt and SL curry powder. Pour in enough cold water so the lamb is just covered. Cover with a lid slightly ajar, and let it come up to a simmer. Turn the heat down and simmer for 1½–2 hours. It is ready when the lamb is so soft you can cut through it with a spoon.

3. While the lamb is cooking, put the potatoes and a pinch of salt in a small pan of cold water. Bring to the boil and cook for 5–6 minutes until very tender. Drain and set aside.

Continued overleaf

DRINKING SNACKS & SHORTEATS

2cm piece of cinnamon stick

½ tsp sugar

1 tsp salt, plus a pinch

2 tbsp SL curry powder
(see page 21)

100g waxy potatoes (e.g.
charlotte or new potatoes),
peeled and diced into 1cm
cubes

100ml coconut milk

¼ whole nutmeg, grated

½ tsp meat powder
(see page 21)

For the coating

100g panko breadcrumbs

1 tsp ground turmeric

250g plain white flour

1 tsp salt

3 large organic or
free-range eggs

200ml milk

200ml water

100ml vegetable oil,
for shallow-frying

4. When the lamb is cooked, get a small, clean saucepan ready. Using oven gloves, place the saucepan with the lamb on a heatproof surface on a table. Tilting the pan a little, use a ladle to scoop out the curry liquid and transfer it to the small saucepan. Place the small saucepan over a medium-high heat and let it gently bubble away for 10 minutes to thicken the curry. Add the drained potatoes and coconut milk to the curry liquid, and stir in the grated nutmeg and meat powder. Return the thickened curry to the lamb, stir gently to combine. Remove the cinnamon stick. Cover, and set aside.

5. To make the coating, put the panko breadcrumbs in a little bowl and mix through ½ teaspoon of turmeric. Crush the breadcrumbs up a little with your hand so some of them get a bit smaller, but not all.

6. Put the flour, the remaining ½ teaspoon of ground turmeric and the salt in a large mixing bowl. Break the eggs into it and whisk them in, then gradually add the milk, little by little, until the mixture is smooth. Add the water about one-third at a time, and whisk in too.

7. Place a small frying pan, about 15cm wide, over a medium heat. Add a little vegetable oil by dipping a piece of folded kitchen roll into the oil and spreading it over the base of the pan. Heat for 1–2 minutes. Test to see if it's hot enough by adding a little batter to the pan; it should sizzle. Pour enough batter into the pan so that it's about 2mm thick and swirl it around, letting it cook for about 30 seconds. Don't flip the pancake. Transfer to a plate, cover with a lid or plate to keep warm, and repeat until you have about 8 pancakes. Keep the leftover batter in the bowl. Get a clean plate ready next to the pancakes.

8. To make the rolls, take one warm pancake and place 2 tablespoons of the lamb mixture in the middle. Fold and roll the pancake around the mixture like a tightly folded burrito. Press the edges of the roll down so it seals, using a bit of the leftover pancake batter to glue it down a bit if it doesn't stick. Repeat with all the rolls.

9. Now, use one hand to dip a roll into the bowl with the remaining batter in it. Place it in the bowl with breadcrumbs, and use the other hand to coat it really well in breadcrumbs, getting it into all the nooks and crannies. Use the breadcrumby hand to place it on the clean plate. Repeat with the rest of the rolls.

10. To fry, get a medium-sized saucepan or heavy-based frying pan over a medium heat and pour in the oil to a depth of about 1cm. Test to see if it's hot enough by dropping a little leftover batter into it; it should sizzle immediately. Place 2 mutton rolls in the pan, and cook them for about 2 minutes on each side, using tongs to hold and turn them, so they get evenly golden all over. Repeat with the rest of the rolls. Keep warm in a preheated oven at 150°C/Fan 130°C/Gas Mark 2. Serve with some hot sauce or Sriracha.

Tinned fish croquettes with dill sambol

This is a very quick, easy snack which Sri Lankans call 'cutlets'. This one is great to make if you are a bit scared of handling fish, because tinned fish are often boneless and cooked already so you don't need to worry about undercooking them.

Makes 10

For the filling

100g waxy potatoes, peeled and halved

1 tsp ground turmeric, plus a pinch

1 tsp salt, plus a pinch

2 tbsp coconut or vegetable oil

1 red onion, peeled and finely sliced

10 fresh curry leaves, sliced

200g tinned fish, e.g. mackerel, sardines or tuna, drained

4 or 5 green chillies, deseeded and finely sliced

1 garlic clove, peeled and minced

2cm fresh root ginger, peeled and minced

1 tsp sugar

1 tsp crushed black pepper

1 tsp cumin seeds

1 tsp mustard seeds

2 limes

For coating and frying

1 large organic or free-range egg

250g panko breadcrumbs

½ tsp ground turmeric

500ml vegetable oil

For the sambol

60g fresh dill

60g fresh coriander

1 tsp cumin seeds

1. Put the potatoes in a large pan of cold water along with a pinch of turmeric and a pinch of salt. Bring to the boil and cook for 6–7 minutes, or until the potatoes feel tender when you poke them with a fork. Drain well and allow to cool.

2. Heat the oil in a saucepan over a medium-high heat and fry the onion, stirring occasionally, until beginning to go golden. Add the sliced curry leaves, and after 30 seconds, stir in the 1 teaspoon each of turmeric and salt. After 2 minutes, add the rest of the filling ingredients except the limes, and stir well, cooking for 4–5 minutes so the fish takes on all the flavours. Remove from the heat, squeeze the limes into the mix and allow to cool.

3. Smash the cooled potatoes using your hand. You don't want them too fine. Stir the smashed potatoes into your fish mixture. Then, using wet hands, make 10 little balls with the fish and potato mixture, each about 2.5cm wide. Place on a plate in the fridge to cool and set for 30 minutes.

4. Meanwhile, make the sambol by blitzing the ingredients together in a mini food processor with a splash of water, until smooth. Spoon into a dipping dish.

5. When the croquettes have chilled, make a breading station. In one medium-sized bowl, beat the egg. Pour the panko breadcrumbs into a second medium-sized bowl, add the ground turmeric and stir through.

6. To fry the croquettes, take the chilled balls out of the fridge, dip one in the egg and then coat thoroughly in the breadcrumbs. Place it back on the plate and repeat with the rest of the balls. Pour the oil into a heavy-based saucepan to a depth of about 5cm. Place over a medium-high heat. The oil is hot enough when you add a pinch of the breadcrumbs to the oil and they sizzle. Use a slotted spoon to carefully lower 3 croquettes at a time into the hot oil. Cook for 1–2 minutes, until golden, then remove from the pan and drain on a plate lined with kitchen roll. Repeat with the rest of the croquettes and serve with the dipping sambol.

Minced beef patties

I once did a language course in Rio de Janeiro, and one day after class we clambered up to the fantastic tiny bar at the top of the Urca peninsula. During the days, I was amazed at how many Sri Lankan Tamil words – *almeira* for wardrobe, *janela* for window, even *pão* for bread – were loans from Lisbon; and then in the afternoons and nights, my new friends and I tried out our broken Portuguese in the city's old bars and cafes.

It was my round, and so I made my way to the front of a stressful, frenetic queuing experience to buy ice-cold *cervejas*, and er, okay yes, *pastéis*, as usual not really knowing what I'd ordered. A little pile of delicious fried patties arrived and I bit into one to be suddenly teleported straight into Sri Lanka. Here in my hands, so far away from our small island in the Arabian Sea, were the Amazonian incarnations of Sri Lankan patties: those small, hot, golden pasties, flaky and fried and crimped down the middle, filled with darkly spiced curried minced beef or smoky black pork or fennel-heavy tempered potato, and one of my favourite Sri Lankan shorteats.

There is a lovely Brazilian song, *Alvorada*, that I listened to a lot during those few weeks, about how glorious the light is in the hills of the *favelas*, about feeling lifeless and out of luck – but, isn't that breaking light beautiful, *que beleza*? When I listen to it, I think of that moment looking down into the shadow of Sugarloaf Mountain, into the ocean with its happy swimming bodies, thinking about Sri Lankans and Brazilians. What an unlikely brotherhood of bonds between countries so far away from each other, that endured the same colonial occupations. What undimmed ingenuity of cooks from the Rio's Lagoa Rodrigo de Freitas to our Jaffna peninsula lagoons, as they endured the hands of violence and theft and slavery. What sad and wonderful variations on the same Portuguese source material. Beef is my favourite kind of patty but you can equally do these with minced lamb. Frying the patties is traditional for crispier, crunchier dough, but baking is easier and lighter.

Makes 16

2 tbsp vegetable oil

1 red onion, peeled and finely chopped

10 fresh curry leaves

Optional: 4cm piece of pandan leaf

300g minced beef, at least 10% fat

2 tbsp SL curry powder (see page 21)

50ml coconut milk

1. Heat the oil in a deep-sided frying pan over a medium heat. Fry the onion, until starting to brown. Add the curry leaves and pandan leaf, if using, and cook, stirring occasionally until the onion is golden brown. Add the minced beef, SL curry powder and enough water to just cover the ingredients. Reduce the heat to a simmer, and with the lid ajar, cook for about 40 minutes.

2. Add the coconut milk and cook for 3–4 minutes. Switch off the heat and stir through the meat powder and a squeeze of lime. Leave aside with the lid on.

3. Meanwhile, make the dough by sifting the flour, bicarbonate of soda and salt into a bowl. Using your hands, mix in the butter, then gradually add the milk, about 2 tablespoons at a time. Continue to work the dough until it is soft and pliable; you may need to add a little water (up to 4 tablespoons). Shape the dough into a large ball and rub with a little extra butter.

Continued overleaf

For the dough

600g plain white flour, plus more for dusting

1 tsp bicarbonate of soda

1 tsp salt

3½ tbsp butter, softened, plus a little extra

250ml milk

4. Preheat the oven to 190°C/Fan 170°C/Gas Mark 5. On a lightly floured surface, roll out half the dough to a thickness of 3mm. Cut out 10cm circles with a pastry cutter or glass. You should make about eight. Spoon a heaped tablespoon of the filling into the centre of each circle and fold in half. Use your fingers to press the edges together, brushing the edge of the dough with a little water if necessary to help it stick. Re-roll the offcuts and repeat with the remaining dough and filling. You should end up with about 16.

5. Place them on a baking tray lined with baking parchment. Bake for 25–35 minutes until golden, rotating the tray halfway.

Hot butter cuttlefish

HBC is one of the island's best-loved drinking snacks. It is rarely made at home and is more a snack to eat at a bar or to kick off a meal, preferably facing the sea, where it will arrive alongside some drinks. The mix of rice flour and cornflour in the batter creates light, crispy rings of cuttlefish, which are then tossed in a buttery, garlicky sauce, hot with chilli flakes, Turkish peppers and fresh spring onions.

Serves 2–4

300g cuttlefish or squid
(cleaned weight – ask your
fishmonger to do this)

100ml milk

150g rice flour

150g cornflour or instant
polenta

500ml vegetable oil,
for deep-frying

For the hot butter sauce

120g butter

1½ tbsp chilli flakes

A bunch of spring onions
(5–7 stalks), finely sliced on
the diagonal

1 green Turkish pepper or a
yellow banana pepper, sliced
about 1cm thick

1 tsp salt, or to taste

4 garlic cloves, peeled
and minced

1. Remove the tentacles from the cuttlefish or squid and slice the bodies into 1.5cm rings. If you want to make the cuttlefish or squid into little flowers, make small slits, 2–3mm long, along one side of each ring using kitchen scissors or a sharp knife. Put all the rings and tentacles into a bowl and cover with the milk, then chill in the fridge for at least 30 minutes and up to 9 hours.

2. When you're ready cook, make the hot butter sauce. Melt the butter in a frying pan over a medium-low heat with the chilli flakes, spring onions, Turkish pepper, salt and garlic, giving it a swirl. Once the foam has died down, watch it very carefully and keep swirling gently; as soon as the butter at the bottom goes brown and it smells nutty, tip it all into a bowl to cool.

3. Mix the flours together in a mixing bowl. Pour the oil into a large, heavy-based pan to a depth of 3–4cm. Set it over a medium-high heat. It is hot enough when a tiny pinch of flour sizzles when it hits the oil.

4. Drain the cuttlefish or squid well. Take 3 or 4 pieces in a handful and fully coat them in the flour mixture. Shake off any excess flour. Use a slotted spoon to lower them into the hot oil. Fry for about a minute, until crispy and light golden, then transfer to a plate or bowl lined with kitchen roll to drain. Repeat with the rest of the cuttlefish or squid.

5. Before serving, put the cuttlefish or squid in the pan with the hot butter sauce on a low-medium heat, just to warm it through, and coat well.

Black pepper beef

This recipe was given to me by my dear friend Joe Lenora's mum, Auntie Patricia. Patricia and Joe hail from the seaside city of Negombo. Negombo is a good-time town on Sri Lanka's west coast, with a big chunk of coastline, a port, a lake, a sixteenth-century maze of canals and, consequently, a whole lot of boats, many of them filled with happy young people dancing to Sri Lankan reggae and swimming in the water.

Negombo also has many beautiful white stuccoed churches and a high density of Sri Lanka's small but mighty Christian community. Sri Lankan Christians have, in my experience, evaded several common Sri Lankan phenomena. They have tended to evade religious extremism. They tend to have the only short names on the island (an advantage they largely squander by instead having five or six Christian names). And most joyously of all, they seem to have largely evaded Buddhist and Hindu guilt when it comes to alcohol.

And so invariably – like at Auntie Attidiya Panagoda Liyanage Dona Josephine Mary Patricia's family home in Negombo – you will find rosary beads in the homes of those who produce the island's best drinking snacks. Auntie P. says that people have eaten drinking 'bites' with alcohol at parties ever since she can remember, and she was born in the 1930s. In Sri Lankan English, a bite is a big snack, an appetiser, something that should cajole you into a bigger evening than you had planned, to turn your one drink into seven, your quick appetiser into an unnecessary and spontaneous dinner. The key to these is to buy great-quality beef and use a really hot pan so it is cooked perfectly, still pink inside.

To paraphrase Ecclesiastes, go eat your black pepper beef with gladness, and drink your beer with a joyful heart.

Serves 4

300g beef fillet

1½ tsp salt

1½ tbsp freshly ground black pepper

3 tbsp coconut or vegetable oil

1 red onion, peeled and finely sliced

10 fresh curry leaves

2 green chillies, sliced

2 lemongrass stalks

2cm fresh root ginger, peeled and crushed

2 tbsp apple cider vinegar

1. Slice the beef into thin strips and marinate in the salt and black pepper for 30 minutes.

2. When ready to cook, set a heavy-based frying pan over a high heat and add the oil. When hot, stir-fry the beef for 30 seconds. Add the onion, curry leaves, chillies, lemongrass, ginger and any juice from the marinade. Stir-fry for 1–2½ minutes, slicing through a sample piece of beef to check how you like the pinkness of the meat. Add the vinegar, then remove from the heat and allow to rest for 3–4 minutes before serving.

DRINKS & SWEETS

Milk toffee

In our neighbourhood in Jaffna, if you say, 'no sugar please!' to a person making you coffee, they'll look confused, ask if you're ill and put in a few anyway. We are an island of sugar junkies, and though it embarrasses me to admit it, my addiction is so bad that I need some kind of hit every day after both lunch and dinner, and am always excited by something sweet.

Few things are more exciting to me than Sri Lankan milk toffee, a spiced condensed milk cashew nut fudge made with ground cardamom. Milk toffee tends to spark pure childlike joy for Sri Lankans, whatever their age. It is, however, ludicrously sugary, so I recommend you keep yours in a tin, to be enjoyed in small doses, washed down with coffee (sugar optional).

Makes about 12 pieces

80g raw cashew nuts

60g unsalted butter, plus more for greasing

400g tin of condensed milk

120g caster sugar

2 tsp sea salt

1 tsp ground cardamom

1. Put a medium-sized heavy-based saucepan over a medium heat. Add the cashews and cook for 3–5 minutes, until golden, stirring every so often to stop them burning. Transfer to a bowl to cool. Grease a 20cm-square baking tin with butter.

2. Pour the condensed milk into a cold saucepan. Half-fill the empty tin with water, swill it out and pour it into the saucepan as well. Add the sugar. Set over a medium heat and keep stirring the mixture vigorously for about 5 minutes until the sugar dissolves. Add the salt, ground cardamom and butter. Keep stirring the mixture for about 15 minutes; it will begin to bubble and boil and darken in colour.

3. When the mixture is the colour of a dark, strong tea, remove from the heat, stir in the toasted cashews and, using a palette knife or a spatula, quickly spread the milk toffee into the greased baking tin. Let it cool for about 10 minutes before scoring into 4cm triangles or diamonds. Let it cool completely, then break into pieces. If you stash it in a sealed container in a cool place, it should keep for up to 2 weeks.

Love cake

Love cake is a dense teatime treat, the consistency and golden colour of a blondie, made with cashew nuts, semolina and rosewater. Crunchy on the outside and moist on the inside, the origins of love cake are unclear and often attributed to the Portuguese. I suspect the cake has Arabic rather than European roots, given its similarity to Egyptian *babousa* and similar sweets eaten all over the Middle East, where instead of cashews they use ground almonds. Traditionally, the recipe requires a lovely pumpkin preserve, a candied winter squash called *puhul dosi*, but I find with a little extra fragrant spice – cinnamon, cardamom and nutmeg – the cake stands up beautifully without it. Whatever the origins, I hope you like it as much as we do in our family. Wrap some up for your friends for a little teatime love.

Serves 9–12

250g butter, plus more for greasing

500g caster sugar

6 large organic or free-range eggs, 5 separated into yolks and whites

1 tsp ground cinnamon

1 tsp ground cardamom

4 cloves, crushed in a pestle and mortar

1 tsp grated nutmeg

2 tbsp rosewater

2 tbsp honey

300g raw cashew nuts, very finely chopped

250g semolina, lightly toasted in a dry frying pan and cooled

Optional: 1–2 tbsp icing sugar, to serve

1. Preheat the oven to 170°C/Fan 150°C/Gas Mark 3½. Line the base and sides of a 20cm round or square cake tin with baking parchment. Grease the paper with butter.

2. Beat the butter and sugar together until pale and creamy. Add the whole egg and egg yolks one at a time, beating well before adding the next one. Add the cinnamon, cardamom, crushed cloves, nutmeg, rosewater, honey, chopped cashews and semolina to the bowl. Mix together thoroughly.

3. In a separate clean mixing bowl, whisk the egg whites until soft peaks form. Scoop a quarter of the egg white mixture into the batter and stir it once. Then fold in all the rest of the egg whites. Be careful not to overmix it at this stage.

4. Pour the cake mixture into the prepared tin and bake for 1 hour, until the cake is golden brown on top. Let it cool in the tin for about 15–20 minutes before slicing and serving dusted with a little icing sugar, if you like.

Banana and Milo icebox cake

In Point Pedro market, there is a booth with a banana seller who looks reassuringly like he's eaten a lot of bananas. He stocks almost all of the twenty-seven different varieties on the island, still on their gigantic banana tree branches that he lifts like a sumo wrestler to apportion your bunch. Sri Lankan bananas are mostly petite, around 10cm long, and come in yellow, red and green. There's *kathali*, a small, sweet, cheap, boy-next-door of a banana, fragrant like jasmine and honey. This one has many sub-varieties: honey *kathali*, rose *kathali*, *kathalis* in different pretty girls' names in various delightful flavours. There is *kappal*, which means boat banana, one of the fancier island bananas, cute and fat and rotund with a dense, ice cream-like texture, less fragrant but still a posh noseful of vanilla and brown sugar. Luxe-est of all is the red banana, that Gucci of Sri Lankan bananas. Rare and expensive and totally out of this world in flavour, red bananas have a meaty, creamy texture, smell almost like the Indian sweet *jalebi*, and taste delicate, something like a little floral maple syrup.

If you're not in Sri Lanka – I'm sorry! To sex up your mediocre bananas, please furnish with Milo and biscuits à la the recipe below. This easy pudding is a fridge cake, or as my Canadian cousins would call it, an icebox cake. Milo is huge in Sri Lanka, and the malted note in it gives it an incredible umami flavour.

Serves 10

150g Milo malt chocolate drinking powder

A generous pinch of salt

240g double cream

3–4 tbsp water from a recently boiled kettle

200ml whole milk

200g ladyfinger savoiardi biscuits

4 bananas, 3 peeled and sliced about 0.75cm thick, 1 left unpeeled

1. Line a 900g loaf tin (approx. 21 x 12cm) or a medium-sized bowl with clingfilm, leaving at least 10cm hanging over the ends.

2. Pour 100g Milo powder and the salt into a bowl and pour in a little of the cream. Whisk for about 30 seconds. Keep going, adding the cream a little at a time, until all the cream is added. Keep whisking until stiff peaks form. Keep to one side.

3. In a small clean bowl, add the remaining 50g Milo powder and just enough hot water to cover the powder. Stir thoroughly, pour in the milk, and stir together.

4. To assemble your icebox cake, dip each ladyfinger in the Milo milk for 1–2 seconds (don't leave them too long, or they'll get soggy!) and arrange a single layer of dipped ladyfingers in the bottom of the loaf tin or bowl. Spread one-third of the Milo cream over the top, then a layer of sliced banana. Spread with Milo cream, then another layer of dipped ladyfingers and sliced bananas. Finish off with another layer of ladyfingers. Keep the rest of the Milo cream aside in the fridge. Wrap the clingfilm ends over the whole pudding, and chill in the fridge for at least 6 hours.

5. To unmold the pudding, peel away the clingfilm from the top. Place a serving plate on the top of the loaf tin or bowl, and flip the whole thing over. Ease off the tin or bowl and peel away the clingfilm.

6. Rewhip the remaining Milo cream and spread on top of the cake. Slice the final banana into round slices or lengthways, and arrange on top before serving.

DRINKS & SWEETS

Jaggery mess with coconut and cardamom

I made these vegan meringues for a dinner I was invited to cook at the venerable Quo Vadis restaurant in London. It's a Sri Lankan play on Quo's signature mountains of meringue, cream, fruit and fun. You can make all the ingredients ahead of time, plating just before you serve. I haven't managed to get aquafaba meringues to hold their structure as well as regular ones, so don't bother piping them; you can just dollop the mix into the oven with spoons. When they're done, crack them open and dish up by adding coconut cream, passionfruit, jaggery syrup, cardamom and toasted coconut chips. It makes for a delightful, crunchy pile of sweetness at the end of your meal.

Serves 6

400g tin of chickpeas

½ tsp cream of tartar

200g caster sugar

1 tbsp cornflour

400ml tin of coconut milk, chilled overnight in the fridge in its tin

To assemble

4 whole passionfruit

250ml jaggery kithul syrup (or maple syrup)

100g toasted coconut flakes

1 tsp ground cardamom

1. Drain the chickpeas, reserving the liquid. Place the chickpeas in an airtight container and refrigerate for another use. Chill the liquid for 2 hours or until cold.

2. Preheat the oven to 170°C/Fan 150°C/Gas Mark 3½ and line two baking trays with baking parchment.

3. When the chickpea liquid is cold, transfer to a clean large bowl, or the bowl of an electric stand mixer fitted with the whisk attachment. Add the cream of tartar and whisk for 8 minutes or until the mixture reaches soft peaks.

4. Add the sugar gradually, about a tablespoon or two at a time, whisking continuously for 15 minutes, until it's all thick and glossy and the sugar has dissolved. Whisk in the cornflour.

5. Using 2 heaped tablespoons of the mixture per meringue, shape into 10cm rounds on the lined baking trays to make 8–10 meringues spaced around 3cm apart.

6. Place the trays of meringues in the oven and immediately reduce the temperature to 120°C/Fan 100°C/Gas Mark ½. Bake for 2 hours, or until the meringues seem dry and firm (don't open the oven for the first hour!). Turn off the oven and leave the meringues to cool in the oven, with the door closed, for at least 30 minutes.

7. Meanwhile, make the coconut cream. Open your chilled tin of coconut milk and scoop out the solids in the top into a clean medium-sized bowl, discarding the liquid underneath. Whisk to as stiff peaks as you can.

8. To assemble, crack each meringue onto a plate with your hands. If you have any extra, crunch them on top. Spoon a little coconut cream on the meringues. Halve the passionfruit, scoop out the seeds and spoon over the cream. Drizzle kithul jaggery syrup over and scatter with coconut flakes and a pinch or two of ground cardamom.

Ravana cake

I love chocolate devil's food cake and for a Sri Lankan chocolate cake, I didn't just want a devil like any other. I wanted the King.

Ruler of Ancient Lanka, the demon-king Ravana wasn't just a garden variety devil with a red trident and fire, hopping from foot to foot like he needed the toilet. Ravana was the kind of hot demon your husband is stressing out about you meeting for lunch. He did have ten heads which is a little freaky I'll concede – but he was also a magnificent musician, a warrior, a scholar and – by the rhapsodical account of ancient Tamil poet Kamban – a very good-looking guy with a lot of cool statement jewellery. Ravana wrote: 'Eating beef causes to infect ninety-eight new diseases to human beings' and if this bit of 2000 BCE veganism wasn't ahead of its time, I don't know what was. King Ravana was a lover and a fighter, most famous for kidnapping the beautiful married Princess Sita (under the pretext of asking her for lunch) and keeping her in Sri Lanka trying to persuade her to cheat on her husband. And so this recipe is an imagining of a devil's food cake with Ravana's kind of irresistible sexiness, the kind designed to tempt the most loyal of wives. Strawberries for passion, chocolate for hotness, coffee for the late-night musician and coconut for an island boy environmentalist with a love of plants. I mean Sita, WHEW* am I right??

Sita never overlooked the consent issue of being kidnapped and didn't ever break her marriage vows.

Serves 10–12

For the cake

125g coconut oil, plus more
  for greasing

250g plain white flour

225g caster sugar

50g cocoa powder

1 tsp salt, or to taste

1 tsp baking powder

1 tsp bicarbonate of soda

350ml freshly brewed
  strong coffee

2 tsp kithul jaggery syrup
  (or maple syrup)

2 large organic or free-range
  eggs, lightly beaten

1. Preheat the oven to 180°C/Fan 160°C/Gas Mark 4. Grease two 20cm sandwich tins with coconut oil, and line the bases with baking parchment.

2. Put the flour, sugar, cocoa powder, salt, baking powder and bicarbonate of soda into a large bowl, and whisk to combine and add air to the dry ingredients. Make a well in the middle.

3. Brew the coffee and pour it into a large jug. Allow to cool for a minute or two, then stir in the 125g coconut oil and let it melt. Then mix in the kithul jaggery syrup. Slowly pour the coconut coffee into the well you made in the flour mixture and whisk together until everything is combined.

4. Add the lightly beaten eggs a little at a time, whisking until it's all used up and you have a thin batter.

5. Divide the batter between the two cake tins. Although this feels weird, drop each tin a couple of times onto your kitchen counter or floor from a height of about 30cm. It forces the air in the mixture to come to the surface.

6. Bake for 25–30 minutes, until a skewer inserted into the middle comes out clean. Remove from the oven and place on a cooling rack still in their tins.

Continued overleaf

For the icing and filling

250g coconut butter or coconut 'bliss'

500g icing sugar

250g fresh strawberries, green tops removed, halved

150g coconut flakes

7. While the cakes are cooking, make the icing. Beat the coconut butter until softened and then whisk in half the icing sugar. When smooth, add the rest of the icing sugar and whisk again, until all the sugar is combined and it's nice and thick and smooth. Add a little more icing sugar if it's too loose or a little more coconut butter if it's too thick for your liking.

8. When the cakes have cooled completely, carefully turn them out of their tins and peel off the paper.

9. To assemble, spread just less than a quarter of the coconut icing on top of one of the cakes. Cover in fresh strawberry halves. Place the other cake on top and spread with a layer of icing, then cover the sides as well. Coat with coconut flakes.

Watalappan tart

This is an homage to the Sri Lankan pudding *watalappan*, which is pronounced exactly like asking 'what'll 'appen?' if you drop your aitches. *Watalappan* is a lovely steamed custard, hailing from the Sri Lankan Muslim community, probably with origins in Indonesia. A spiced wobbly caramel pudding, it is made with cardamom, coconut milk, jaggery and cashews. I find the bain-marie method of making it a little tricky, easily resulting in a kind of curdled, eggy mess. So, instead of the traditional version, this is a *watalappan* tart, a kind of marriage between a perfect Portuguese custard tart and the Sri Lankan classic. It combines the easy, reliably silky texture of a pastel de nata with most of the flavours of the original.

For a Sri Lankan pudding to get together with a European pastry feels a little odd because for centuries, Sri Lanka and Europe were in an abusive relationship. By the time of its independence in 1948, Sri Lanka had been invaded and overrun by Europeans for over 450 years, a process which got started by Portuguese colonisers in 1505. I wasn't taught this in school, but the kings of Sri Lanka had not given in without a fight. The island's separate kingdoms: Colombo, Kandy, Jaffna and Vanni, had fought bravely and cleverly. Some had engaged in ingenious guerrilla tactics, like King Vimaladharmasuriya II, a King of Kandy, and the last ever Tamil king in Sri Lanka, King Pandara Vanniyan.

The north of the island had been ravaged by Portuguese rule, who destroyed almost all the ancient Hindu temples in Jaffna, the massive Saraswathy Mahal library in Nallur full of precious scripts, and taxed the population so heavily that the people of Jaffna were reduced to utmost misery. The Dutch and British had begun their own occupations. King Pandara Vanniyan, whose kingdom spanned Anuradhapura and Puttalam, fought back so hard and so strategically that he seized British forts and cannons. But eventually the great hero was fallen, his bravery remembered by the people, immortalised in folk song.

I think of this tart as – at last – a chance for Sri Lankans to take something from the Europeans. What will happen? A small slice of healing and redemption, I hope. To the lost warrior kings of Sri Lanka, to most of all, King Pandara Vanniyan: this one's for you.

Serves 10–12

For the tart case

175g plain white flour, plus more for dusting

70g caster sugar

90g unsalted butter, roughly chopped and slightly softened, plus a little extra for greasing

1 large organic or free-range egg yolk

1. To make the pastry, sift the flour and sugar together into a large bowl. Using your fingertips, rub in the butter until it forms a breadcrumb texture. Add the egg yolk and keep mixing with your hands until it comes together into a smooth dough. Add a little cold water if it's too dry. Shape it into a ball then cover with a damp clean tea towel and leave to rest in the fridge for at least 1 hour or up to overnight.

2. While you're waiting for the pastry to chill, grease a 25cm-diameter, 5cm-deep tart tin.

Continued overleaf

For the filling

7 large organic or free-range egg yolks

40g caster sugar

100ml double cream

400ml coconut milk

40g grated jaggery or kithul syrup (or if you can't get any use dark muscovado sugar)

1 tsp ground cardamom

2 tsp icing sugar

3. Preheat the oven to 200°C/Fan 180°C/Gas Mark 6. On a lightly floured surface, roll out the pastry so it's quite thin, about 0.5cm. Slide your rolling pin under the pastry and then lift it up and use it to help you place the pastry over the tart tin. Press the pastry down lightly to line the tin, then roll your rolling pin over the top of the tin to remove any excess pastry that is hanging over the side. Chill the shell in the fridge for about 15 minutes.

4. Tear off a sheet of baking parchment roughly 30cm long and scrunch it up into a ball. Open it out again, and place it in the pastry case, along with some baking beans, uncooked dried beans or uncooked rice to weight it down. Blind bake the pastry for about 30 minutes, until it is golden and crisp. Remove from the oven and allow it to cool in its tin, taking out the paper and beans. Reduce the oven temperature to 160°C/Fan 140°C/Gas Mark 3.

5. While the pastry cools down, make the filling. In a large bowl, beat the egg yolks and caster sugar together until fluffy and smooth.

6. Pour the cream and coconut milk into a medium-sized saucepan, and add the jaggery and cardamom. Place over a medium heat and stir slowly until the jaggery has dissolved. When there are no more lumps of jaggery, stop stirring and when little bubbles appear at the edge, take the pan off the heat.

7. Get yourself ready to whisk with one hand, and pour from the hot pan with the other. Whisking all the time, slowly pour the hot cream in a thin, slow stream onto the eggs.

8. Carefully pour the custard filling into the pastry case. Cook in the oven for 1 hour 25 minutes, or until the custard has set all the way through. The filling should be slightly firm but still with a little wobble. Remove from the oven and allow to cool completely at room temperature.

9. Just before serving, sift icing sugar lightly over the top and place under a hot grill for 5–10 minutes to give it a little crunch as you bite into it.

Mango fluff pie

For British-Sri Lankan parties in the Nineties, the aunties would get together and help each other out by making an array of desserts. Fluffs were big in those days, a kind of cult British-Sri Lankan dessert, an absolute must-have on the pudding table. In homage to our aunties, this dessert is an easy mango and lime curd pie with a throwback mango fluff topping. The fluff refers to a marshmallow icing, which is easy to make and makes for a puffy, blouse-y dessert that looks glamorous on the table.

Serves 10

For the base

120g unsalted butter

250g digestive biscuits

50g caster sugar

¼ tsp ground cardamom

A pinch of salt

For the filling

2 large organic
or free-range egg

3 large organic or free-range
egg yolks (keep the whites
for the fluff topping)

6 tbsp caster sugar

300g tinned mango pulp

1½ tbsp cornflour

Juice of 4 limes

85g cold butter, chopped into
4 pieces

For the fluff topping

3 large organic or free-range
egg whites

180g caster sugar

¼ tsp cream of tartar

40g golden syrup

¼ tsp salt

50g tinned mango pulp

1. Preheat the oven to 190°C/Fan 170°C/Gas Mark 5. Line a loaf tin, about 20 x 12cm, with baking parchment.

2. To make the base, melt the butter in the microwave or in a small saucepan over a low heat. Blitz the digestive biscuits, until fine. Mix the biscuit crumbs, melted butter, sugar, cardamom and salt together in a bowl. Use your fingers to press it down evenly into the base of the loaf tin. Bake in the oven for 10 minutes until firm. Remove from the oven, but keep the oven on.

3. To make the filling, in a heavy-based saucepan, beat the whole eggs, egg yolks and sugar until they're just combined. Stir in the mango pulp, cornflour and lime juice, then the butter. Place it over a medium-low heat and stir constantly until it has thickened enough to coat the back of the spoon. Remove the pan from the heat and allow it to stand for 5 minutes, then give it a quick whisk until smooth.

4. Spread the curd onto the biscuit base. Bake for 10–15 minutes or until the filling is just set. Remove from the oven and leave to cool. When it has cooled to room temperature, chill in the fridge.

5. When you are almost ready to serve, make the fluff topping. Pour some water into a medium-sized saucepan until it comes a quarter of the way up the sides. Bring to a very gently simmer over a low heat. Put the egg whites, sugar, cream of tartar, golden syrup and salt in a clean heatproof bowl. Place the bowl over the pan of gently simmering water, making sure the bottom of the bowl doesn't touch the hot water. Whisk constantly for at least 8–10 minutes, until thick and opaque. Once the sugar has dissolved (you can test this by rubbing a bit of the egg white mixture between two fingers; you should not feel any graininess) whisk it on high (ideally using an electric whisk) until the egg whites hold stiff peaks; this usually takes about 5 minutes. Very gently fold in the mango pulp, and whisk hard for about 30 seconds. If it goes a little too soft, it should seize up again if you leave it for a few minutes.

6. Spread the fluff over the pie to make it as fluffy and high as you can. Eat as soon as you can.

Rambutan and rose frozen falooda

When I first slurped on a falooda, I was nine and I was in Faluda House on Colombo's Galle Road. It must have been a crazy genius who had invented it, I thought in wonder. A falooda is a well-loved pink unicorn of a dessert, a big fat Sri Lankan ice cream-milkshake-sundae. It is made with rose syrup, sugar, soaked rice noodles and a variety of other mad and glorious jellies and customisations. The whole lot is topped up with gloopy, crunchy *falooda* or basil seeds, which are meant to cool you down if you are floundering in the heat – and give you the curious sensation that your sweet rose milk float has been peppered with some sort of delicious tiny eyeballs.

Faludhaj, the Persian precursor to falooda, is said to be the world's most ancient sundae, and the first ever frozen dessert. Born around 400 BCE, and still eaten all over the Middle East, it was brought to India sometime in the Mughal era and reincarnated as falooda. It then arrived in Sri Lanka pretty late, first put on a menu in the 1940s by an Indian entrepreneur called Mr Dawoodbhoy, at his Royal Sweet Mart in Keyzer Street (which, by the way, is still there). The Dawoodbhoy family is one of the oldest Bohra families in Sri Lanka, a community of Shia Muslim traders, entrepreneurs and merchants from Gujarat, who began to arrive in Sri Lanka in the 1830s. They built many of Colombo's long-running businesses and beloved shops, particularly in downtown Pettah.

Falooda took a long, meandering route to Sri Lanka and I seem to have taken a long, meandering route to tell you that this recipe is my frozen tribute to the Colombo classic. You start with a very easy no-churn condensed milk ice cream made with crème fraîche. And then a granita, not too sweet, which is basically little crystals of raspberries, rose and my favourite: tinned rambutans. The whole shebang is topped with soaked seeds – if you can't find basil seeds, chia will do, but don't skip them, otherwise you won't get that eyeball-y crunchy feeling to really get you to falooda nirvana.

Ingredients & method overleaf

Serves 8–10

For the ice cream

300ml double cream

500ml crème fraîche

375ml condensed milk

For the sherbet granita

100ml water

90g granulated or caster sugar

Optional: 375g tinned rambutans

500g fresh raspberries

Juice of ½ lemon

½ teaspoon rosewater

To serve

Optional: 2 teaspoons dried rose
petals

Optional: 2 tablespoons basil
seeds (or chia seeds), soaked
in water

1. To make the ice cream, pour the double cream into a large bowl and whisk until it forms stiff peaks. Spoon in the crème fraîche and condensed milk, and fold together until combined and smooth. Transfer the mixture to a freezer-proof container with a lid and freeze for 8 hours, or overnight.

2. Pour the water into a small saucepan and add the sugar. Set over a high heat and bring to the boil, stirring continuously, until the sugar has dissolved. Simmer for about a minute to thicken it a little. Remove from the heat and set aside to cool, which will take about 25 minutes.

3. Drain the rambutans, if using, over a bowl and keep the liquid. Blitz the raspberries in a food processor with the lemon juice, then strain through a sieve to remove the seeds. Add the raspberry pulp and rosewater to the cooled sugar syrup, along with 2 tablespoons of the rambutan canning liquid, if using, and stir together.

4. Transfer to a shallow freezer-proof container with a lid and freeze for 2–3 hours, until clumps form and the edges are solid. Drag a fork through the ice clumps to separate the crystals and freeze for another 30 minutes. Repeat the action with the fork, then freeze for another 30 minutes. Repeat once more with the fork and freeze for a final 30 minutes.

5. Remove the granita from the freezer and place in the fridge for 10 minutes before serving to loosen it up a bit. Place a scoop of ice cream at the bottom of 8–10 small glasses. Top with granita, rose petals and basil (or chia) seeds, and whole rambutans, if using.

Arrack egg muttai coffee

I never knew Mum's dad, Ammappa, because he died before I was born. But it sounded like we would have got along great. He ran his own business and, by all accounts, told a lot of bad jokes and liked his food and drink too much. On Fridays, most Hindus are vegetarian, which means strictly no meat, fish or eggs, and so a stressed-out Ammappa would wake his young children at the break of dawn. Mum and her sisters and brother would rise, bleary-eyed at 5 a.m., to be faced with a delicious egg coffee. Ammappa felt any rule violations before the sun came up didn't really count.

Muttai kopi is made by whisking fresh eggs into hot coffee, which makes a delicious thick consistency. It is sweetened with sugar, and sometimes a little cardamom and ginger is added for deliciousness. When we were small, Mum always made it when we are ill, although I'm not totally sure raw eggs are great for sick kids, nor sleeping ones for that matter. This version is an adults-only egg coffee. It is fantastically rich and tasty, and is wonderful with a dash of arrack, apparently my grandfather's afternoon tipple of choice.

Makes 2 cups

¼ tsp ground cardamom

3 tsp caster sugar

1cm fresh root ginger, peeled and crushed

120ml freshly made strong coffee (about 4 shots of espresso)

2 large organic or free-range eggs

200ml boiling water

Optional: 2 shots of arrack or brandy

1. Add the cardamom, sugar and ginger to the black coffee and allow to sit for about 5 minutes.

2. Meanwhile, whisk the eggs in a bowl until super-fluffy.

3. Top up the coffee with the boiling water. Then, beating the egg with one hand, pour the hot coffee into it, little by little, until it has a fluffy, rich texture. Add the arrack or brandy if using, and pour into two cups.

Condensed milk spiced tea

In ancient Sri Lanka, the central hills were called Mayarata, which means the land of illusions. The area teemed with Sinhalese kings, forests and spooky tales until one day in the 1860s it came to an abrupt end. The British decided to clear the trees, pack up the ghouls and grow coffee; and when that failed, tea. It worked like gangbusters.

Sri Lanka's emerald plantations now produce some of the best tea the world, and bring in £1bn in exports a year, almost none of which goes to the people who pick it. Back in the nineteenth century, the British needed workers for their plantations, and so they brought in indentured labourers from South India. The system of being indentured labour was a sort of a slavery catfishing exercise. It looked like you were being offered a nice job somewhere sunny, but then when you got there it turned out the job was unpaid and you had to work in horrible conditions until you died. As many as one million Malayaha or estate Tamils were living in the island by the time the British left. Today, around one million of their descendants live in Sri Lanka, and many still work the plantations. They aren't technically indentured anymore, but unless they work in a Fairtrade or organic plantation, they generally get paid £1–2 a day and suffer horrible working conditions.

Tea in Sri Lanka, like its politics, is sold in varying degrees of broken-ness. The system for grading teas depends on the quality of the tea leaves. Amongst the biggest leaves and fanciest tea are TGFOP, which stands for 'Tippy Golden Flowery Orange Pekoe', or as the old colonial joke goes, 'Too Good For Ordinary People'. The grades get less 'tippy' – which means fewer delicate silver or golden tips – and flowery as they go down in quality; then there are all the Broken Orange Pekoe grades, where the leaves are broken, but still exquisite. Finally, at the bottom of the whole lot, are the most broken still. These are the tea dust grades: strong, tannic and cheap.

This recipe is for Sri Lanka's tea plantation workers, who cannot afford to drink superior grades of the stuff they have been plucking with such skill for centuries. This is the tea that they and most working Sri Lankans drink, made from tea dust, which is also probably the cheap filling for your teabags. In Sri Lankan shops or kades, tea is often drunk 'plain' which is to say, black, with some calming ginger or sometimes a little liquorice. My personal favourite is the way my neighbours make it, with condensed milk (although whole milk is a good substitute), with cardamom, cinnamon and ginger. You must add sugar; we will all be very confused and offended if you don't. Please buy your Ceylon tea from a Fairtrade or organic source.

Makes 4 cups

1 litre water

3 cardamom pods, lightly bashed in a pestle and mortar

4cm piece of cinnamon stick

4cm fresh root ginger, peeled

4 strong black teabags

4 tsp condensed milk

1. Pour the water into a saucepan set over a medium heat. Add the cardamom, cinnamon and ginger, and bring to a boil.

2. Add the teabags and turn the heat to a low simmer for 3 minutes. Stir in the condensed milk, then bring it back up to a boil and simmer for 2–3 minutes until it's bubbling. Strain into mugs, pouring from a 10cm height if you want that frothy effect.

Lemongrass and lime soda

When I left home, my parents left the UK in the winter to go back to Sri Lanka, staying for longer and longer periods each year. They now live in the lovely village where they were born, and where so many of their childhood friends and family are still neighbours. I try to visit often, to sort of detox from life in London and drink organic goat's milk from the herd and eat juicy black mangoes from the tree.

But, despite Jaffna's warm and witty welcomes, cute little kids and other-worldly food, after a week or so I inevitably start to count down the days until I return to The Big City. Rural Sri Lanka sounds idyllic in theory, but in real life I get rudely woken up by screaming cockerels, psychotic dogfights and unfeasibly chirpy neighbours shouting 'AH, HELLO' into their mobile phones outside my bedroom at 5 a.m.

About ten years ago, I decided I needed to try and make my own friends in Sri Lanka if I wanted to have an adult relationship with the place, and so I embarked on a series of friendships. 'Oh great, another diaspora Sri Lankan trying to get in touch with her roots,' deadpanned Janeen when I was introduced to him, who welcomed me in anyway alongside Daniel, Amita, Harshi, Arun, Widya, Nim and Chanch among others. And with their help I have lightened up a little and learned to enjoy some of Colombo's metropolitan charms. An ice-cold lemongrass and lime soda at the magnificent Barefoot Gallery and Cafe is chief amongst them, and this recipe is an homage to my favourite drink in my favourite cafe in all of the world. If you get there, you must also try their beef rolls, peruse the bookshop, enjoy the art, and settle in for Sunday afternoon jazz.

Serves 2

150ml water

300g granulated sugar

5 lemongrass stalks

Zest and juice of 6 limes

Ice

300ml soda water

1. Pour the water into a deep saucepan and add the sugar. Bring to a boil, stirring until all the sugar is dissolved. Then add 3 stalks of lemongrass and the zest of all the limes. Remove from the heat, and allow the syrup to cool down in the pan completely. When cool, leave to infuse in the fridge overnight, in a bottle or covered jug.

2. When ready to drink, fill your glasses with ice and add a lemongrass stalk each as a garnish. Strain 3 tablespoons of lemongrass and lime syrup into each glass, and then add the juice of 3 limes to each glass, using a sieve or strainer to catch the pips. Top with soda water and stir to combine.

Cool Drinks

There's a sort of familiar script when you make a house visit in Sri Lanka, at least when guided by the fading maps of memory that reside in your parents' heads. First, you ring the bell and something unpredictable happens – maybe a really overheated-looking Alsatian comes out of nowhere, goes berserk and tries to kill you. Maybe some lovely giggly young girls open the gate, say 'Oh hello, Uncle,' warmly to your father and hug everybody, and then after twenty minutes your parents realise it's the wrong family and you've never met these people. Maybe you circle around an address that doesn't make sense because the street name was changed from Worcester Avenue to Shri Bogdunmagenumu because fuck the Empire, but no one you ask for directions calls it either name. Perhaps the house number you're looking for is '22 upon 6' and you think existentially, what *is* 22 upon 6? Until a neighbour helpfully shouts over to you that the house has been bombed or turned into luxury flats or your family members emigrated to Japan or got a new luxe pad in Borella or popped out to the temple or died or have been 'disappeared'.

And then at some point eventually, the person you came to see appears. And your dad says a warm 'HEL-LO!' and they grin back broadly, and your mum lies 'we were just in the neighbourhood passing. . .' although, in fact, you planned your whole day around this very moment.

Whereupon the person starts to look stressed and runs around his house to switch off the blaring TV, switch on the fan, put on the lights, put on a shirt, open windows, wash his face, wake his wife up rudely from her afternoon nap, splash on some eau-de-cologne, fix up, look sharp. You, meanwhile, stand around awkwardly, the hot Alsatian has not forgotten you, looks beady eyed if you think about moving, growls.

Eventually you have survived the dogs, taken off your shoes, you are sitting down, you've definitely forgotten who everyone is, you reply, 'Oh for my A Levels it was actually history and physics' to no one listening, and people start offering you delicious things to eat. Some love cake (page 288) or hot *vadai* fritters (page 262), crispy vegetable rolls stuffed with spiced potato, perhaps 'Hawaiian' or lemon puff biscuits, all thoughtfully arranged on little trays. And you start eating them hungrily like an amateur, noticing your parents are refusing to eat anything for at least a polite thirty minutes after you were all invited inside.

And every single time all of this happens, you will be offered 'Cool Drinks' on a tray. In my experience, it is a firm rule of Sri Lankan hospitality that no one ever says, 'Would you like a drink?' without first specifying the temperature. Someone will break off from a stream of Tamil and say,

'Cool Drinks?' – or if they're being well, cool, just 'Cool?' And you'll think, 'It's honestly very hot and I'm suddenly very thirsty and I can't imagine anything I'd like more than a Cool Drink, so thank you very much, yes.'

––––––––––

Cool Drink would also be the term I would choose to describe Sri Lanka's most famous cricketer, that smouldering, thirst-quenching sporting legend that is Kumar Sangakkara.

In Sri Lanka, cricket – like drink – is a nice thing people enjoy, impeded in lots of annoying ways by politics. Just as you might order a nice cool gin and tonic on the island and not realise that you have just committed a crime (because (a) you're a woman or (b) it's a full moon day), when you witness the deep love Sri Lankans have for cricket, you may not realise it has a dark and sometimes criminal underbelly. Sri Lankan cricket can still be a deeply classist sport, it has suffered corruption, it historically has discriminated against Tamils and Muslims, and every single appointment to the national squad still has to be personally signed off by the Sports Minister, which brings with it a maelstrom of archaic bullshit. And yet, from Dondra Head to Point Pedro, from Wembley in London to Wentworthville in Sydney, Sri Lankans love the game. The island is absolutely cricket mad, with little kids of all ages, classes and ethnicities, playing on every scrap of beach and quiet stretch of road they can get hold of. The national team is mobbed whenever they are spotted in public. And the cricket legends are regarded as rock stars.

––––––––––

Cool Drink would also be the term I would use to describe Sri Lanka's most famous cricketer, that smouldering, thirst-quenching sporting legend that is Kumar Sangakkara.

––––––––––

There have been many great Sri Lankan players: Sanath Jayasuriya, Arjuna Ranatunga, Muttiah Muralitharan, Aravinda de Silva. But if we're judging by who draws the biggest crowds, Sanga is perhaps the biggest rock star of all. I should say as a disclaimer here that I am no kind of expert: I hardly ever watch cricket, and I don't a hundred per cent understand what a wicket is, no matter how many patient cousins have tried to explain it to me. But even I have absorbed the cult of Kumar. Here's what we all know: Sanga is one of the greatest batsmen and wicketkeepers of any country, of all time. He is Sinhalese, he's a left-hander, he's from Kandy, he's a trained lawyer, he's got a very cool and stylish wife, he writes, he endorses and he invests. I'm sure the guy has flaws, but I sure don't know what they are. More than any of that, Sanga has become an ambassador for a different kind of cricket, and maybe even a different kind of Sri Lanka. He talks with passion about the legends who have moved beyond its colonial past. He talks about including all Sri Lankans in what can still be an exclusive sport, whether you're rich or poor, Tamil, Muslim or Sinhalese, whatever area you're from or school you go to. He advocates for Sri Lankans moving on from an obsession with snobbery and school-level cricket, to embrace our Sri Lankan-ness, and to do it with excellence, professionalism and pride. He dreams of an island where in his own words, Sri Lankans 'compete without self-doubt or fear, to defy unhealthy traditions and to embrace our own Sri Lankan identity'.

In other words, Sanga is the people's prince of cricket, and the whole world knows it. He has been described breathlessly in the sports media, both at home and away, as 'classy', 'erudite', 'charming', 'whip smart', 'razor sharp', an 'intellectual', a 'man with a plan', a 'true Jedi of a batsman' and the maker of 'the most important speech in cricket history'. In the words of my favourite sportswriter, Andrew Fidel Fernando, '[Sanga has his] audience. . . besotted. [He] could unbuckle his belt and moon them. . . and still they would all come away enchanted.'

––––––––––

If it is a full moon, Sanga's or not, when you're next in Sri Lanka, you might yet be able to try all of Sri Lanka's cool drinks. Booze is illegal on Buddhist *Poya* days, but you can often get hold of it somehow anyway – bartenders, like cricketers, doing their best to work around the system. In my dad's village and many other villages, you can get toddy, a fermented palm tree sap that starts the day sweet and gets progressively rougher and more dangerous as the day goes on. A refined, distilled toddy produces arrack, an ancient spirit called *sarayam* in Tamil that tastes like a kind of coconut bourbon or a strong, sort of woody cognac. It's great on its own on the rocks, or in an arrack sour or an arrack-and-ginger. As a leftover from British Empire, there is plenty of gin in Sri Lanka too, drunk as gins and tonics or in various gin cocktails.

Whatever the day, you can definitely get hold of Sri Lanka's soft drinks, which is what people saying 'Cool Drinks' usually mean. There is lovely fiery homemade ginger beer, with one of the best served at the Barefoot Cafe in Colombo. Made from real ginger, sweetened with fat juicy sultanas and mildly fermented, it is mind-bendingly refreshing and completely delicious. There are the neon-coloured sugary classics like bright green *Nelli Crush, Necto, Cream Soda*, and many others. Sri Lankan coconut water is the best I have drunk in the world; sweet, refreshing and best drunk roadside, from a young orange or green coconut. And there is excellent iced tea in Sri Lanka, from the delicate tippy tea grown in the island.

Ice Sangakkara

For a great boozy Cool Drink for this book, I got thinking about the legendary US golfer Arnold Palmer. His favourite was iced tea, lemonade and a little vodka after a hard day's teeing off. If that guy gets his own drink, I feel like our guy should get one too. So, this is a Lankan variation on an Arnold Palmer, for cooler-than-cool, ice-cold, Kumar Sangakkara. Instead of iced tea with vodka and lemonade, it is Ceylon iced arrack and a lime soda, with a little pandan cordial which gives it a warm, subtle coconut flavour. It is spiked with not vodka, but Sri Lankan arrack, an everyman spirit that rich and poor enjoy alike; smoky, woody and complex. Arrack is cool, it is ancient, it is indigenous and it was variously banned and controlled by Dutch and British colonisers. I feel it represents a proud Sri Lankan outlook that doesn't look towards Europe or the Empire. Like the man, this cocktail combines excellence, cosmopolitanism, and Sri Lankan pride. I hope you make it for your house visitors, unannounced or not.

Serves 4

200ml Ceylon arrack

4 Ceylon teabags, or 4 tsp
  Ceylon tea

8 tbsp pandan syrup (see below)

Juice of 2 limes

Ice

400ml soda water

Optional: 1 large pandan leaf,
  to garnish

For the pandan syrup

100g granulated sugar

4 whole pandan leaves, sliced
  into 1cm pieces

A pinch of salt

100ml water

1. To make the pandan syrup, put the sugar, pandan leaves, salt and water in a small saucepan and bring to a boil. Turn the heat down to a simmer, and allow to cook for 5 minutes. Switch off the heat, and let the syrup cool down in the pan completely. When cool, cover with a lid and allow to infuse overnight in the fridge. Strain into a glass bottle; it will last for 1 month in the fridge.

2. When you're ready to make cocktails, pour the arrack into a small bowl or mixing glass and add the tea. Set a timer, and leave to infuse for 8 minutes, then strain into a jug or second mixing glass.

3. Take four highball glass and add all cocktail ingredients except the ice and soda. If using, slice the garnish pandan leaf on a bias, so it is just slightly taller than your glasses. Add enough ice to half fill each glass. Top up each drink with your soda and gently stir to combine the ingredients. Garnish by placing your pandan leaf straight down the side of the glass.

Suggested Menus

A quick Sri Lankan weekday meal for two or three people might include one or two curries from the first two chapters, one of the rice, roti, hopper or dosa accompaniments from that chapter, and one or two sambols. For a bigger spread, for say five or six guests, you could start with a dip from the pickled dishes chapter on page 160 or a snack from the shorteats chapter on page 242, then serve a rice dish, two vegetable dishes and perhaps one meat or fish dish, finishing up with a pudding.

A midweek dinner

Roast pumpkin curry (page 30)

Coconut dal with kale (page 40)

Daikon, mint, carrot and kohlrabi sambol (page 164)

Coconut and onion pol roti (page 218)

OR

Prawn curry with tamarind (page 106)

Burnt cabbage varai (page 56)

Green mango sambol (page 178)

Plain boiled rice

A big feast

Burnt aubergine sambol with coconut milk (page 162) and poppadoms

Yellow rice (page 206)

Pickled pork curry (page 128)

Parsley and fresh lime sambol (page 176)

Fried aubergine vinegar moju (page 198)

Watalappan tart (page 298)

OR

Vadai doughnuts (page 262)

Fried sweet plantain curry (page 42)

Black coconut pineapple curry (page 44)

Fried chickpea and yoghurt sundal (page 186)

Thin godamba roti (page 220)

Plain boiled rice

Jaggery mess with coconut and cardamom (page 292)

OR

Apple acharu (page 196)

Slow-cooked lamb red curry (page 120)

Plain boiled rice

Cashew nut curry (page 74)

Tempered crunchy fried potatoes with turmeric (page 86)

Fresh pineapple sambol (page 180)

Ravana cake (page 294)

A Sunday brunch

Plain dosas and tomato thokku sambol (page 236)

Black sesame sambol (page 184)

Arrack egg muttai coffee (page 308)

OR

Seeni sambol, egg and cheese sandwich (page 134)

Condensed milk spiced tea (page 310)

A Summer barbecue

Grilled ambul fish (page 96)

Corn sundal salad with lime, coconut and curry leaves (page 188)

Lamb chops and mint sambol (page 118)

Fresh pineapple sambol (page 180)

Coconut and onion pol roti (page 218)

Cucumber sambol with salted spiced mor yoghurt (page 200)

Conversion Tables

WEIGHTS

Metric	Imperial
15g	$^1\!/_2$oz
20g	$^3\!/_4$oz
30g	1oz
55g	2oz
85g	3oz
110g	4oz / $^1\!/_4$lb
140g	5oz
170g	6oz
200g	7oz
225g	8oz / $^1\!/_2$lb
255g	9oz
285g	10oz
310g	11oz
340g	12oz /$^3\!/_4$lb
370g	13oz
400g	14oz
425g	15oz
450g	6oz / 1lb
1kg	2lb 4oz
1.5kg	3lb 5oz

LIQUIDS

Metric	Imperial
5ml	1 teaspoon
15ml	1 tablespoon or $^1\!/_2$fl oz
30ml	2 tablespoons or 1fl oz
60ml	4 tablespoons or 2fl oz
90ml	6 tablespoons or 3fl oz
120ml	8 tablespoons or 4fl oz
150ml	$^1\!/_4$ pint or 5fl oz
290ml	$^1\!/_2$ pint or 10fl oz
425ml	$^3\!/_4$ pint or 16fl oz
570ml	1 pint or 20fl oz
1 litre	1$^3\!/_4$ pints
1.2 litres	2 pints

LENGTH

Metric	Imperial
5mm	$^1\!/_4$in
1cm	$^1\!/_2$in
2cm	$^3\!/_4$in
2.5cm	1in
5cm	2in
10cm	4in
15cm	6in
20cm	8in
30cm	12in

OVEN TEMPERATURES

°C	°C Fan	Gas Mark	°F
110°C	90°C Fan	Gas Mark $^1\!/_4$	225°F
120°C	100°C Fan	Gas Mark $^1\!/_2$	250°F
140°C	120°C Fan	Gas Mark 1	275°F
150°C	130°C Fan	Gas Mark 2	300°F
160°C	140°C Fan	Gas Mark 3	325°F
180°C	160°C Fan	Gas Mark 4	350°F
190°C	170°C Fan	Gas Mark 5	375°F
200°C	180°C Fan	Gas Mark 6	400°F
220°C	200°C Fan	Gas Mark 7	425°F
230°C	210°C Fan	Gas Mark 8	450°F
240°C	220°C Fan	Gas Mark 9	475°F

Vegan recipes

Potato white sodhi curry (page 28)

Roast pumpkin curry (page 30)

Roasted aubergine red curry (page 32)

Coconut dal with kale (page 40)

Fried sweet plantain curry (page 42)

Black coconut pineapple curry (page 44)

Breadfruit curry (page 48)

Green mango curry (page 50)

Coconut milk greens curry (page 52)

Roast beetroot dry varai curry (page 54)

Burnt cabbage varai (page 56)

Squash sambar spicy wet curry (page 58)

Carrot, parsnip and peas avial curry (page 62)

Cucumber and turmeric white curry (page 64)

Cashew nut curry (page 74)

Chickpea spicy red curry (page 76)

Green beans white curry (page 78)

Spinach puttu with fenugreek milk (page 80)

Tomato rasam broth with leek and coriander
(page 84)

Burnt aubergine sambol with coconut milk
(page 162)

Daikon, mint, carrot and kohlrabi sambol aka
slambol (page 164)

Parsley and fresh lime sambol (page 176)

Green mango sambol (page 178)

Fresh pineapple sambol (page 180)

Raw carrot sambol salad (page 182)

Black sesame sambol (page 184)

Corn sundal salad with lime, coconut and curry
leaves (page 188)

Apple acharu (page 196)

Fried aubergine vinegar moju (page 198)

Coconut rice kiri bath with lunu miris (page 208)

Flaky paratha (page 216)

Thin godamba roti (page 220)

Hoppers (page 230)

Plain dosas and tomato thokku sambol
(page 236)

Devilled party cashew nuts (page 256)

Potato and leek spicy stuffed roti (page 258)

Vadai doughnuts (page 262)

Jaggery mess with coconut and cardamom
(page 292)

Lemongrass and lime soda (page 312)

Ice Sangakkara (page 318

Vegetarian recipes

(in addition to the listed Vegan recipes)

Fried chickpea and yoghurt sundal (page 186)

Cucumber sambol with salted spiced mor
yoghurt (page 200)

Turmeric rice pongal with eggs and beetroot
acharu pickle (page 210)

Coconut and onion pol roti (page 218)

Curry leaf rava dosa (page 234)

Milk toffee (page 286)

Love cake (page 288)

Banana and Milo icebox cake (page 290)

Ravana cake (page 294)

Watalappan tart (page 298)

Mango fluff pie (page 302)

Rambutan and rose frozen falooda (page 304)

Arrack egg muttai coffee (page 308)

Condensed milk spiced tea (page 310)

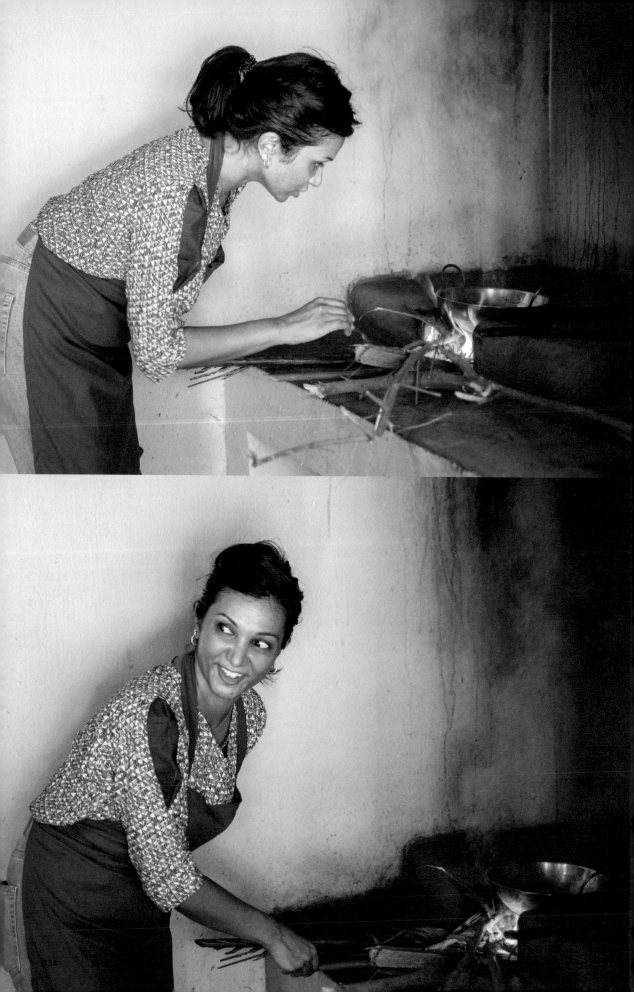

Thank you

This book just wouldn't exist without my family, who gave me all the best recipes and stories in it. Thanks to Mum, Dad, Amu and Vathany, and our big extended clan, especially Liliya, Thierry, Charlie, Cinnauntie, Mark, Ganesh Anna, Thevy Auntie and Gaya. All my gratitude to those whose time has come: Athappa, Suntharam Mama, Sri Anna and most of all, Ammamma.

A cookbook, I have discovered, is a team effort and I got lucky with an absurdly creative one. From the bottom of my heart, thanks to Rowan and Lena my editors, for your faith in me, and for welcoming me into the extraordinary stable of cooks and writers at Bloomsbury. To other Bloomsbury legends: Laura Brodie; Ellen; Don and Rose, for such tenacity and hard work in getting us there. To Ben, my agent, for being there every step of the way, I must have done something good in a past life to deserve you. To Laura Bayliss for your endless patience and good humour in turning a unwieldy stream-of-consciousness into a real recipe book; and Sally for such diligent proofreading. To Dave for designing this mighty beast with all my mad ideas – it's gorgeous. To Dilukshan for supplying several beautiful photos of our homeland. To the shoot team: Sam, the most thorough and thrillingly talented a cook as I ever met, for your glorious food styling and testing and developing. To Songsoo, our assistant stylist, for championing the book with your beautiful spirit (and killing big boiii). To Rachel, our prop stylist, for masterminding the style of the photos. And most of all to Alex Lau, our photographer. What a magnificent view into Sri Lankan life and food these pictures are, my friend. They are full of your sweetness and your light and your humour.

Finally, a big thank you to my friends, my chosen family, who saved me from going completely nuts through a lonely long year of writing and cooking. To Laura Baynton and Shanth for giving me the idea in the first place. To my Sri Lankan chosen family, Harith, Dani Akka, Don, Firi, Vicky, Kattai Appappa, Savan, Daniel, Chanch, Lakshmi and Pushpa Auntie, Tony, Rasa Uncle and Auntie, Liz and her granny, Auntie Patricia, Auntie Ianthe, Muthu, Ruwanthi, for letting me cook in your kitchens and sharing your dishes. Joe, thank you for being my anchor and going over every word and picture with me. Thanks to my Rambutan restaurant dreamteam, Shanika, Volker, Colin, Charlie, Iqbal Wahhab and Nitharshan. And to the people who pulled me through: Louise, Bren, Alex Gezelius, Geri, Sarah, dearest Richard, Anokhi, Jack, Alex F Webb, Louis, Mohamed, Duncan, Ollie, Katja, Nishna, Rav, Shamil, George Alagiah: my heart is just full of gratitude for being there for me, at the end of a phone or a long email, reading and turning it all over in your deep, creative minds.

And the last but biggest thanks of all: thank you to all the people of Sri Lanka, wherever you may be, now diaspora'd out across the globe. Thank you to all the Sri Lankan cooks who have gone before me.

About the author

Cynthia Shanmugalingam is a British-Sri Lankan cook who grew up in Coventry, visiting Sri Lanka in her childhood holidays and eating dishes adapted by her Tamil family at home.

She has cooked Sri Lankan food at pop-ups since 2019, including at Asma Khan's Darjeeling Express, Palm Heights in the Cayman Islands, and at Quo Vadis in London. Her work has been featured in *The Times*, *Guardian*, *Monocle* and *WePresent*. She lives in Hackney, and splits her time between London, Jaffna and Colombo. This is her first cookbook.

BLOOMSBURY PUBLISHING
Bloomsbury Publishing Plc
50 Bedford Square, London, WC1B 3DP, UK
29 Earlsfort Terrace, Dublin 2, Ireland

BLOOMSBURY, BLOOMSBURY PUBLISHING and the Diana logo are trademarks of Bloomsbury Publishing Plc

First published in Great Britain 2022

A catalogue record for this book is available from the British Library

Library of Congress Cataloguing-in-Publication data has been applied for

ISBN: HB: 978-1-5266-4657-6; eBook: 978-1-5266-4660-6

10 9 8 7 6 5 4 3 2

Project Editor: Laura Bayliss
Designer: Dave Brown, apeinc.co.uk
Photographer: Alex Lau
Food Stylist: Samantha Dixon
Prop Stylist: Rachel Vere
Map illustrator: Sarah Locher
Indexer: Vanessa Bird

Printed in China by RR Donnelley Ltd

MIX
Paper | Supporting responsible forestry
FSC
www.fsc.org
FSC® C144853

To find out more about our authors and books visit www.bloomsbury.com and sign up for our newsletters